# Good Housekeeping

OCTOBER 1935 · ONE ... NETT ·

Beginning R.C.Sheriff's new novel
· GREEN ... ATES ·
REVIEW OF NEW ... ER FASHIONS

# Good Housekeeping

OCTOBER 1936 · ONE SHILLING

## SPECIAL BOOK REVIEW SUPPLEMENT

Marguerite Steen · Clare Sheridan · Ethel Smyth
A.J. Cronin · Elizabeth Goudge · Florence Kilpatrick
"Education by Wireless" by Joyce Wedgwood

# Good Housekeeping

APRIL 1935 ONE SHILLING NETT

## SPRING FASHIONS FOR EASTER

Sheila Kaye-Smith : Florence White : Dr. Maude Royden
Victoria Sackville-West : Countess of Oxford and Asquith

# Good Housekeeping

FEBRUARY 1937 ONE SHILLING

"SWEET CONTENT...
"SOME OF MY CONTEMP...
Kathleen Wallace Ae...
Ezie Linklater James...

# Childhood Memories

# A Prayer by Edmund Leamy
## Drawing by C·B·Falls·

DEAR God in Heaven, of Your pity
　　Help the poor children of the city;
　　The little youngsters of the slums
　　To whom Your blessing rarely comes;
The little tots who run and play
In crowded, dirty streets each day;
Who dream not song of bird and tree
Nor star and field and sighing sea;
Who are denied and do not know
Their birthright of the long ago—
The clean, sweet wind, the grimeless sun,
Wide spaces, health, and wholesome fun.
Oh, help them that at last they find
And know You, good and dear and kind:
That each wee heart may thrill and sing
With happiness and wondering.
And keep them ever in Your ken,
Safe from all hurt and harm.　Amen.

# Childhood Memories

## Growing up with Good Housekeeping
## 1922 – 1942

*With contributions from:*

**H G Wells ✦ Vita Sackville-West ✦ Ernest H Shepherd**

**Lady Violet Bonham-Carter ✦ Ogden Nash**

EBURY PRESS
LONDON

Published in 1991 by Ebury Press
an imprint of the Random Century Group
Random Century House
20 Vauxhall Bridge Road
London SW1V 2SA

First impression 1991

British Library Cataloguing-in-Publication Data
Childhood memories: Growing up with Good
Housekeeping, 1922-1942. – (GH nostalgia series)
I. Braithwaite, Brian II. Walsh, Noëlle
III. Series
649

ISBN 0-85223-981-5

Printed and bound in Great Britain by Butler & Tanner Ltd, Frome and London

# CONTENTS

# FOREWORD

## ADVERTISING INTRODUCTION

There was no problem in selecting advertisements apposite to children from the pre-war pages of Good Housekeeping. The little mites and tots appear constantly as a stream of clothing, toy, remedies and food advertisements were directed at them – or, rather, to their doting mothers. Good Housekeeping took its children seriously and, even with the smaller pre-war families of the 1920's and the 1930's, offspring represented an important and lucrative market to the advertisers.

Even a guilt complex was introduced by the nagging Children's Encyclopaedia on page 13. (OK, so what does become of the light when it goes out?) Some of the advertising was directed at the mother of the weaning infant, with Ovaltine declaring that Breast Fed is Best Fed and Virol claiming life-saving properties (page 35). Blue Band margarine made out a strong case for fat (page 51) and some of the extant food manufacturers such as Oxo, Horlicks and St. Ivel were advertising their products for healthy children. Norwegian Cod Liver Oil (page 84) espoused the cause of their oleaginous product to counter the trend of horrid children – it could be malnutrition.

There were more abstruse arguments for the health of the family as promulgated by Hoover, Fridgidaire, Radiation and Valor. And Gibbs were on the familiar toothpaste trail, a piece of daunting copywriting (page 24) – enough to send you straight to your toothbrush. The treatment was obviously efficacious because by page 132 the children had become 'gay, young people'.

The toy companies were mining a rich vein with the Good Housekeeping children. Hamleys (page 34) made a universal appeal with toys for both (but different) sexes and all ages with dolls and prams for girls and a model motor car for boys. (This was 1924 when the sexes knew their places.) And their Cat-in-a-Milk-Can toy probably produced apoplexy in many an unsuspecting, visiting relative when the feline suddenly appeared out of the can and licked its lips to a delightful melody. The ubiquitous Meccano is here (for boys again) and, of course, Hornby Trains on page 111 – nostalgic equipment and prices even if the illustration is confusingly out of scale.

Maternal pride would have been stimulated and challenged by Pretty's announcement on page 38 of the handsome prize for a photograph of your pride and joy – the only condition being the insistence on wearing one of their Fleeci bodices. And musical education was not eschewed with the proposition of the Pianola on page 96.

As always, advertisements were a wonderful and enterprising reflection of the times. So many of the advertisers are still with us today – others have been cast aside and lost forever like our own toys and games of innocent childhood!

BRIAN BRAITHWAITE

# EDITORIAL INTRODUCTION

Ever since Good Housekeeping was first published in 1922, the family has been at the heart of its existence. Children – how to feed them, clothe them, care for them, discipline them and keep them healthy and happy – were the subject of grave discussion and hearty argument. The language may sometimes have been overly sentimental – 'There is, perhaps, no greater joy on earth to a true woman than the knowledge that her love has been crowned and that she has handed on the torch of life' – but the underlying sentiment, as today, was one of good commonsense.

The twenties were a time of great debate about the proper rearing of children; no more so than in the pages of Good Housekeeping, where the different shades of opinion were allowed free rein. The debate concerning the age at which children should start school, for example, prompted by proposals to raise it from five to six, caused Charlotte Cowdroy, Headmistress of Crouch End High School, to declare (page 12): 'The deadening influence begins as soon as the child, still but a baby, is sent to school. What a child of that age needs is to be loved and to be let alone.' Ah, but who is to do the loving? This brings us to the wider debate of the twenties – working mothers – as Ms Cowdroy continues: 'But we are told that if the little children cannot go to school, their mothers cannot go out to work. This alone would be reason enough for raising the age for beginning school. Children have an absolute right to the attention of their own mothers in their own home. If public opinion were healthy, any able-bodied man who let his wife turn breadwinner would be treated with the contempt he deserves, while the woman who would let any outside work prevent her giving her own personal service to the children of her body would be regarded as the unnatural freak she is.' Never let it be said that Good Housekeeping, then or now, was afraid to give voice to controversial opinions!

Two of the most popular series, which continued all through the twenties, were entitled *Things You Don't Learn At School* and *Things You'll Like to Know*. Some of the contents show the mark of time but others provide much-needed answers to the relentless questioning of young minds, such as 'Why does the wind blow?'.

Some of the greatest writers of this century chose Good Housekeeping as the vehicle for expressing themselves on the subject of children. From HG Wells on *The Launching of Sons and Daughters* (page 30) and *The Servant Question* (page 18) where Violet Bonham Carter looked back to her own childhood for answers to the vexing question of the twenties, to *Is it Right to Pass On One's Experiences To One's Children?* by Vita Sackville West and *The Story of the Gardener and the White Elephants*, a short story for children by Richard Hughes, author of *A High Wind in Jamaica*. Then, as now, Good Housekeeping covered the issues of the day in an intelligent, well-researched and well-written way.

Perhaps the one statement with which today's mothers would wholeheartedly concur is left to the final page of this book when a mother, among a whole host of people, is asked what she would hope for her child when he grows up. Her reply – 'There will be true peace, not just an interval between two wars.' The date is 1941.

NOËLLE WALSH

1922

# SPRING

Childhood's heart grows light with the smiling advent of soft blue skies and days of sunshine. Happy Children!

Health was ever the twin of Happiness. The boundless good spirits, the glowing radiance of happy kiddies, are sometimes

### A SURPRISE

to those parents who have not yet discovered the secret of healthy childhood. It is just made up of fresh air, plenty of sleep, proper dress, and good food. What more nourishing than custard made with eggs and milk? REAL eggs, not powdered substitutes! The effect

### ON THE KIDDIES

is very evident. You can build up sturdy little frames with "PETER-KIN"—the nutritious delicacy children love. Its rich creaminess, delicious flavour, and real nourishment make and keep healthy, happy childhood!

*Give Them*

## PETERKIN
### REAL EGG CUSTARD

**THE K.O. CEREALS CO., LTD.**
London      Greenock      Glasgow

"Eat more REAL Custard - - It helps Health"

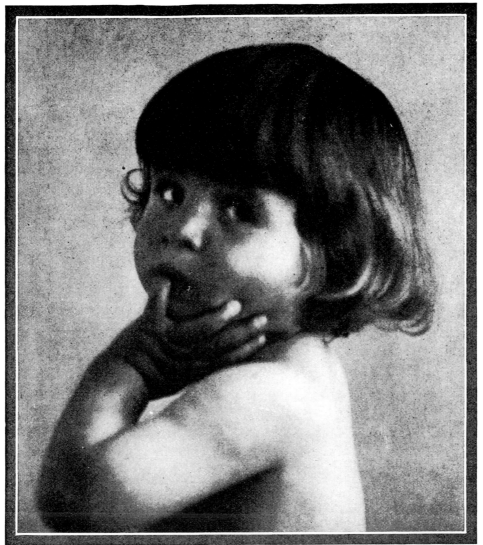

*Photo: Marcus Adams*

# Our Children's Heritage

## "GOOD HEALTH"

### By Margaret Hallam

THERE is, perhaps, no greater joy on earth to a true woman than the knowledge that her love has been crowned and that she has handed on the torch of life.

But infinitely sweet as the clinging touch of baby fingers is, it brings with it a sense of care and responsibility. The thinking mother realises that the old order has changed, and the transition stage through which we all must pass before we arrive at newer and better things is a difficult one.

Economic conditions have altered completely during the last few years, and How to do the very best for my children under existing circumstances? —when means are often straitened and children born with delicate constitutions owing to the strain the parents have been through—is a problem that confronts the fathers and mothers of to-day.

Fortunately, the possession of riches is not necessary to a child's well-being and happiness—indeed, the finest men and women are those who have had their own way to make in life—but what is known as *Good Health* is. And by *Good Health* is meant the possession of a sound mind in a healthy, well-formed body, and a well-balanced character.

Almost anything is possible to the man and woman who enjoy really good health. They are usually happy and successful; they have a clear sense of proportion and are not easily thrown out of their stride.

What every mother should do is to take infinite care and pains for her child's welfare from babyhood onward, and to establish its health and train its mind—to endeavour, in fact, to achieve perfect unity between the conscious and subconscious self. The task is not so stupendous as it seems, for the methods which have been proved to be most satisfactory in the long run in child training are *simple* and *fad-free*.

Three of the factors necessary to a child's physical well-being are Fresh Air, Food, and Exercise. It must also be taught obedience and self-control, and its mind carefully trained—for mind and body react on each other; but it is of the physical side that this article will chiefly treat.

It is an acknowledged fact that a child cannot well have too much Fresh Air, but many children, although they live a more or less out-door life, do not get a sufficient supply of oxygen into their little lungs because they do not breathe correctly, and, unless the lungs are properly filled and emptied, the blood is not thoroughly purified and the child has not got an adequate supply of pure blood to nourish body and brain, its growth is checked, and its mental development often arrested.

Furthermore, the child who does not breathe correctly has a narrow, contracted chest, *Continued overleaf*

## Our Children's Heritage
*(Continued)*

and usually suffers from adenoids and throat troubles.

So one of the very first things a mother ought to ascertain is whether her child is using its lungs to their fullest capacity or not, and, if not, to teach it some simple breathing exercises, of which the two following are good examples.

In order to test whether a child has the habit of breathing correctly or not, place the hands lightly on its body just above the waist. Tell it to close its lips tightly and to breathe slowly in and out through its nose. If it breathes through its nose easily and the ribs dilate under the light pressure of the hands, the mother may be satisfied that her child's lungs are in good working order, and that it will get sufficient breathing exercises when it is running about and playing and shouting out of doors—for shouting, though it may prove trying to grown-up ears and nerves, is one of Nature's ways of strengthening children's lungs, and should, therefore, not be discouraged.

If, however, the child has difficulty in breathing through its nose, and its ribs do not expand properly, breathing exercises must be used.

Make the child stand upright, its feet slightly apart, its hands by its sides ; tell it to shut its lips quite tight. The mother should then take hold of its little arms, raise them sideways above its head and down again. As its arms are raised, tell it to take a deep breath in through its nose. As the arms are lowered, tell it to breathe out again. The movements should be very gentle and even, and made interesting to the child. A little child will enter into the spirit of the thing if it is told it is a bird, and its arms are the wings flapping.

The passages of the throat and nose may be kept clear if children are taught, when quite tiny, to close their little lips very tightly and take three breaths first through one nostril and then through the other, the mother closing the nostril not in use by holding her finger firmly pressed against that side of the nose.

While on the subject of Fresh Air, a mother should remember that while well-ventilated rooms are necessary for children, draughts and raw damp air are extremely dangerous, and many ailments children suffer from nowadays are due to the modern craze of outside air at any cost, no matter of what quality. Also, it should be borne in mind that little children if delicate should never go out of doors in a strong, biting wind.

Next to Fresh Air comes the all-important question of food and feeding.

It is not only the children of the poor, but the children of the rich, who suffer from malnutrition. A child may have three or four meals a day, and yet be insufficiently nourished, because it does not masticate its food or it is not food that it can easily digest.

The child who suffers from malnutrition falls an easy prey to every passing ailment, and usually has an impaired constitution all through life.

In thinking out a diet for her family, a mother has to take the fact into consideration that not only has the child to eat to sustain life and repair wasted tissues as grown-up people have to, but it has, in addition, to manufacture the extra tissue needed by growth to build up bone, muscle, nerve, etc.

Children's fare should be of the simplest description, but of the best quality possible —well cooked and well served. English meat should always be given, and the best butter—whatever the parents may eat themselves. And the children must be

## Our Children's Heritage

taught to masticate their food very thoroughly.

All mothers should make a study of food values in order to provide their children with a variety of suitable food. It is not possible to give a comprehensive diet list here, but, roughly speaking, the following articles of diet, advised by a well-known doctor, are suitable for those who are growing fast.

Milk should form the staple diet all through childhood. Fresh cream, obtained by letting the milk stand all night, is of great value if eaten with mashed potatoes and stewed fruit. Eggs lightly boiled or poached are excellent. Fresh meat should be given once a day, and be underdone and either shredded or cut up very finely. Chicken is excellent. *White* fish, such as sole, turbot, cod, etc., are good as a change from meat. Bacon fat and small pieces of bacon are good for breakfast.

Small quantities of well-cooked potatoes and green vegetables may be given. Fruit juice, and baked apples, and stewed fruits should be taken. Milk puddings are excellent; bread and butter, sponge cake, biscuits, fruit jellies, and sweets in moderation, if eaten just after and not between meals, are good for the little ones.

In regard to exercise, children should have sufficient to ensure their eating and sleeping well, but should not be allowed to walk too far or get over-tired.

As the child grows, a mother must keep a sharp look-out to see that it is growing straight and strong, and not developing bow legs, knock knees, or ankles that turn over. Slight curvature of the spine and signs of flat-foot should be watched for. If tendencies to deformity are taken in time they can usually be checked, and slight cases cured ; too often they are not noticed till too late.

Eye-strain must also be taken into account, for it is at the root of much childish and after-life misery.

Teeth are all-important, and should receive careful and constant attention.

So-called growing pains should be treated at once: they are one of the signs of rheumatism, and rheumatism is a deadly foe to the young, even more than to the old.

All mothers should notice the mental development of their children: whether they are unduly backward or unduly precocious, each case needs prompt and special training.

Above all, if the children are to be healthy, happy, and normal, they must not be fussed over or experimented with. Since children and child-study have become the fashion, the child has been taken out of its proper place in the home. Children want infinite care and love, but they do not want to be made self-centred. The less a child thinks about itself, the better. Provided that a child eats and sleeps well, and keeps about the right weight a child of its age and height ought to be—a fact which mothers can ascertain for themselves by procuring one of the excellent tables published—there is no need to worry about that child's condition.

All children should have learnt to be obedient by the time they are three years old, and should have laid the foundation of habits of self-control and consideration for others at a very early age.

For the Heritage of Good Health is not a matter of physical fitness only.

# The Geddes Axe *and* the Babies

## By CHARLOTTE COWDROY

*Author of " Thwarted Women," etc., and Head Mistress of Crouch End High School*

**1922**

ONE of the proposals of the Geddes Economy Committee was that children should not be admitted to the State schools before the age of six. As they had been compelled to attend on reaching the mature age of five, this alteration would save many thousands of pounds, and this would mean a slight lifting of the tax-payer's burden. The right of the tax-payer to consideration is great, for the existence of the country depends upon him. But the future of the country depends upon the child. And for years the child has been worse treated than even the unfortunate tax-payer.

To-day it is lamented that we have no outstanding men, no men of genius: that the reign of mediocrity is here. Yet mediocrity is the exception and not the rule with the young child. Parents are often astonished at the profundity of the thoughts expressed by quite young children, and are laughed at for repeating them or accused of exaggeration. I know of one father who was approached three times by his tiny daughter. She was playing at ball, and each time dropped it to propound to him an idea that has been the central thought of a whole separate system of philosophy.

The imaginative powers, the poetry in the soul of the young child who has been left to develop freely, will be wonderful to those who have no personal experience of one that has so far been unspoilt. Such a child weaves romances round the commonest facts of daily life. The little one has the key to "magic casements opening on the foam of faëry lands forlorn" until we take that key away, hang the curtains of the commonplace before those casements, and then swear they cover only a blank wall.

The deadening influence begins as soon as the child, still but a baby, is sent to school. What a child of that age needs is to be loved and to be let alone. It is pitiful to see the little things that were bubbling over with chatter, roaming round the room on the quest of adventure, scribbling over books, and otherwise behaving as babies should, at the end of a few months reduced to "order," sitting passively in their places and accepting the school routine as if it were a law of nature.

When children are let alone knowledge comes with delight in conscious power, just as a baby pulls itself to its feet and toddles a step, crowing with joy at discovering its gift of independent movement. The harm done by the ignorant nurse in putting the child upon its legs too soon is patent enough, but it is as nothing compared with the evil result of the too early stimulation of the child's

brain. Unfortunately that harm is not on the surface, but I believe it to be largely responsible for the general dead-level of mediocrity, for a certain lack of mental equilibrium, and for much of the modern increase in lunacy. The little child is obliged to "attend" when attention, unless voluntarily given, even for the shortest time is an undue strain. It is not natural. Let the grown-up think for one moment how tired he feels after listening attentively to a twenty-minute sermon. Let him then compare the powers of a child of five with his own, and then perhaps he may begin to realise the cruel demands made upon the child brain. We shall be told that the child is in the hands of a trained teacher, that the attention is won by arousing its interest, not by exciting its fear. It is just that artificial awakening of interest

> THE proposal of the Geddes Economy Committee to exclude children from the State schools until they are six may benefit the tax-payer, but infinitely more it will benefit the children who escape the "deadening influence" school life exerts on the very young child. The personal care of its mother is the child's first right, yet one of the reasons advanced by the Education Department for sending a child of five to school is that its presence at home prevents the mother from going out to work. If public opinion were healthy, any able-bodied man who let his wife turn bread-winner would be treated with the contempt he deserves. While the woman who would let any outside work prevent her giving her personal service to her children would be regarded as the unnatural freak she is

that is so exhausting to the delicate nervous system of a being so immature.

The child is often taught to read long before it actively wishes to do so. When that time comes it will hardly need teaching, so great will be its own interest and mental activity. This I have frequently found. In my own case I can perfectly remember a period when I wondered what people found to look at in the books, the pages of which looked all alike, and I looked at them and tried to see what it was. But I have not the faintest memory of learning to read. It seems as though there was no appreciable interval between when I could not read at all and when I could read quite well. Many other people have had the same experience who learned to read before going to school.

No gardener would pull open the

petals of a bud and set them to his own pattern. Yet how seldom are the petals of the child mind left to disclose themselves in their own true time, their own order, individuality, and beauty.

We are told the young child will suffer if left in its own home—that the homes are unsatisfactory, unhygienic, and many other "uns." To many officials a child's worst enemy is its mother, only useful to bear the child until some system of State incubators can be devised; a person to be separated from the baby—to give life to which she has herself gone down to the gates of death—at the earliest possible moment. By severing the home ties and the natural bonds of love she may indeed in time be rendered as bad as they would make her out. Yet a tenth-rate mother is infinitely better for any child than the average trained teacher.

We may smile at the wealth of love and adoration poured out by the mother on some awkward and unattractive child. May it not be that her eyes are clearer than ours, that she sees something divine we cannot see? And the child too—may he not look with purer eyes than ours and see something of the Madonna where we materialists see only the overworked, time-scarred, or often sordid exterior? The "trailing clouds of glory" are non-existent to the official mind. No! The child must be driven to school. It is not enough that "the vision splendid must fade into the light of common day" as time passes. The official aim is to anticipate that period and "provoke the years to bring the inevitable yoke."

The right of the child to home life also implies that of playing in the home with others of different ages. The Education Department seems to think that Nature has made a big mistake in not arranging that the young of man should be born in litters, sets all of an age. So it tries to rectify that error by gathering the children into regiments, all of the same age, thus replacing the little loving and natural activities of the home by the pushful and self-assertive elements in the classroom or playground amongst equals. In the humblest home one can often see beautiful love and care shown by the child of seven to the five-year-old, by the five-year-old to the baby of two.

Even from the standpoint of health alone the child has a right to remain with its mother till it is at least seven. I have heard workers in the East End of London remark how robust and bonny the children look playing happily about in the sordid streets. They seem uncared-for to one accustomed to the nurseries of the well-to-do, yet seem to flourish in the open air while often the cared-for *Continued*

## The Geddes Axe and the Babies

darlings fade. Their rough-and-ready mothers show great fondness for them, and they seem promising enough. Then they reach school age, or sometimes are sent before five. And at once there is a change for the worse. They lose their pretty colour, their roundness, and their gaiety. They begin spending the brightest part of the day within four walls, and they start running through the diseases incidental to childhood, which are exchanged at school long before they have developed sufficient power of resistance to cope with them.

But we are told that if the little children cannot go to school their mothers cannot go out to work. This alone would be reason enough for raising the age for beginning school. Children have an absolute right to the attention of their own mother in their own home. If public opinion were healthy, any able-bodied man who let his wife turn breadwinner would be treated with the contempt he deserves, while the woman who would let any outside work prevent her giving her own personal service to the children of her body would be regarded as the unnatural freak she is. The driving of the young children into the schools has had much to do with a general moral deterioration on this point. The woman's natural and God-given occupation, the occupation which should be her pride and pleasure, which should fill her life, the occupation by which she can best serve the future of her country, is taken from her. She fills the vacant time with outside work and gradually the centre of her interest is shifted from the home.

For the child's own sake no child should be permitted inside a school till it is six years old, and compulsory attendance should not begin till seven, if not later. Unfortunately the gospel of freedom from officialdom is against the law of the Scribes and Pharisees. If the children were set free it would mean financial loss to interested persons, and these denounce the real child-lovers. They talk of the school door being "banged in the face of the children"! They talk about a relaxing of compulsion, a less forcible hounding of the unfortunate children into herds, as "banging the door in their faces!" Nothing could show more plainly how they have lost touch with the mothers of the children. These officials also tell us in moving terms that numbers of assistant mistresses must be dismissed if the age is raised. It is a little unreasonable that the poor children are to be put within four walls and have their poor little bodies denied the freedom of the home for the sake of providing employment to assistant mistresses. But why should not these assistant mistresses receive their salaries in full till their numbers are used up automatically by filling future vacancies from their ranks? The good to the nation will be well worth the outlay, and in the long run the tax-payer will benefit by stoppage of addition to the number of assistant mistresses. The large number of class-rooms that would be set free could be used to relieve overcrowding and to save fresh building.

Few public acts would so immediately benefit the whole nation mentally, morally, and physically, while at the same time (though this is a mere detail) saving the tax-payers many thousands of pounds, as the raising of the compulsory school age to the age of seven.

# The *Hygiene* of Children's Clothes

## BY MURIEL WRINCH

*National Froebel Union Higher Certificate, Organiser of the " Jack and Jill " Camps for People under Eighteen*

1922

THERE was a time in the world's history when we clothed ourselves in woad, painted ourselves, in fact a cheerful, uncompromising — though perchance monotonous—blue. A strange travesty of clothing this; even Eve knew better when she made Adam a fig-leaf waistcoat. But fig leaves proved, no doubt, disappointing, for they were not tough enough. We have travelled far since then in the matter of dress, though we still adorn ourselves with furs reminiscent of the days when skins were the only clothing, and still wear the beads primitive woman was the first to introduce for her adornment.

Can't you imagine her sitting in her cave stringing necklaces of the teeth of great animals to thread through her dark hair and to hang round her neck and wrists and ankles? But can't you imagine, too, how when a necklace proved particularly successful she would take a peculiar delight in dropping those beads over the head of her little daughter instead of over her own?

Civilised woman has the same instinct to adorn her children. But she has more knowledge to help her and more chance of applying it than had her primitive sisters.

Woad and skins were all right in their way—they served as a protection from the elements, which, after all, is one of the chief functions of clothes —but wool and silk and the numerous other materials we have to-day are infinitely better. In fact, there are so many materials it is difficult to choose always the most hygienic and healthful. The three representative materials which at once present themselves to the mind are cotton, wool, and silk. Wool and silk have very decided advantages over cotton: where wool is slow to let heat pass from the body, cotton is a very good conductor of heat; where the relatively coarse mesh of

ALL normal children take an interest in their clothes, from the baby who displays his new shoes with pride to the chance visitor, to the little girl of eight who has definite ideas on the choice of colours for her new frocks. In this instinct for dress the child develops an appreciation of beauty. The practical side of children's clothes is also fully dealt with in this article by Muriel Wrinch, who will write next month on " Work and Play for People Under Five "

wool or silk allows free natural ventilation, the tight warp and weft of cotton impedes the passage of air within or the passage of perspiration out. Cotton garments should for this reason never be worn next the skin. In hot weather they become moist, and on drying become hard so that they chafe tender skins; while in winter they let heat pass away quickly from the skin, leaving it chilled and blue.

Wool is the best material for children. Not the scratchy wool which so much irritates a child that one little girl I knew used to pay her elder—and fatter! —sister a penny a week to wear her new combinations and stretch them for the first day after they came from the wash! —but the real, old-fashioned, fleecy, comfortable wool. Knitted garments are much more reliable than woven ones —they are softer and warmer because they entangle the air and warm it within their meshes, whilst the majority of woven material is in these days lamentably far from being " pure wool."

One material should never be worn— even as an outside garment—the rubber amalgam of which children's mackintoshes are so frequently made. It is, of course, of very great importance that children should be kept dry and warm; damp feet and wet hair are responsible, not only for the trivial colds and coughs which frequently result from a wetting, but also for the more serious " internal chill " which, because it has no obvious symptoms, is seldom noticed, although it may lower a child's health for several weeks. It is, however, more satisfactory to regard the mackintosh as an extra covering for wet weather rather than as a garment. It should be made of oiled silk, and if made of this material it need be only a feather-weight to carry. With the old-fashioned rubber mackintoshes, in which it is not uncommon to see hapless children dragged out for their morning walk, there are all the disadvantages of a non-ventilating

*This is the type of romper that will please your baby, because he can button it himself. A pattern (size 2-4 years) for making this hygienic garment may be obtained for 1s.*

*A type of gymnasium frock, made in all materials, which is being worn in the larger modern girls' schools. Patterns (sizes 6-8 and 8-10 years) cost 1s. each, and may be obtained from Paper Pattern Department, " Good Housekeeping," 1 Amen Corner, London, E.C.4*

material (even though there may be artificial ventilation beneath the arms), a very thick material, and one with a smell peculiarly objectionable to quite a large number of children.

With regard to the number of garments a child should wear, there are two facts to be considered. In the first place, two thin garments are much warmer than one thick one. This is because air becomes entangled between the two layers of clothing, becomes warmed from contact with the body and thus forms a third—and intermediate— layer of covering for the skin. Not only does it form a warming layer round the body, it forms also a ventilating layer, a current of moving air circulating and sweeping the pores free from dust and the " stickiness " to which children object so much.

It must be remembered also in this connection that when we heap a child with clothes, with the very praiseworthy intention of keeping him warm, we frequently—by excess of enthusiasm— defeat our own ends. When the skin, in consequence of too many clothes being worn, becomes too hot, perspiration ensues, the body making a valiant effort to regulate the temperature by moistening the surface of the skin. But it is an elementary fact in physics that when a substance turns from liquid to vapour, it abstracts a certain amount of heat—540 calories in the case of water turning to steam—in order to do this. This heat, called " latent heat," is taken from the body when perspiration, excreted in the form of moisture, is given off as vapour. A child perspiring freely because he is over-clothed is therefore losing heat instead of gaining it, and in the process giving up valuable energy, which might be devoted to other activities.

Girls are more frequently the victims in this matter of overclothing than boys; they are frequently burdened, for instance, in *Continued*

# The Hygiene of Children's Clothes

1922

the natural shape of the body. Modern parents do not dress their children in clothes tightly fitting at the waist. They have had awful examples held up to them in the shape of the little Victorians, whose poor little bodies were so much compressed that the ribs were twisted and contorted into the shape of the fashionable bodice, while the lungs, poorly aerated because there was no room to breathe, fell easy victims to the tubercle bacillus. Children's clothes are now slung from the shoulder, and hang loose—or at the most, slightly caught in at the waist—from neck to hem. It is, however, not uncommon to find unnoticed constrictions in children's clothes. It is for instance no rare thing to see a red mark round a child's chin after the hat has been removed. This is due to too tight a hat elastic, and produces lack of circulation in a particularly important region, since there are at least three large arterial and venous trunks in the region of neck and chin. It is common also to find tight elastic round the knees, either to keep stockings up or to keep the knicker edge from slipping down. A constriction at this point has the obvious effect of cutting off the circulation to the legs and feet. This in itself is serious, leading as it does to chilblains, chapped skin, and cold feet, and a thousand minor discomforts in winter-time —but there are greater ills to which constriction in this region may lead. Down the body, from midway between the hip and thigh to the ankle, runs the longest column of liquid in the whole body, the great sciatic vein. The blood in this column is normally driven by the pumping action of the heart upwards to run into the femoral vein. The blood is therefore running in direct opposition to the influence of gravity, and even normally tends to run back and accumulate in the little valves with which the walls of the veins are furnished. When a tight garter is placed in the path of this blood, a further influence causing the blood to tend to run backwards enters, and the blood will in this case almost inevitably do what it tended to do before—accumulate in the valves of the vein, giving rise to the very painful "Varicose veins" seen so often in people of middle age.

So much for the physical hygiene of the child's dress. A more interesting point perhaps is the way in which his dress may play its part in the child's development— a question of mental hygiene. The *whole* of a child's daily life is an education to him; he learns, in the small tasks which he does for his mother, in the small obstacles which he overcomes for himself, quite as much as he learns during his school hours. His animal pets, his garden, teach him of nature, showing him, unconscious as his knowledge may be, the part played by the great science of physiology in every life; his work in the toolshed teaches him simple mechanics and mathematics; his walks with his nurse may lay the basis for an appreciation of the principles of geography. The careful consideration of his clothes may teach him not only hygiene, but the *æsthetic appreciation of colour, the principles of designing, and the art of weaving and dyeing.*

The colour of a child's clothes may be perfectly exquisite or it may be hard and glaring and cheap. It depends upon whether the mother is content to buy readymade clothes dyed with aniline dyes, or whether she wishes to cultivate the child's taste and to utilise and to find expression for the unconscious artistry which is in him. I met the other day a small boy attired in a simple smock of one of the most beautiful shades of brown it has ever been my good fortune to meet. I admired the smock, seeing from the child's eyes that he too took a delight in it. "Now guess," said the mother triumphantly, "just how we obtained that particular shade of brown." I tried to remember where I had seen that autumn brown before—but could not. "Tell her then, Charlie," prompted the mother gently. "Dipped it in the pot on the beach the brown sails for the ships are dipped in," said Charlie with a shy, fat chuckle. On further inquiries I learnt that the mother had made the smock and that the baby had chosen the colour himself, that even now he was executing a beautiful dye at home—with beetroot and mountain ash berries boiled in water and strained. Logwood, saffron—all these natural objects yield exquisite colours with which children can dye their own material.

And for the designing on the finished clothes—babies of four or five can do charming designs with only little squares or triangles in different positions as the basis. While girls of nine and ten, who refuse to do embroidery or any kind of handwork whatever, have eagerly begun a piece of embroidery with which to adorn a dress! One little girl of eight embroidered a little dress for herself with Noah's ark animals running round the hem and over the pockets.

It is educationally sound that children should, as far as possible, work for themselves. Boys and girls up to eleven and twelve are living more or less at the stage when man is an individualist—they belong to an age when he was his own carpenter, his own baker, his own hunter; they are not developed to live in an adult society where one man is the better carpenter, one the professional baker, another the butcher by trade. This is the reason why, at one very advanced school, the children now actually weave their own material for frocks and stockings and gloves. Actually to weave the material is, of course, not possible in the circumstances of an average home, even though there are now delightful little children's looms which will keep a child busy and happy for many hours. There is, however, always the possibility of making charming garden hats, which most children will delight in, and which involve only quite a little material. In dress, as in everything else, allow your child to educate himself in co-operating with you. And in the pattern and fastenings of his dress follow the advice of the modern educators who have said, on bigger issues than this question of clothing: "Study the child. Aid his development by *never* doing for him anything which it is possible for him to do for himself."

1922

# Breast Fed is Best Fed

**N**ATURAL feeding is the duty of every mother and the birthright of every child. A medical authority states : "*Maternal nursing is not merely one method of feeding an infant—it is the only right way.*"

To ensure an adequate supply of milk and to enable the mother to maintain her strength while nursing, "Ovaltine" should be regularly taken throughout the entire nursing period. With much advantage it may also be taken before the birth. The baby will become robust and healthy and more immune from infantile ailments.

A nurse writes :—"Four recent patients who took 'Ovaltine' before the birth of their babies have each had a beautiful baby and in each case the mother has been able to breast-feed her little one."

"Ovaltine" is a delicious beverage containing the concentrated nourishment extracted from malt, milk and eggs.

*"Ovaltine" gives Health to Mother and Baby!*

# OVALTINE
### TONIC FOOD BEVERAGE

**Enables Mothers to Breast Feed their Babies**

*Sold by all Chemists and Stores at 1/6, 2/6 and 4/6*

**A. WANDER, LTD., 45 Cowcross Street, London, E.C.1**

P. 125 A

Dishes decorated with nursery rhymes make happy meals for children

1922

# *To Please* The Children

IT will always give pleasure to the children of the household when some new and attractive dish is made for their special benefit. With a little thought and ingenuity the simplest food can often be made to look both pretty and tempting; it may only be in the manner of serving or in the little bit of decoration added. For the tiny tots there is a good choice of china to be had in the shops: mugs, plates, cups and saucers, porridge bowls, and even egg-cups, all with funny pictures or nursery rhymes, and a child is always delighted to have his or her own little set. For the older children, too, one can buy many pretty dishes at a moderate price, and it is very important to accustom them to seeing their food daintily served.

The following dishes are all easy to make; this month they are principally sweets; but try them on the children and we feel sure they will be hailed with delight.

## Fish Scallops

This is an inviting way of serving the remains of cooked fish, and the children will like them. The natural scallop shells can generally be obtained from the fishmonger, and they should be chosen as deep in form as possible. Wash and scrub the shells and, when perfectly clean, grease them with a little butter or dripping. Put into each some flakes of fish, free from skin and bone, and then cover with suitably seasoned white sauce. Have ready some cooked potatoes, mash them with a little milk, and season with salt. Pile this on the top of the fish, mark with a fork, and place the shells in the oven until brown and thoroughly hot. Garnish with a sprig of parsley.

Minced meat may be put in the shell instead of fish, or hard-boiled egg cut in slices.

## Banana Surprises

*Required:* Bananas, Pastry, Jam, Cake or Biscuit Crumbs.

Peel as many small bananas as required, coat them with a little jam or fruit syrup, and roll in cake or biscuit crumbs. Roll out some pastry very thinly, and cut out rounds large enough to enclose a banana. Wet round the edges, lay a banana in the centre, and fold over. Press the edges well together, brush over the pastry with a little milk or water, sprinkle with sugar, and bake on a greased tin in the oven from fifteen to twenty minutes. These

Banana Surprises

may be served hot or cold. They are very good for the school luncheon and for picnic parties.

## Cocoa and Marshmallow Pie

| Pastry | 2 tablespoonfuls Sugar |
| 1 pint Milk | Vanilla Essence |
| 2 oz. Cornflour | ¼ lb. Marshmallows |
| 1 tablespoonful Cocoa or Chocolate Powder | 1 tablespoonful Cocoanut |

Line a flat dish or tin with any simple pastry, and bake it in the oven. Meanwhile, prepare the mixture for filling the pie. Heat most of the milk in a saucepan, and mix the cornflour and cocoa smoothly with the remainder. Add the

Scalloped Fish

mixture to the hot milk and stir over the fire until boiling. Simmer slowly about ten minutes, and add the sugar and flavouring. Put this into the pastry case and place the marshmallows, cut in halves, over the top. Sprinkle with cocoanut and brown the pie in the oven or under the grill.

Marshmallows are great favourites with children, and this pie is sure to be enjoyed.

## Pancakes with Apples

| ¼ lb. Flour | Sugar |
| ½ pint Milk | Lard for frying |
| 1 Egg | Stewed Apples |
| ¼ teaspoonful Salt | |

Cocoa and Marshmallow Pie

Put the flour and salt into a basin and make a well in the centre. Break in the egg and, with a wooden spoon, mix a little of the flour gradually into it. Then add half the milk by degrees, gathering in all the flour, and beat the batter until perfectly smooth and full of air bubbles. Pour in the remainder of the milk and stand for half an hour. To cook the pancakes: melt a small quantity of lard in a frying pan and, when smoking hot, pour in enough batter to cover the pan very thinly. When brown underneath, toss the pancake over or turn with a knife and brown the second side. Then slip the pancake on to a sheet of sugared paper, put a spoonful of hot stewed apple on one side, and roll up. Keep hot on a plate over hot water and proceed with the other pancakes in the same way. Sprinkle them with sugar before serving. This quantity should make six pancakes.

Pancakes are not new; ever since we can remember we have eaten them; but they need not always be served in the stereotyped way. Fillings of different kinds may be introduced—stewed fruit of any kind, provided it is not liquid, jam, lemon curd, or even a savoury meat mixture; or the pancakes may be served with a sauce, such as orange, lemon, or chocolate sauce; or hot maple sugar or golden syrup may be poured over them.

## Orange Jelly with Cream

| 3 oz. Tapioca | 2 oz. Brown Sugar |
| 1 pint Water | A little Cream or |
| 3 Oranges | Marshmallow Cream |

Use the small tapioca, wash it, and let it soak in the water for half an hour or so. Wipe the oranges, grate off the yellow rind, and add to the tapioca. Cook over a slow fire, stirring frequently until the tapioca turns quite clear. Then add the sugar and the strained juice of the three oranges. When cold this mixture will be set like a jelly. Pile it up in a dish and decorate with a little whipped and sweetened cream.

Custard may be served instead of cream; or marshmallow cream, which is sold in cartons, is very good and less expensive than real cream.

Lemon jelly can be made in the same way; or tapioca jelly, with chopped nuts and vanilla flavouring, will make another nice sweet.

# *The* Servant Question

### By Violet Bonham Carter

WAS there a "servant question" in the past? If there was, I was never conscious of its existence. The servants of my childhood presented no problems. We accepted them, and they seemed to accept one's own family and the points of the compass. They stand out vividly among the earliest landmarks of memory, as institutions — classics — personalities more familiar than those of any friend—and how much more indispensable!

I could never make out why they were called "servants." They seemed to me much more like rulers, each controlling a wide domain with an, on the whole, benevolent absolutism.

It was Susan's white paint on the stairs we were admonished every day not to kick, on our return, muddy-booted, from Hyde Park; it was by the ebb and flow of Mrs. L.'s largesse that our favourite pudding was given or withheld; it was Mr. C. who in a mellow mood would pour us out with a wink a wineglass of ginger-beer, that nectar of childhood, while our governess wasn't looking—and even in a hospitable moment admit us for a short time to the thrilling mysteries of "his" pantry, and to the still greater delights of his conversation (for he was a brilliant talker).

There was no room for discomfort or misgivings in these relationships. Were we taking too much from them? Giving too little? Was their work degrading? Was our dependence more degrading? Were we bloated parasites? Were they slaves? These were questions which it never occurred to us, nor, I honestly believe, to them, to ask. In those days the household seemed a natural unit, a harmonious organism of which they were integral parts, and in which they discharged by far the most important functions.

The white paint on the stairs, if it wasn't Susan's, was in a very literal sense "as good as" Susan's. It was her pride, her joy, her spiritual possession. Hers was the substance of ownership, ours the shadow. The same was true of Mrs. L.'s puddings and Mr. C.'s ginger-beer.

"I could never make out why they were called 'servants.' They seemed to me much more like rulers"

There was, it is true, even in those days a wistful underworld which rarely saw the light of day, those Nibelungs who toiled hidden away out of sight, the "under-servants." They seemed to possess nothing, by spiritual or material right, hardly even an hour of their own time. It was difficult to get into touch with them, to slip between the iron barriers of caste, which seemed to shut them off from the occupants of the "Room," and indeed, apparently, from those of all the other rooms in the house. I can remember being haunted by their plight, by their isolation, by their apparent negligibility and invisibility, and being only consoled by the reflection that they would one day emerge from this chrysalis of servitude, and be magically transformed into one of those great and powerful beings who now controlled their destinies. (All but the ODD man. There seems to be a tragic finality about his status. I don't know what odd men grow out of, but they never seem to grow into butlers.)

But all these things belong to a past order. They are changed now. The great houses are collapsing right and left, and with their fall is crumbling the awful majesty of the Upper Servant.

The war tore up domestic tradition by its roots. Staffs shrank, footmen vanished, "Room" and "Hall" melted into one (a far more revolutionary change this than if "Room" and "Dining-room" had joined forces). The grand old figures began to disappear and with them went much of the close personal relationship between employers and their servants. The whole domestic atmosphere appeared to change. There seemed no fixity of tenure among servants. The houses they inhabited no longer belonged to *them*. They ceased to have roots. When one went to see an old friend, one had no idea who was going to open the door. It was upsetting to be received by a strange, blank face and asked what one's name was. A race of nomadic temporaries drifted through households, refusing to cast anchor, committing themselves for a few weeks at the outside, and then off again, always on the same plea: "I feel so unsettled."

Among employers there was a new, plangent note whenever this subject of servants came up for discussion. The mere mention of them was an appeal for sympathy. "Servant worries? my *poor* dear—there's nothing like them. What an *impossible* lot of people! I never want to see one again," etc. . . . but these muffled wails culminated in a howl of bitter and heartfelt injury, when it was discovered that these "impossible people" were not to be had.

For one thing has not been changed by the war, and that is our complete and helpless dependence on them. It is a form of chronic invalidism without the excuse of disease. For those who have been accustomed to be "looked after" by others (and it doesn't much matter whether it is by two or five or fourteen others, because by some miraculous dispensation two are enabled to perform in some households the duties which it takes fourteen to do in others), it would be easier to part with almost anything. We look to our servants as we would to some great law of nature, operating with punctual power through foul and fair weather for the benefit of the just and the unjust alike, something we

# The Servant Question

have not deserved, but which cannot fail us.

Which of us, if given the choice as to whether the sun or our own servants should fail to rise next morning, would not unhesitatingly give up the sun?

It isn't that we are *incapable* of looking after ourselves. The war showed that many of the most pampered and apparently helpless employers could not merely look after themselves, but other people, with the utmost hardihood and efficiency. It is that we grudge spending time and energy on anything so dull. Servants liberate us. By standing like buffers between us and the leaden routine of daily drudgery, they endow our lives with freedom, spaciousness, and scope. Are we aware that in making these precious gifts to us they are, consciously or unconsciously, abdicating them for themselves? And is it not these very things—freedom, space, scope—that the servants of to-day are beginning to miss and, very naturally, to demand from us?

It is not *work* they mind, as anyone will realise who has tried (as I have) to induce them to make use of labour-saving appliances. Soon after I married I purchased at great cost a vacuum cleaner, mastered its complicated processes with difficulty, explained them with ease. . . . How by gently propelling it, you could mow the carpet of its dirt like a lawn, without ever stooping or using a muscle. How by affixing a kind of elephant's trunk, you could suck the dust from off the topmost bookshelves, the curtains, palmettes, etc., without so much as raising an arm.

The vacuum cleaner rusts and rots in my box-room to this day. It has never once been used. My housemaids have all, without exception, preferred to crawl for hours on all fours across what must seem like acres of carpet, brushing into their own faces a whirlwind of dust, which cannot but settle back again in the selfsame place it originally came from.

No, it is evidently not work they mind. Work is probably lighter now than it was. Wages are certainly higher than they were. And yet a ferment of "unrest" is undoubtedly at work, unrest the more genuine in that it exists and thrives without an organised campaign, without direction from Trade Union Headquarters, without so much as a Press launch behind it. It is, as Mr. Max Beerbohm says in his brilliant essay, "the mere Spirit of Time sneaking down the steps of areas, and leading to an infinite series of spontaneous and sporadic risings in isolated households."

To understand the promptings of this spirit, we cannot do better than imagine ourselves confronted, as some of us have been, as many of us may be any day, with the choice of a career. What are the factors that would deter us from going into service?

In my own case I should reply, first and foremost, lack of freedom and the absence of any fixed limit to one's day's work. In a factory one may work harder and more uncomfortably, but when the hour of release strikes, one belongs to oneself. In the evenings, half the day on Saturdays, and all day long on Sundays, the factory hand is a free woman. In service one

is never free. The black tyranny of the old days is gone, when mistresses forbade "followers," prescribed religions, and vetoed becoming coiffures in their maids; but there are still no defined limits, in terms of time, to the demands which a capricious and exacting personality may make upon them. And apart from the nervous exasperation produced in them by their employers, their relations with their fellow-servants must often be very trying. What would it be like, to be cooped up at close quarters with a chance collection of people, a kind of permanent house-party whose members had been thrown together not by choice or affinity, but by the sheerest accident? I can imagine no greater strain, and the fact that it must exist makes the unshakeable loyalty of servants to one another the more amazing and admirable.

To afford opportunities for frequent escape from this almost intolerably close proximity, and to give more freedom should, I feel sure, be the first aim and effort of all employers. Sooner or later, with or without trade unions, we *must*

---

### DIVORCE

Not easier but *fairer* divorce: It is upon this change in English law that public opinion is at present divided. Read Lady Bonham Carter's brilliant article on the subject next month

---

get to eight-hourly shifts in domestic service as elsewhere. How easily they could be introduced to-morrow but for those hidebound hierarchies of specialists, who will not consent to do "someone else's work." The housemaid who won't open a door, the parlourmaid who won't make a bed, etc., these are throwing away hours of leisure and tracts of freedom for each other and themselves. Abroad this rigid specialism is unheard-of. In France and Italy people live happily with two or three interchangeable and amazingly versatile Jacks- (and Jills-) of-all-trades, each one of whom can make an omelette, clean a room, and wait at table. Even in America, where servants are notoriously unprocurable, though wages are enormous ($800 a year for a good cook and $280 for an odd man), far fewer are kept and there is a far greater elasticity and interchangeability of function, resulting in a wider freedom for all. It is possible that quite the same perfection of execution may not be retained, but if so, this is one of the things we must be prepared to sacrifice.

One other point. The people who talk glibly about the "comfort" of being in service should go over a few London houses, and not neglect a visit to the basement. I think in the great majority of cases they would be unutterably shocked.

At the bottom of lovely, airy houses, flooded with sunshine, sometimes look-

ing out over a wide sweep of green park, you will find a damp, black basement to which daylight rarely penetrates, and in which it would be difficult to ask anything but a rat or a black-beetle to make itself at home. Down below there, separated only by a thin wafer of ceiling from us, who roam above in air and light, there is a community of human beings, to whom we owe the whole comfort of our lives and for whose well-being we are very directly responsible.

Abundant freedom, a standard of comfort which must at least include air and daylight, wages as generous as you can possibly afford to make them (wages are not only the meanest, but also the stupidest, of all forms of economy), these are the essential claims of every worker on his employer. But essential as they are, these things are not in themselves enough to justify the domestic servant. It is vital that the head of a household should establish between herself and her servants that sense of partnership and intimacy which alone can make their relationship a possible one. Mutual affection is the only basis on which domestic service can decently rest. It can never become an impersonal business transaction. And there must be confidence. Servants know so much about one, that if they are to understand one properly, one must tell them more. I never say to my cook, "Eight for dinner." I tell her who is coming. It is more amusing for her to know who is to enjoy the fruits of her labour, and with this knowledge she naturally cooks a far more intelligent meal.

In this connection I always recall a snatch of dialogue between my stepmother and the butler of our childhood. C.: "Lord Spencer called to see you. m'm." "Oh, C., why didn't you ask him to wait?" "I did, m'm, but he couldn't." "Oh, C., if only you had asked him to dinner!" "I did, m'm, and he's coming." This fearless initiative might have alarmed some employers, but it was guided by an unerring *flair* which never blundered. By intimacy and confidence you can enlist brains and hearts, as well as bodies, in your service—and a body working without brain or heart is slavery, whatever the work and whatever the wage.

There is one other aspect of domestic service which must tease a philosophic mind, and that is the question that intermittently haunts every one of us in our pursuit of a livelihood: "Apart from the fact that I live by it, is this work worth doing? Is it worth while spending my life making other people's easier for them? Spending my time and strength in order to save theirs?" I think it all depends on what "they" do with the time and strength thus saved. And it is this spending of strength and leisure and freedom so generously given, that the people of this country, not servants alone, but all who work, are watching more closely and more narrowly day by day.

*Violet Bonham Carter*

# Things You Don't Learn

### *By* Muriel Wrinch

## Animal History

### *At the Beginning of Time*

LONG ago—when time was young, when the earth had split off, a fiery flaming mass, from the big ball of fire from which the universe was fashioned, when it began to cool and to move in its appointed path round the sun—animals and plants began to live on the earth's surface.

It was in the sea that life started first, for that was the coolest place in the world. The water which had collected from the earth's surface—just as mist forms over the window-panes when the room is warm and the air outside is cold—ran down into the hollows on the earth's surface and made the cool seas in which animals could live even so long ago as when the earth began. You, who have had a refreshing dip on a hot day, will know how cool water may be; but the hot sand which scorches your feet is cold in comparison with the burning rock which formed the margins of the ancient seas. I expect the animals had to stay in the sea for a very long time indeed, for if they had tried to crawl on to dry land their damp little feet would have been burned right away.

But when the earth became cooler, some of the animals began to crawl out of the sea and the bodies of some of the queer animal baby-things in the water changed little by little to meet the new conditions of life. These slow changes went on during thousands of years. *But neither you nor I, nor the wisest nor the oldest nor the most religious man in the world, knows where the first animal came from nor how it was born!*

## At The Zoo

### *The Best Way to Enjoy it*

THE Zoo of to-day would never have existed if the first tiny baby animal had not been born in the sea. Such a tiny thing it was that we cannot see it with our own eyes and have to borrow the eyes of a very complicated instrument called the microscope to see it at all. Yet, in one sense, this one little creature was the father and mother of all the animals to come.

I'm sure the striped panther at the Zoo doesn't know this! When I arrived

**The Grey and Brown Squirrel**

at the lion-house, where he lives, he was just looking out for his dinner, which is always served punctually at three o'clock. He kept his big green eyes on the path by which the keeper would approach and every now and then he looked at the clock!

### *Can Animals Tell the Time?*

I wondered if the clock had been put right in the middle of the wall opposite the cages in the lion-house in order that all the animals might see it, but I don't really know whether or not animals *can* tell the time. The animal next door to the panther was a lynx—the sort of person who doesn't like to show he is excited, but he couldn't help it now and then, his meat was so nice.

Zoologists and learned people talk about the number of vertebræ a donkey has, and the cranial nerves of a rabbit. I don't want to spoil the Zoo for you by suggesting you should think about difficult problems like these—but I have a few suggestions by which you can use your own knowledge to make the Zoo a more interesting place.

## Backbones

### *The Difference they Make*

FIRST you can divide the animals into classes containing those which have a backbone and those which have not. Amongst those who have backbones, some are covered with fur; these are the mammals who have their babies born alive and feed them until they are old enough to look after themselves. Others have feathers and lay eggs from which the baby birds come. Others have a covering of scales and they, too, lay eggs. But snakes, instead of looking after their eggs, generally lay them in a nice warm place and leave them to hatch by themselves. The animals with slimy skins with no feathers or fur or scales—the frogs and toads—are called amphibians, *amphi* meaning *both,* since they live both in air and water. And there are the fishes who live entirely in the water and have scaly bodies and gill slits and many other characteristics which show us that they make a special group in the big animal family. The animals without backbones are too numerous and too difficult to classify. The lobsters and crabs make up, by themselves, the group of shell-fish, but all the little families are not so clearly divided.

Below is a scheme you might draw up of the animals you have seen at the Zoo, and you can add to it as you see more and more of the animals of the world. Another thing you can notice at the Zoo is the habits of the animals. By their movements you can tell how they live and where, whether they are accustomed to walk on soft grass or desert sand, in woods or open places. And the animals have definite personalities. Some of them are very courageous, others are very shy, all of them have something to teach us in their own way.

### *Animals With Backbones*

*Mammals*: Tiger, kangaroo, squirrel, etc.

*Birds*: Eagle, sparrow, robin, etc.
*Reptiles*: Snake, slowworm, tortoise.
*Amphibians*: Frogs, toads, etc.
*Fishes*: Cod, roach, perch, stickleback, etc.

### *Animals Without Backbones*

Lobsters, crabs, sea-anemones, earthworms, and snails.

# *At School*

*Decorations*
*By* Elizabeth Montgomery

## Samosaurus

### *A Puppet Dragon*

I WENT not long ago to a puppet show, a little theatre with jointed wooden dolls, pulled on strings, for the actors. The little girls and their dolls at the top of the page are watching them with great interest. There was Harlequin, in his patches, singing his funny songs, and Pimpinella, the modern Columbine, with her round blue eyes and white frock and flaming red hair, and Pantaloon, too, an old old puppet with his long white beard and apple-red face. A pin could have been heard to drop on the floor as these wooden dollies danced; they all seemed alive, yet they were made of wood and no one could see who was pulling the strings! By the time you read this article, the Puppet-show will have moved from London, but I hope this will be the first of many marion-ette theatres which grown-up children, as well as boys and girls, all enjoy. Puppet-shows have been neglected for many years, but a hundred years ago they were the fashion in theatre-land.

### *A Dragon who Plays the Piano*

Samosaurus, the big green dragon, with his wooden scaly back and brown - leather tummy, was my favourite puppet. He has been mentioned in all the grown-up papers and praised for his dewy and pathetic eyes and his doggy expressions. This dragon is learning to play the piano and to sing—or so the showman says—yet his throat and his fingers are, after all, only made of wood! 

The colours on the puppet stage were the kind of colours we should see every-where—clear, bright, and simple. The curtain was orange, the clear orange you get by mixing red and yellow in equal quantities, and the background dull of olive-green—a *basic* colour, artists call it. People are beginning to realise what beautiful effects are obtained by putting on a few clear colours in a dark setting.

## Painting

### *Many Colours from Five*

IF you have enough pocket-money, buy five tubes of watercolour paint, red, blue, yellow, brown, and black. Get them of the best quality you can afford and buy several white saucers, a thick brush, and a brush which comes to a fine point. Then discard your old paint-box and begin your colour work all over again.

If you are to be a real artist you will

### The King of Spain

The King of Spain, with thrice ten thousand men,
Marched up the hill and then marched down again.

"There was an old woman"

Drawings by Lovat Fraser from "Nursery Rhymes"

*By Permission of Thomas Nelson & Sons, Ltd. (incorporating T. C. & E. C. Jack)*

not be content unless you mix your colours yourself. Experiment, and see how many different colours you can obtain from mixing red, blue, and yellow—the three primary colours. Keep your black and brown paint for heightening the effect you produce. If you make a chart showing how different combinations of colours give you colours of different tones and shades, you will have, from a few tubes, a really good paintbox.

There is a drawing by Lovat Fraser in this column for you to redraw and colour yourselves. In the painting, the hillside is bright green and the soldiers red. The advance-guard is yellow, and the flags of the army are red and yellow. This will give you an idea of what the picture should look like when it is done.

## Keeping Pets

### *Making a Hutch*

NOT so very long ago I used to keep rabbits and white rats myself, and my guinea-pigs —I had several families of them— used to live in *flats*! These were made by fitting in shelves, made of wood cut exactly to the size of the floor of the hutch and resting on ledges formed by nailing strips of wood along the side walls. My white rats lived in a wooden box with wire netting in front, and a wooden roof which took on and off. They had black heads and long black tails, and lived on millet and tiny pieces of cheese and meat.

Whatever your pets, remember that every living thing has certain needs. Every animal, big or little, must have suitable food and water given regularly, and a clean house.

You have no hutch? Well, it is simple enough to make one, if you can get a large sugar-box from the grocer. The first thing to remember is that it must be water-tight, so stop up all the small holes and crevices with plasticine, before giving the whole box a coat of solignum. Over three-quarters of the open side tack wire netting, the free edge of the netting being tacked on to a small strip of wood just long enough to stretch from top to bottom of the hutch. A door can be made by taking a piece of wood to fit the rest of the opening.

1923

"Hark-a-bye Baby—"

Western Electric
LOUD SPEAKING EQUIPMENT
for
LISTENING IN

(WHOLESALE ONLY) OBTAINABLE OF ALL HIGH-CLASS DEALERS

When the weather is at all fine serve children's meals out of doors. You can see from the illustration that even the elephant enjoys this

1923

# *Fruit Desserts for Tiny Tots*

THE nursery dessert is a most important part of the midday meal. It ought to be light and digestible and at the same time nourishing enough to form a substantial part of the meal and not be added merely as a supplement. While the fresh fruits are in season it is always well to include them in some form or other in the daily menu.

The chief value in fruit lies in the sugar, acids, and salts it contains; it also cools the blood and corrects any tendency to constipation. The use of raw fruit is also advocated for older children, on account of its cleansing action on the teeth; a raw apple eaten at the end of a meal being as good as the use of a tooth-brush.

The selection and use of fruit for young children demand careful consideration, and it must be used moderately at all times. It is of the utmost importance to have it fresh, ripe, and in good condition. The juice of fresh fruit is, as a rule, perfectly wholesome, and may be used long before fruit in its more solid form is taken. Thus, orange juice and grape juice are given in small quantities to mere infants.

The next stage would be a cooked fruit pulp. Baked bananas or baked apples, for example, will always form a staple part of children's diet, and may be given frequently. An uncooked banana, if perfectly ripe, can also be mashed up with a silver fork and given at an early stage, with a little cream and sugar added. Or the pulp of a baked apple may be beaten up with a fork until smooth, and then a small amount of cream or custard added. Served in a pretty cup or custard-glass this makes a very inviting dish.

With regard to the summer fruits, especially those with seeds and stones, those should always be eaten in moderation by young children, as they are frequently the cause of serious upsets.

It is often safer to use the juice only, or to stew the fruit and make a purée. This juice or purée can be made up in many delightful ways, which will be appreciated by the little ones.

For example, the juice or purée may be made into a jelly by adding to it a small quantity of instantaneous gelatine, dissolved in a little hot water and sugared to taste. With regard to the sugar, it is always better to under-sweeten any mixture, as every child likes to sprinkle an extra supply over the surface. The jelly should be set in small cups or moulds, which can be turned out when required. Custard or cream should be served with the jelly to make it more nourishing, and there might be a biscuit or sponge cake, too.

Fruit juice can also be used as a sauce for any simple pudding, such as a blancmange, custard, or any of the cereals cooked in milk. The juice may be used raw with a little sugar, or it may be steamed until heated through.

A purée of cooked or raw fruit, made by rubbing the fruit through a sieve, may be used for making a "*fool*." The purée should be fairly thick. Mix it with some thick cream or custard, sweeten to taste, and beat with a wooden spoon for a few minutes. Serve in a custard-glass with biscuits. Or a *fruit whip* may be made: Warm the purée for this, and to each cupful allow 1 egg. Beat up the yolk of egg in a basin with a little sugar, and pour the purée on to it, stirring all the time. Whip the white of egg to a stiff froth and stir it lightly in just before serving. Sprinkle with a little pink sugar, and this will delight any child.

A *Children's Fruit Tart* is another excellent dish for summer. First put some stewed fruit in a greased pie-dish. Then cut some sponge-cake in thin slices, soak them in yolk of egg and milk, and

place them on the top of the fruit instead of pastry. Bake in a moderate oven until brown. Whip up the white of egg to a stiff froth, mix a little sugar with it, and pile it on the top of the tart. Return to the oven for a few minutes to set, then sprinkle with sugar, and serve hot or cold.

*Sago or Tapioca with Fruit* makes another light and appetising pudding. Use the fine tapioca or sago, soak the required amount in water, and then cook it until it turns clear. Add some fruit, cook for a short time longer, and sweeten to taste. Sliced apples, picked raspberries or loganberries, peeled apricots or peaches, etc., may be used, or the juice of any fruit may be used along with water for the cooking of the cereal. Serve hot or cold with milk or cream. A variation of this pudding is to cook the sago or tapioca in milk, to let it cool, and then to stir in the yolk of an egg to each half-pint, and a small cupful of fruit purée. Pour this into a pie-dish, make a meringue with the white of the egg and a little sugar, put it on the top, and place in the oven to set and brown slightly.

*Emergency Pudding* is another example of how fruit and a milk pudding can be combined. Simmer ground rice in milk, or cook in a double boiler until soft and rather thick. To each cupful allow 1 white of egg. Beat it up and stir it lightly into the mixture. Cook 2 minutes to set the white, but leave it light and frothy. Put a cupful of stewed or crushed fruit into a pie-dish and pour the white mixture over. Serve warm or cold.

A *Fruit Trifle* makes a pretty dish for a children's party. Slice some sponge-cake and put it into a glass dish or in individual cups. Pour over red fruit syrup to soak the cake, and let it stand. Cover with whipped cream or custard and decorate with small fancy biscuits.

# Your Boy's Ambition

## *Good Teeth will help his Career*

Your boy probably has confided to you his ideas as to what he would like to be "when he grows up." Teach him that whatever this may be, he will have to be strong and healthy, and that good health depends on sound, clean teeth.

Explain to your boy that the surface of the enamel which protects the teeth is formed into millions of miniature waves and facets (visible only through a powerful magnifying glass) which split up and reflect the light just as does a diamond.

This many-angled reflection of light from the hard bright surface of the little facets makes the teeth glisten and look strong and manly.

Of course, if the teeth are not cleaned, the facets get covered with greasy food deposits and could no more shine and gleam than could a diamond covered with mud. Also, the greasy deposits ferment and set up an acid which eats into the enamel and causes toothache and decay. Therefore, teeth must be cleaned thoroughly at least twice a day. For this purpose Gibbs Dentifrice is ideal.

Gibbs Dentifrice washes away all food deposits, polishes the enamel without scratching the delicate facets, ensures a life-time of good teeth, and keeps the mouth sweet and wholesome always. Leading British Dental Authority endorse this fact.

Let your boy experience for himself the refreshing benefit of Gibbs Dentifrice. Buy him his own case to-day.

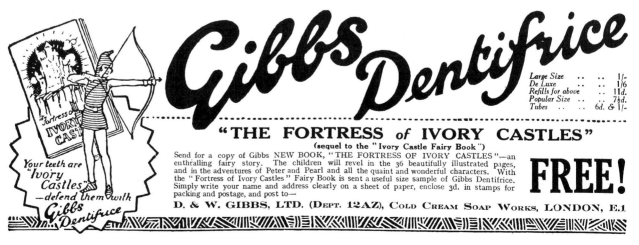

# *Polly Pratt* Goes to the Seaside
### *By* Sheila Young

1923

1924

# Now for the last Effort of the Day

There's no "please carry me" with CHILPRUFE youngsters. They glory in every exercise of their strength, and keep happily on until the very moment their heads touch the pillow. The sure protection of CHILPRUFE against the effects of cold and damp keep them always splendidly fit—cosy, comfy and contented by night and day.

# CHILPRUFE *for* CHILDREN

CHILPRUFE consists solely of the Purest Wool, finished by a secret process. This renders CHILPRUFE infinitely more protective than any other form of wool. Made in a complete range of undergarments, skilfully cut, daintily trimmed, embracing every requirement from the tiniest tot upwards.

### RENOVATIONS SERVICE

If you have any out-grown CHILPRUFE garments, or garments worn in places, send them to us—we can increase the size and repair the weak places at very little cost.

For SPRING AND SUMMER WEAR, ask for No. 436, the same unparalleled quality, but lighter in weight to meet the demands of the warmer weather.

**Ask your Draper for a copy of the Chilprufe Price List.**

*If unable to obtain Chilprufe, write addressed to the firm for name of nearest Agent.*

THE CHILPRUFE MANFG. CO.
(John A. Bolton, M.I.H., Proprietor)
LEICESTER

# Books to Read

## " *The Pedlar's Pack* "

**H**ERE is a book written specially for you by the mother of the famous Mr. Baldwin. Hers is a well-known family, and her famous son may well be proud of his ancestry. One of Mrs. Baldwin's sisters married the father of Mr. Rudyard Kipling; another married Burne-Jones, the great pre-Raphaelite painter; yet a third is the wife of Sir Edward Poynter.

It is Lady Poynter who first heard the fairy-tales in the "Pedlar's Pack," for she was the interested little listener when in nursery days her older sister spun these tales.

And very good tales they are—" The Giant's Baby," a story of the big baby who drained a cup of milk at a draught and roared for more, will amuse you mightily. But it was not so amusing for the poor labourer who had found the baby screaming under the hedge on a cold winter's night, for the child drank as much in one sip as Dick, a boy of eight years old, took at a meal. But it all ends up quite happily, and so do the eight other fairy-stories. A youth with cheeks as " red as apples, and grey eyes shining like stars, and a head covered with fair curls," and a king, and a prime minister, and princesses and twins and shepherds figure in the noble company. Truly—

> " *There's that within this book that*
> *suits young and old.*
> *In choice of wares a very Pedlar's*
> *Pack !* "

(*The Pedlar's Pack*, by Mrs. Alfred Baldwin, with coloured illustrations by Chas. Pears. Chambers, 6s.)

## *Jolly School Stories*

" Jan of the Fourth " and " Captain Cara " are very nice girls indeed. Christine Chaundler tells you all about them in these two books, published by Nisbets at 6s. each. " The Only Day Girl," by Dorothea Moore, published by the same firm in the same edition, is also well worth reading.

" ' BEING A GOOD NOTICER IS TERRIBLY IMPORTANT ' "
*From " The Voyages of Dr. Dolittle "*      *J nathan Cape*

# Dr. Dolittle

## *A Great New Book*

**D**R. DOLITTLE, of whose voyages I have just been reading (*The Voyages of Dr. Dolittle*, by Hugh Lofting; Jonathan Cape, 7s. 6d.) must have been a very wonderful doctor indeed. He had quite a good practice at one time, but as he would insist on keeping so many animals about the surgery, his patients gradually left him.

Polynesia, the parrot, and the cats-meat man between them managed to launch the doctor on his new career as an animal medical man. And Chee-Chee, the traveller, whom you see arriving home in the picture, was a wonderful help too.

The doctor learnt the language of the shell-fishes, and he knew when sick horses wanted spectacles, and he had a private Zoo with little stone houses with locks on the inside, so that the animals

### DOLITTLE FARM

**Read how to make this little Farm**

could go and shut themselves in at any time they wanted, to get away from the annoyance of other animals and people who might come there. " In my Zoo," says Dr. Dolittle, "every animal stays here because he likes it, not because he is made to."

One of the reasons all Dr. Dolittle's animals are so happy is that he does notice things so. He knew all about tiny things that might make an animal unhappy. As Polynesia said to Tommy Stubbins, the cobbler's son, who wanted to learn as much about animals as Dr. Dolittle did—" Being a good noticer is terribly important.'

The doctor was so observant that if he saw two cock-starlings on an apple tree he would be able to tell them apart next day if he had only taken one good look at them.

Most of you will envy Tommy Stubbins, the doctor's assistant, when you read this book. He was, indeed, a very fortunate boy.

Tommy didn't go to school like ordinary little boys—he learnt everything from the Doctor and Polynesia, his lessons including most of the animal languages.

You are sure to enjoy all this, not to mention the story of the voyage of the *Curlew*, with its stowaways, disasters, and adventures, and the very strange things that happened on Spider-monkey Island.

# Dolittle Farm

## *Keeping Wooden Animals*

**D**R. DOLITTLE would certainly have done better to keep his animals in a special farmyard instead of just letting them wander into every room in the house in the way they did. If only he had done so he would not have frightened away the paying animal patients sent by their fond owners for medical treatment. However, that's a bit of the story, and you can read it for yourself. What I want to explain is how to make a farmyard for the animals you have made yourself as described on the previous page.

First of all, take a piece of cardboard, or better still of wood, square or oblong in shape, as big as the lid of a hatbox. The first thing to do is to make a fence to enclose the yard all round. This can be cut out of cardboard painted green, which should be cut as shown in the illustration, and if it is bent at the dotted line can be glued firmly to the base.

Then you must decide where your sheep and cows are to graze, and here you can glue down a square of Turkish towelling, which if brushed up and painted green can be made to look very like grass. With cardboard paling round the edges they will be made into fields. If you want a pond in your field, cut a round hole in the towelling before you lay it down, and put a square of glass underneath.

Cowsheds and pigsties can be made of plasticine with red roofs—made sloping so that when it rains the animals don't get wet, the water pouring off the roof as it does with our houses. The construction of these I will explain more fully next month. But you will need no directions as to how to make humpy fields and valleys by putting lumps of plasticine or heaps of sand beneath the green surface of your fields. Don't forget to put the sheds of the grazing animals near the fields in which they live during the day.

Trees can be made of sprigs from the garden, or with moss and twigs, or drawn on cardboard and mounted like the toy animals.

" A TRAVELLER ARRIVES."
*From " The Voyages of Dr. Dolittle "*      *By Permission*

1924

# Things You Don't

*Decorations by*
*Elizabeth Montgomery*

## Kaffir Toys

### Farms of Clay and Stones

FAR away in South Africa, three weeks' journey over the sea, live the little Kaffir children. They are very happy little people, playing all day long in the sun, and always, in spite of the fact that they have never been given toys, they have plenty of playthings. The little Kaffirs make their own toys, and very fine some of them are too—much better than many found in our shops.

Yet they only use rough materials—clay and sticks and stones, and pieces of bark.

The little boys make horses and cattle from clay, and build them a pen of stones for their home, driving them into the fields in the morning and back home at night, just as they see their fathers do. They make fine whips of sticks, with leather thongs attached, and good outhouses of mud and old pieces of matting.

### Dolls and Dolls' Houses

The little girls, too, make houses for their dolls. They take some broad flat stones, set them in a circle, and cover them with cow-dung to make a little round hut similar in shape to the mat huts in which their parents live. Sometimes they can find an old deserted anthill, and scooping the inside away make a little home for their dolly.

The doll herself is often made only of a piece of bark. She has a gay rag tied round her shoulders, as a cape, secured with a thread, upon which one or two beads left from the mother kaffir's head-work have been strung.

The dolly has cooking utensils made of clay, a little bed of hay and a windscreen. There is no end to the things which can be made for her.

The boys and girls who read these pages can easily make toys like these.

## Seeds

### How Seeds leave Home

IT is Autumn, and many little seeds are setting out to begin life on their own. Tiny feathered seeds, big winged seeds, seeds with prickles—all these we find as we ramble through the country.

Some have beautiful feathering tufts which waft them over the meadows. Such are the seeds of the dandelion, and when you blow the "clock" to tell the time, you are helping the dandelion plant to distribute its seeds.

The big "winged" seeds can also fly some distance. The sycamore "keys" have a splendid journey as they flutter along in the breeze, and so do the twisted green fruits of the ash as they travel gaily over the lawn.

The tall poppies keep their round black seeds in the case, which alone remains of the poppy flower in the autumn. Gently the stalk sways to and fro, and the little seeds get thrown out through the holes round the top of the seed case and so set up in life some distance away from their parent.

The mistletoe has lovely silver-white berries of which the thrush is very fond, but the gummy seeds inside the pulp stick fast to his beak so that he must rub it very hard against the rough bark of the oak or elm to get them off. That is why in winter we can see green bunches of mistletoe hanging high amidst bare branches.

## The Wishing-Ring

### One Million Pounds

ONCE upon a time there lived a poor farmer, who was very much worried about his farm. He had barely enough money to buy his seeds, and he owned such a tiny piece of ground that had all the crops yielded a hundredfold he would not have been rich.

One day as he was sitting beneath a hedge a witch passed by. "Hey! why so sad?" said she, and dug him in the ribs with her broomstick. "My house needs repair and my wife needs a new hat and I have no money," said the farmer. "That is soon settled," said the old lady briskly. "Under yon tree there lies a wishing-ring. Find it and you shall have one wish."

So the farmer set out for the big tree the witch had pointed out. It was farther away than he thought. His knees ached and his feet were sore by the time he got there. But all the trouble was worth while. In a little golden box under the tree lay the golden ring.

The farmer slipped it on his finger and started for home. But he was an inquisitive fellow, and as he passed the goldsmith's shop he went in to inquire the value of the ring.

"No value at all," said the goldsmith.

"Oh, yes," said the farmer, nettled. "It is worth more than all you possess. With this ring on my finger I can have anything I wish for."

### In the Night

The goldsmith was an avaricious man. After a little conversation he offered to put the farmer up for the night. The goldsmith took care to give him a good supper and a good bed, and the farmer slept so soundly that he felt nothing when late that night the host took the ring from his finger and put one exactly like it in its stead.

"Oh," said the goldsmith, in high glee, "now for my wish." He slipped the stolen ring on his finger and, trembling with eagerness, locked himself in his store room. "I want one million pounds," said he eagerly.

Then, "plonk," came the first coin. He tried to reach the door, but could not, and the gold fell so fast that it buried him and he fell through the floor into the cellar.

And in the morning, "How very sad," said the goldsmith's friends when they found the still figure beneath the heap of coins.

# Learn At School

## By
## Muriel Wrinch

**1924**

## Good Luck

### Through Hard Work

BUT our little farmer, rising refreshed in the morning, tramped away home to tell his wife about the wonderful ring. There it gleamed upon his finger. He had no suspicion it was not the real one.

"Shall you wish for a little piece more ground?" said his wife eagerly, seeing prosperity before them. "I think I could get that if I work," said the farmer. "It is a pity to waste this one wish." And he did work, and made enough money to buy another small piece of ground.

Next year his wife said: "What about wishing for a horse? Then I could drive to market in fine style to sell my eggs." For you see by this time the farmer had been able to buy her a fine new hat, and naturally she wished to show it off.

"I think I could get that if I work," said the farmer; "it is a pity to waste the one wish on that." And he worked and made enough money to buy a horse.

The next year it was the same, and the next. The farmer's wife suggested a herd of cattle, a flock of sheep, a litter of pigs, and each time the farmer saved up his wish till he could decide what he wanted most, and worked instead to buy the cattle or the sheep or the pigs.

### The End of the Ring

The years rolled by. The farmer was a rich man. He drove to church every Sunday in his own carriage and had Sunday dinner of roast beef and Yorkshire pudding with the squire.

And still the years rolled on and the wish was not wished. But the farmer was more prosperous than ever.

At last, when the farmer and his wife were very old, God blessed them by allowing them both to die on the same day.

The farmer's sons saw the ring on the father's finger. "Let's take it off," said one. "No," said the others; "our father loved that ring. Leave it with him. Perhaps our mother gave it to him when she was young."

And so it came about that no one ever knew the ring had been changed. But that didn't matter, for you see the farmer's ring had brought him luck, although it wasn't the magic luck he thought he wanted.

## Crystal Grasses

### Preserved by Alum

IN September all the grasses are ripening. Dip some of the grasses in a strong solution of alum and leave to dry.

Crystals will form on the grass-heads, which will make pretty decorations, especially if a little red or blue ink has been added to the solution.

The Witch of the Wishing Ring

## The Wind

### Why Does it Blow?

WHEN air becomes warm, it takes up more room than when it is cool. It becomes lighter and rises, while fresh colder air blows in and takes its place.

That is why there is usually a breeze at the seaside. The land grows warm in the sunshine, while the sea remains comparatively cool, so there is generally a flow of cooler air from the sea taking the place of the warm air rising from the land. These differences of temperature occur all over the world. Big areas of land and water become unequally hot and thus make the layers of air above them unequal in temperature.

## A Letter

### To Boys and Girls

I HOPE many thousands of boys and girls are reading "Things You Don't Learn at School" each month. There are thousands of grown-up readers of GOOD HOUSEKEEPING, so that I hope there are thousands of readers of this "Magazine in Miniature" too. I should like to have letters from all of you. I should like to know the dates of birthdays, so that I can send you "Many Happy Returns." I should like to know about pet guinea-pigs and rabbits, and about your postage stamps and other hobbies. I should like to know how you are getting on at school, about the lessons you like best, and what you want to be.

### How I can Help You

I, in my turn, can help you. I can advise you what to do for your pets when they are ill; I can tell you about the profession you want to follow—how long it takes to become a doctor, or a teacher, or an engineer, and what you have to do to become a chemist or a nurse; I can explain about objects you find in the field and do not recognise. I love getting letters and answering them, and if you write to me as you would to any other friend, I shall feel I know many boys and girls I could not know otherwise.

Congratulations to Mea Allen, who sent me a very nice letter from Glasgow, giving all the answers to the Posers in the June Number. Does she or anyone who learns Chemistry at school know the reason one can make crystal grasses as described in column five? There is a fine subject for a letter. I shall expect a very full post-bag this month.

# The LAUNCHING of Sons And Daughters

## By
## H. G. Wells

*What is the role of the modern father and mother? How are they to control their instinctive possessiveness, their sometimes too-aggressive solicitude?*

Illustrations by F. E. Hiley

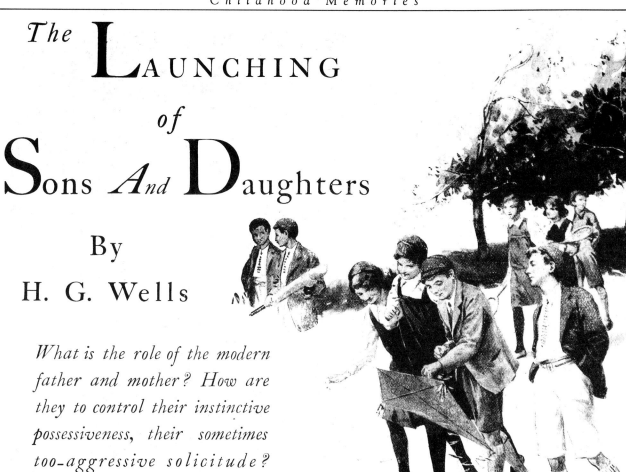

HOW far is it wise and desirable that the modern parent should direct and control the start in life of son or daughter? We no longer think of keeping them in tutelage until our deaths release them. That may have been wise and even necessary in the larger, more self-contained family life of the past. Now parents live longer and are reluctant to become venerable. They travel, they dine abroad, they dance, they refuse to differentiate themselves from youth. A brighter, more varied and active world is more and more impatient of the homely wits of home-staying youth. Everything conspires to push the young out to independence and self-reliance.

If reverence and obedience diminish between father and son and mother and daughter under the new conditions there open out new possibilities of friendship and co-operation. What is the rôle of the modern father and mother? How are they to control their instinctive possessiveness, their sometimes too-aggressive solicitude for their children? Where lies the golden mean between affectionate fussiness and a too-perfected indifference?

The attitude of the parent in the simple past was purely one of ownership. It was "*my* son" or "*my* daughter"; the young people were told just exactly how to think and behave, and if they were recalcitrant they were disinherited and disowned. The modern parent is reminding himself continually that "this boy belongs not to me but to himself." There is a quickened conscience nowadays about parentage. "I have launched him into the world with my weaknesses of soul and body. It's my duty to see he has a fair chance." But is it giving son or daughter a fair chance, just to push him or her out into the world with an allowance and freedom to make every possible blunder? A good many of us nowadays do that; we shirk our responsibility with a fine air of generosity. It isn't so simple a business as that.

The problem for the parent is to contrive such an amiable detachment that the wonderful, the almost divine Daddy of childhood, and the resourceful, all-providing Mummy, may

**At an early age—fourteen or fifteen say— the parent who can afford it should let the son or daughter have a banking account**

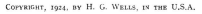
1924

In a more varied and active world everything conspires to push the young out to independence and self-reliance

*Lizzie Caswal Smith*

*1924*

gradually be converted into the nearest, best, and most trusted of friends. The problem for the parent is to let this apparently almost inadvertent launch slide safely into safe waters, and to remain near at hand and trusted sufficiently to be consulted in doubt or trouble.

This is not a natural process. There is no instinctive tendency for an adult son to be his father's close friend; nor for a daughter to become her mother's intimate companion. In the past they were kept under, resentful enough in many cases. Modern psychology tells us that an almost instinctive antagonism develops between father and son and mother and daughter as adolescence is approached. Parental pride does not exclude an almost hostile overbearingness and a distrustful restraint. Through all the ages, so soon as the phase of passionate care and protection is past, the parent has stood in the way of the maturing young, a kindred being already in full possession of everything they would grasp and take. The primitive factors make for final conflict and separation:

that was Nature's way. The ancestral animal, the old man of the herd, was a killer of insurgent sons, the daughter was her mother's rival, and all the fundamental human institutions, the life of law and co-operation that has replaced the small patriarchal herd, are framed on the mitigation and sublimation of these primordial impulses.

A generation or so back, this deep-lying, hidden, and forbidden con-

Our civilised life to-day is built in this matter, as in most elemental issues, upon suppressions.

flict was not realised. Its influence was felt; it led to strange incoherent reactions, but all established sentiment and tradition was

*Continued overleaf*

It is very magnificent for a son to be given an automobile, but it is far better that the boy have the education of buying it

1924

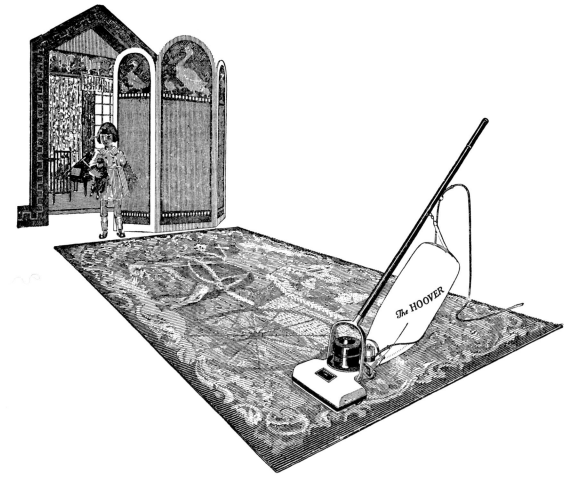

# If Only For Your Children's Sake

More and more as winter comes your children must play indoors—with the nursery carpet as their playground.

And often little hands and knees will be in close contact with that carpet; and sometimes little fingers that have pressed deep into its pile will make dangerous acquaintance with their owner's mouth.

Are you sure of the absolute, hygienic cleanliness of your carpets?

Surface sweeping will not effect that. Only the Hoover can guarantee it, because only the Hoover *beats* out all the dangerous, germ-harbouring dirt, from the depths of carpets, as it sweeps them electrically and suctions away all this loosened, swept-up dirt and dust into its dust-proof bag.

And the Hoover does all this in one easy, rapid operation which scatters no dust, to filter into your children's lungs, and cause mysterious illnesses.

A "Servant to the Home," the Hoover's thorough, sanitary cleaning is needed most of all in the nursery. Act now. Any Hoover dealer will gladly give you a demonstration of the Hoover on your own carpets. It commits you to nothing—that is understood—but you will be amazed at the quantity of dirt, dangerous dirt, the Hoover extracts from a carpet usually cleaned by other methods.

Only £3. 19s. down and 31s. a month for a short time pays for the Hoover while you use it. There is also a larger model for hotels, clubs, offices and large residences. Write for illustrated booklet and names of nearest Hoover dealers.

Hoover Limited, 288, Regent Street, London, W. 1,
and at Birmingham, Manchester, Leeds and Glasgow

# The HOOVER

## It BEATS.... as it Sweeps    as it Cleans    REG. TRADE MARK

# The Launching of Sons and Daughters

*(Continued)*

against its open recognition. It seemed right and proper that parent and child should go on in close contact and mutual interdependence far into the adult life of the latter. Multitudes of people did so prolong the family relationship, and fought earnestly within themselves to ignore the mutual vexations and limitations that arose. But we belong to a clearer-minded generation, living in an age of comparative light, and we perceive that it is as natural and necessary for adolescents to get away from their parents as it is for little children to cling to them. We have, we realise, to give these wonderful variations upon the themes of ourselves the utmost freedom from ourselves, if they are to make the fullest best of their lives. Then, with the longer, better-preserved lives that science has given us, we may hope to establish a relationship novel in the world, unknown in the briefer, more passionate, and violent ancestral life, the relationship of friendly, intimate understanding with these younger equals of our own blood and quality.

A day may come, if the Socialist has his way, when there will be little inheritance of property from parents to children. Even as it is, taxation, death duties, and so forth, chip the ample inheritances of the past. The whole tendency of our time, under such fiscal pressure, is to shift forward the transfer of property to the young in the lifetime of the parent. Less and less are people disposed to keep their sons and daughters waiting about uncertainly for the great day when the will is read, and more and more they are launching their offspring into independence, fairly and handsomely, retaining for themselves, with a free mind for their own complete spending, all that is necessary for their own freedom and comfort. Almost all of us who have children coming on are thinking about and planning for this release as they grow up. A multitude of interesting experiments are being made. I can imagine no more fascinating symposium —I make my editor the present of the idea —than to ask a range of modern parents with growing sons and daughters what they are doing in this respect or, if they are sufficiently experienced, what they have done and how it seems to be working?

For my own part I think it is of very great importance that the modern youngster should be early accustomed to the use of money. The power and tyranny of the old-fashioned parent has been very largely due to his money power; he was the magical, unexplaining giver. But even from childhood I think that children should have definite allowances, not merely for pocket-money but for minor necessities. They should not be given railway-tickets, bicycles, articles of clothing and so forth; they should be given the money to pay for these things themselves. At quite an early age— fourteen or fifteen, say—I think that the parent who can afford it should let the son or daughter have a banking account. It need not be a private and secret account; it can be a "joint and several" account between the parent and the individual child, so that the parent can watch how things go. The youngster can then pay clothing bills, holiday charges, school fees, and so forth, by cheque. He or she can begin to realise what it costs to live. And all big, unpriced gifts are to be avoided. It is very magnificent, of course, for a son or daughter to be given a car, for example, but it is far better that the boy or girl should have the education of buying it. Presents are bad parentage. There should never be vague desires and demands

between children and their parents. The son of a prosperous father who wants a car ought to come along to his father with a clear statement of cost and be prepared to state what sacrifices in other directions he is prepared to make to get what he wants. A bicycle, a motor-bicycle, or an automobile are excellent things in the training for autonomy; all the running expenses—tyres, repairs, oil, and petrol— should be absolutely the owner's private affair paid for out of that banking account; there should be no communism in the parental garage about such things.

But that "joint and several" banking account is only an educational phase. By the time a son or daughter is one-and-twenty, a new phase of detachment should be reached. The parent should be an interested consultant rather than a director of the new career. He should end all discussions of the outlook with the reminder: "It's your affair, not mine." One of the most successful parents I know did this for his three sons. He was not a very rich man; he was a schoolmaster; and as each son came of age he explained to him that there was a thousand pounds invested for him. He could leave it alone for a bit to accumulate, or draw and spend the income. Or he could spend it right out to establish himself in business or what not. But in all probability it was all that the son would ever get. If he wasted or lost it there would probably be no more for him. This method worked very well in all three cases. Two of the sons are successful lawyers. The third wanted to write—that fatal, terrifying proposition. The father had a great dread of the literary adventurer's uncertainties; there was a good proprietary school in the family and a successor was wanted for it. He protested. He begged his son to take the school. But he stuck to his valiant resolution; it wasn't his life he was dealing with but his son's, and he recognised his son's right to fail, if it was to be failure, in his own fashion; the young man went to London with five years' maintenance in the bank. For two years he had a hard, disappointing time. That is where the wisdom of not keeping him on an allowance, that might have been stopped under discouragement, came in. He is now one of our most brilliant and successful English writers and his father's most grateful and affectionate friend.

I think that is a very good example of the art of modern parentage. I know other such cases of gift and free release, but I do not know any that have failed. Young people take responsibility gravely when they are fully responsible. And in all the cases I know the independent launch of the sons or daughters was not the result of a sudden impulse; it was prepared for over a number of years. Of course there must be failures; reckless sons or daughters who are caught by some strong passionate or sensual impulse, or who are credulous or too adventurous. There is the type that would go wrong if it suddenly came into money, and which will go wrong just as certainly when it comes into freedom. Even then, has it not the right to fail in its own fashion and in its own time? Does the controlling, restrictive parent do more than delay the downfall? I know several people who were "saved from themselves" in their heady youth. None of them are more than thwarted creatures with crippled wills. I know a man whose circumstances were such that he was left in uncontrolled possession of twenty thousand pounds at eighteen. It was before the days of automobiles and flying; he bought race-horses, and he had a

# Preparing for Christmas

*Hamleys have it!*

1924

**Dolls—Motor-Cars—Trains—Bears —Footballs—Toys and Games of every description to please the hearts of children of every age.**

Hamley's toys are all stoutly made, yet inexpensive—designed for the hard use that kiddies give them, and Hamley's century-old experience in designing unbreakable toys ensures the little ones perfect satisfaction.

### BOY'S MODEL MOTOR-CAR

Stoutly constructed and suitable for boys from 4 to 10 years. A most realistic model, with adjustable wind-screen, driving-mirror, horn, stop-and-go mechanism, tool box fitted with tools, four lamps, hood-cover, enamelled dashboard, and starting-handle. Rubber-tyred wheels and pedals. May be had in various colours. Price **£4:19:6**

### DOLL'S PERAMBULATOR

The most delightful present of all for girls. The inexpensive model illustrated has plated fittings, with long tubular handles, leather-lined hood, apron, and outside Cee springs, and is in every way an exact model of an up to date baby carriage. Price **52/6**

### A CUDDLY DOLL FOR THE KIDDIES

A charming china doll which "Little Mother" can undress and "put to sleep."

Dolly has a complete set of clothes, including a silk dress and coat and a pretty bonnet. The kiddies will love her. Price **35/6**

### CHARMING FELT DOLLS

We hold a large selection of these dolls, price from **11/6** upwards. Their colouring is life like, they are all beautifully dressed, and are practically indestructible. Each doll is completely clothed, and all are dressed in pretty and delightful colourings

### "FELIX KEEPS ON WALKING"

A well-designed model of "Felix" made in black plush. The novel feature of this toy is that it has no clockwork mechanism to be wound up, but by simply running it backwards and forwards on the floor, the model will then walk under its own power. Price **18/6**

### MINIATURE ELECTRIC TABLE RAILWAYS

An entirely new departure in railways. The complete outfit will fit a small dining-room table, and comprises a reversible electric locomotive, 3 coaches, "figure of eight" track, station, signals, etc. The engines and rolling stock are coloured, lined and lettered in the correct colours of the new companies. Price (excluding battery) **25/9**

As above, but with large track, including points. Price **39/6**

### THE CAT IN MILK-CAN—

A highly amusing and entertaining toy. A milk-can of polished aluminium, from which, on being wound up and the lid taken off, a mischievous white cat rises and commences to lick its lips, a delightful melody playing at the same time. Wonderfully entertaining. Price **39/6**

### AND THE SQUIRREL IN TREE

This is another version of the cat and the milk-can: a squirrel rises from the centre of an oak-tree and bobs about, a pretty melody playing at the same time. Price **37/6**

## MAH-JONGG SETS

**The World's Most Fascinating Game**

Hamley's, foreseeing a great public demand, obtained supplies that are complete in every detail and practically inexhaustible.

Original Chinese Bone and Bamboo Sets (as illustrated), complete in cabinet with counters, dice, etc. Price **55/-**
Other cabinets from 69/6 to £50

A special offer of perfectly carved Bamboo sets complete for . . . . **17/6**

Mah Jongg in playing-card form, from 4/6 a pack.

*Write for our new Illustrated Mah-Jongg catalogue—free.*

### MONKEY ACROBAT

Working on the gyroscopic principle, by touching the monkey's head he will turn somersaults either backwards or forwards with remarkable cleverness. Monkey made in felt in brilliant and lasting colours. Price **5/6**

Postage 6d. extra.

*Send a p.c. for fully illustrated catalogue G.H.2 of fascinating games, sports, and toys.*

# Hamleys
*Estd. 1760*
**·HAMLEY·BROS·LTD·**

MAIL ORDER DEPARTMENT, G.H.
**200/202 REGENT STREET, W.1**

*Also at*

86/7 High Holborn, W.C.1
27/8 Ludgate Hill, E.C.4
512/4 Oxford Street, W.1
59 Knightsbridge, S.W.1
23 George Street, Croydon

*Goods post free unless stated. Motor-car and perambulator carriage free within 30 m. of London.*

## The Launching of Sons and Daughters

1924

tremendous time before the money was exhausted. He also bought much wisdom. He had been rather badly educated and trained; he learnt himself and how to correct himself in those spendthrift years. He was young enough to learn. At two-and-twenty he was beginning life again in an office, and he is now one of the shrewdest and ablest of London business-men. Had he come into that money at thirty-two, say, he would probably have still satisfied his craving for race-horses and have been too old to learn from his experience.

Perhaps my belief in youth is abnormally strong, but I confess myself altogether of the modern persuasion upon this issue. There is a fresh interest in the outlook before one at twenty-one that will not last. Let your sons and daughters have their lives in their own hands in that bright, inspiring phase. Let them begin life with full freedom and open opportunity where it should be begun—at the beginning.

## Good Wishes

*A Merry Christmas*

FIRST I must wish all who read these pages a very bright and happy Christmas. May there be many crackers and parties and stories round the crackling fire.

I think Michael England was the first reader of these pages to send me a letter. Michael is six and just starting lessons. I hope he will let me know how he gets on this term. Mary Towny wrote to tell me all about her camping-out holiday. From John Gow, who is nine, I heard all about the robin called Dinky-Doo and the little lizard he sees on the way to school. Ivor Richards wrote and told me of his puppy and canary.

*Hobbies and Ambitions*

Constance Gow, who is twelve years old, collects the tops of match-boxes; Gwyn Williams collects engines' names.

Our readers have many and varied ambitions for the future. Toby Devitt, who is fourteen, wants to be a photographer. May Clarke, from Edinburgh, is going to an art school. Mona Warren, who is fifteen, wants to be a veterinary surgeon, and Muriel de Vinney is hoping to go to the Froebel College or to the Norland Institute.

1925

## Trees of London

### *Where to Find Them*

NEARLY every Londoner can direct you to some glorious tree or trees he knows. But this is not quite enough, if you don't want to miss the best. In case you don't possess a charming little book by Mr. Walter Johnson called *The Nature World of London,* in which many details can be found, we will take some news from his pages for you.

When you are next at St. Paul's, go round to the north side and you will find a green, glossy fig-tree. Right amidst the roar of the city, there it grows serenely, and if you go round to Cheapside in Wood Street you will see an old, old plane, which was the home of the last of the rooks that nested in the City.

### *Mulberries and Ash Trees*

It is rather fun, when you are riding on the top of a 'bus, to count all the different kinds of trees you can see. The mulberry tree may be found at the Charterhouse, right down by Smithfield Market, and there are some beauties at Battersea, while Hogarth the painter's mulberry at Chiswick is still flourishing. There are fine specimens of ash trees in Holborn Churchyard and St. Dunstans in the East; but when you are next shopping with Mother round about Oxford Street, get her to let you call on the noble ash tree in Cavendish Square.

Of course there are lovely trees in all the London parks. Mr. Lucas, in his jolly book *A Wanderer in London,* says that if we will go into Kensington Gardens in winter we shall see a beautiful picture made by the naked branches holding and loving the blue winter mists.

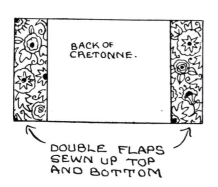

BACK OF CRETONNE.

DOUBLE FLAPS SEWN UP TOP AND BOTTOM

## Snowballs

### *And Snowflakes*

HERE is something very important to remember. I expect you have often rushed out to make snowballs when it was freezing, and have been disappointed that the snow was powdery, and would not bind. Try next time when it is beginning to thaw. Hard snowballs can be made by squeezing snow together then. By the way, have you ever looked carefully at snowflakes? They are made up of little stars, and there are six rays in every star. Every crystal is different, but they all have six rays or six sides.

## Nursery Books

### *Making a Catalogue*

Get a note-book with stiff covers, and cut out the edges of the pages to make it look like Mother's address-book.

Cut a strip of cretonne just larger than your books, and hem the rough edges top and bottom; then turn the short ends of the stuff over for about 2 inches and sew up at the top and bottom to the cretonne. The book will slip into this pretty cover. Stretch the cretonne over the book before turning in the ends, to get it taut and neat.

Enter your books under the name of the author. Thus *Grimm's Fairy Tales* should not be catalogued under F for Fairy, but under G for Grimm.

## A Story

### *The Tidy Dog*

DOWN to the house of Mr. Jeremiah Trevor in a Dorset village came his little niece and nephew, Betty and Colin, to spend all the Christmas holidays.

Jeremiah's house was the house of a very fussy old bachelor. It was extremely neat, and Brisk, the Cairn terrier, who lived with Mr. Trevor, was a very wise, tidy dog indeed.

But very soon the parlour, which was made into Colin and Betty's nursery for the visit, got all topsy-turvy. The table was strewn with Christmas presents. There were toys of all kinds heaped upon it.

"Tut, tut," said Jeremiah, peeping in.
"What next?" sighed the worried old housekeeper.
"Very queer indeed, by my paws and basket!" thought Brisk, the terrier.

### *He Hates a Muddle*

One day it rained, and Betty quarrelled with Colin. They went to bed quite cross. Colin said that he hated most of his Christmas presents, and that people had sent him the wrong things. Betty threw a doll on the floor. Early in the morning, before anybody was down, Brisk went into the sitting-room and saw the doll.

"What's this?" he asked himself, for his master always put Brisk's food on the linoleum floor. "What's this? A bone for me?"

The rule in that house was that anything on the floor belonged to Brisk, except, of course, the mats. Nothing was put there but Brisk's food. But this wasn't a bone; it was a dolly, all in pink and pearls. Brisk knew odd things mustn't lie about on linoleum. So he took the doll in his mouth, and went out of doors, and there, across the road, outside the poor cottage opposite, was a little girl called Mabel, cleaning the step.

### *Little Cottage Mabel*

"Must get rid of this," thought Brisk, and trotted over, and laid the doll at Mabel's feet. She took it up and kissed it.

"Oh, fine!" said she. She hadn't ever had a dolly like that.

Back went tidy old Brisk, and on the sitting-room floor found a little picture-book, dashed down by Colin, carelessly.

"I don't think this is a bone either," said Brisk to himself, and he took it in

# Like To Know

### By
### Marjory Royce

1925

## Brisk's Gifts

### And the poor little girl

his mouth and crossed the road and laid it also at Mabel's feet. She was simply thrilled. She hadn't had a new book for ages.

"Look, Mother! Oh, if I could only keep them!" she cried, running in to her mother. "That young lady and gentleman over there have had thirty-two presents between them, the housekeeper was saying. If they could only spare me those——!"

"What's that dog doing?" exclaimed the mother, for Brisk had been back, and had found a new soft silk handkerchief of orange and rose colour pitched down on the floor by Betty, who said she hadn't anything to wear with it that would match it.

"Why, this is just what I'd love," sighed the mother, who had not had anything pretty and gay since she was married. "But we're honest folk. Here, doggy, take it back home again, all of it."

And she called in Brisk and did not see Betty and Colin signalling at the bathroom window, watching the whole thing.

Brisk stood on the cottage doorstep, very puzzled.

### Putting it Right

Inside, Mabel was crying, salt tears splashed over Dolly's face. She was quickly trying to read the book, fast, fast, before it had to go away for ever.

Downstairs, opposite, rushed Betty and Colin with no clothes on, save each a towelling dressing-gown. They dashed across to say, "Please, please keep the things!" The idea of giving the doll and hankie and book made them tingle with joy.

"Tut, tut," said old Jeremiah, peeping out of his window as he slowly rose from bed, and seeing Betty give Mabel a hug.

"With their bare feet too, across the muddy road," sighed the housekeeper, open-mouthed at the front door. "What next?"

"Very queer indeed," thought Brisk, who was being violently patted and praised. "By my paws and basket, I was only doing my duty."

## A Fairy Poet

### Fairy News

HAVE you all heard of Rose Fyleman? She's a real person, and she knows lots and lots about fairies. I was thinking the other day of all the news she had brought chil-

The Fairies' cooking pots on the telegraph poles

dren from fairy-land. You will find it in her books; in *Forty Good-Night Tales,* in the *Rose Fyleman Fairy Book,* in *The Fairy Garden,* and one book is even dedicated to the Queen of the Fairies. Think of that! I expect the Queen keeps a copy in the special bookcase that stands beside her bed of gossamer.

Now then, for some of this news. Have you ever noticed people say that it won't rain if there's enough blue sky to make a cat a pair of trousers?

That all came from something that really happened, Miss Fyleman says. There was a poor cat who wished to go to the Fairy Queen's party, and he was obliged to coax the weather clerk to give him some sky for a party suit. Then did you know that if you're in danger from a fairy crocodile, it's a very good thing to throw him a bag of caramels so that his jaws may stick together? I thought you didn't.

## Cooking Pots

### Fairy Toffee and Jam

THESE little white things on the top of the telegraph poles are the fairies' cooking-pots! It's almost the biggest news Miss Fyleman's brought us, I think. The humming you hear in the pole is the toffee and the jam singing in the pots as they boil.

Lovely to think of when you're coming past, hungry! Also, Miss Fyleman happens to have found out what fairies buy when they go to market. Grown-ups have thought this so important, that they have often sung a song about it, and you may have heard that Fairies buy fish, coloured birds, winter gowns (lined thistledown), and gentle mice.

Miss Fyleman lives in a fascinating house above a post-office. I know she does. She told me so. It's a lucky thing, as if any fairy news comes to her which she wants to post on immediately to the great waiting world of children, she doesn't ever feel she can't possibly buy a postage stamp.

### Be Careful !

By the way, pillar-boxes have been known to go for walks, so do be careful to find one ready to take all the thank-you letters for Christmas presents you'll soon be writing.

The best plan with letters just after Christmas is to have a special time each day to write two or three of them; then, very soon, every one gets thanked for the nice things they have sent you.

1925

1925

*Indoor Occupations for
Little Boys and Girls—*

"What can I do *now*, Mummy?"
is a question that may become too
familiar during a wet November

# On Rainy Days

*By* MURIEL WRINCH

"WHAT can I do *now*, mummy?" is a question which may become all too familiar to mothers during the wet and foggy days of November. It is a wonderful question, revealing as it does the ceaseless activity of the mind of the child, the desire to be always doing, the reluctance to waste even one moment of the waking hours. Yet it is a question which should not be heard too often in the nursery—the child should be *doing* rather than wondering what to do. Nor is it the mother's business always to suggest the line of action—early in life the child must learn to make decisions for himself.

The games which mother and child make up together should be such that they lend themselves easily to modification. The mother may suggest the outlines of some such games as are described in this article, and the child, if he has not been accustomed to too much entertainment nor spoiled by too much attention or too many toys, will add many ideas of his own and occupy himself happily and busily for hours.

The years between three and seven have been said to comprise the Dramatic Age of childhood. This is the age when a piece of marvellously fluffy cotton-wool is a far greater treasure than a ruby ring; this is the age when, as Robert Louis Stevenson says, it is "the child's whole profession to take a tub for a fortified town and a shaving-brush for a deadly stiletto." Mothers of little children, therefore, should encourage them to use imagination in their play. They should avoid giving the child too many materials lest he grows to depend upon elaborate toys for

THERE will be no dull days in your nursery this winter after you have read Muriel Wrinch's article in which she helps you to plan the work and play that make up a happy child's day. Any special problem that you may have concerning child care and training should be sent to Children's Department, "Good Housekeeping," 153 Queen Victoria Street, London, E.C.4. State exactly what you want to know, and enclose a stamped addressed envelope for the reply

effects which, by a little ingenuity, he could as well produce for himself. To give a child a highly finished toy is to encourage him to desert the Land of Make-Believe, to allow the artisan who manufactures to kill the artist who creates.

But although the five- or six-year-old is such a little dreamer that he sees gold in orange-peel and fairies in every tree, he also has a great thirst for knowledge and a healthy desire for *facts*. His play must be practical as well as imaginative. For this reason I advocate such games as the shop-game or that of the "Word Dictionary," described in this article. The child learns much that is valuable to him in these games—the boy who can by no means be taught to read the simple sentence. "The cat sits on the mat," will soon recognise such words as "sugar" or "rice," or even "tapioca," when these are painted on gay tin canisters in his own shop; and he who cannot be persuaded to learn the ready-made weights and measures table positively aches to make up his own when he has a real balance to weigh his own goods.

I advocate the game of shop for another reason also. Any game requiring

a certain amount of exactitude, such as that involved in weighing or measuring, is particularly valuable for the six-year-old. Fine work, necessitating minute actions of the hands, should be avoided, but it is never too early to begin to teach a child to work and play *well*. The power to *act* truthfully comes before the power to talk truthfully. Mothers of small sons and daughters of five and six know how much they tend to "romance," but perhaps they do not realise that truthfulness in deed may be easily established at this age. The child who builds carefully and truthfully, laying one brick exactly on top of another, will grow to appreciate accuracy in life as the untrained child will never learn to appreciate it.

I have in mind as I write this article a little boy of six who *loves* the foggy days he spends indoors. He is happy and busy all day long, and mounts the stairs singing when bedtime comes without showing any of the flashes of bad temper which we sometimes see in children who have been confined to the house for twelve hours at a stretch.

Of course Michael rejoices in a mother who loves children—that is a *sine qua non* for childish happiness. Equally, of course, he has many companions of his own age—that again is a necessity if small children are to develop healthily *as* children and not as miniature adults. But Michael's material for work and play are simple and inexpensive enough. He has very few playthings, but they are *right* playthings, for all of them give opportunity for constructiveness on the part of the child who plays with them, and his education.

1925

Young ambition's ladder . . . His foot is sure upon the first rung who has stamina . . . The after-climb comes easily to him who started well . . .

The nightly glass of Horlick's Malted Milk—delicious, tempting, containing all the good of pure milk, wheat and malted barley—will build body and brain and give overplus of energy to draw upon.

Thus is the future made sure.

## HORLICK'S
### THE ORIGINAL
## MALTED MILK
MADE
IN ENGLAND

**Ready in a moment with hot or cold water**

At all chemists, in four sizes, 2/-, 3/6, 8/6 and 15/-
The tablets also in flasks, 7½d. and 1/3d.
A liberal sample for trial will be forwarded, post
free, for 3d. in stamps.

**Served in restaurants and cafés of standing**

Horlick's Malted Milk Co., Slough, Bucks.

1925

# The Used-To-Be

### By Harry Lee
*Decoration by Arthur E. Becher*

Little Boy grown tall,
    Little Boy grown tall,
Could you know how much I miss you,
You would leave your fame and all—
Just to take the old road homeward
Just to sit awhile with me,
Droning over, dreaming over,
    Little things of Used-to-be.

Little Boy grown tall,
    Little Boy grown tall,
The yellow cloves are blooming
And the spring-birds call—
The plate you always loved so,
With the blue, bent tree,
And the birthday cup I gave you
    Wait for you across from me.

Little Boy grown tall,
    Little Boy grown tall,
Spring changes into summer
And summer to the fall;
Then comes the time of winter,
And it has come to me—
Oh, take the old road homeward,
    Bring me back the Used-to-be.

1925

### By M. Grant Cook

# What does
# *Your Child*
# READ?

*Illustrations by*
*Ernest H. Shepard*

**Children will rather hear a**

THE self-sufficiency of the modern child is startling. He is not nearly so much influenced by the suggestions of his elders as was the child of, say, twenty years ago. What with the widespread, if erroneous, knowledge of Freud and infantile psychology, the preoccupation of his shingled mamma with dancing and other amusements, and the general post-war tendency to regard extreme youth as in itself a nearly perfect state, the child of to-day is largely left to his own sweet will in a number of matters that once were carefully presented to him without any alternative. He may choose his games, his accomplishments, and to a certain extent the subjects that he prefers in school. In some schools, indeed, complete freedom is the only rule, and the child may attend or absent himself from classes according to the degree of interest or boredom they make him feel.

In nothing is the present-day child more independent than in his reading. Parents may tell him with what rapture they enjoyed Dickens, Kingsley, and Scott, when they were his age, and wonder that he does not snatch them from the book-case, and he turns but a languid ear. "Mummy is always saying how much she loved old Walter Scott when she was young, and *Westward Ho!* and things," a young person of ten remarked to me. "We had to do *Ivanhoe* for a holiday task, and it *was* dull. I hate all those old hoes. I wouldn't read books like *that* for fun!" Pressed as to what he would read—with pleasure—he answered judicially: "I really like a clever murder better than anything else. One with lots of wrong clues, and a very good detective, and hardly any silly love. I know you have to put in a little," he added reasonably. This child belongs to an intellectual family, and the nursery and schoolroom are stocked with the usual suitable books of fairies and

adventures; but he prefers the detective fiction on which his literary father relaxes his brain. He is quite typical of his generation, which feels a positive need for violence in one form or another.

A holiday party of children, mostly from a vicarage, all gentle and well brought up, and whose parents had made constant efforts to form their literary tastes on the soundest models, were read a "thriller" on a rainy evening by a wicked aunt. The effect was almost intoxicating, even on the shivering smallest and mildest girl, who was heard to say: "I think it is very bad and awful, but oh, I *love* killing!" In this connection a similar story is told of John Masefield's daughter Judith when she was a little girl at school. She and a number of her companions were asked what sort of books they liked best to read, school stories, or fairy-tales, or poetry, or adventures. Little Miss Masefield replied with ardour: "Oh, I like stories with lots of blood."

It all seems very bad and awful, as the vicarage child remarked, but anxious parents who cannot get their boys and girls to read good and noble books, or even books that supposedly might help to form a moderately good taste in literature, may take heart of grace from the experience of Mr. A. S. Neill, whose sound and practical and varied knowledge of children makes his books on child-psychology so delightful as well as so helpful to anyone in close association with children, and specially to parents and teachers.

In his international school, formerly at Hellerau, where his original ideas on education are carried out, he tried to interest a group of five English-speaking children in *King Solomon's Mines* which he read aloud to them. One by one they fell asleep, and none of them wanted him to continue to the end. He decided that they were bored because "their

egos had no display in the story"—in other words they could not in imagination act a part in it. So he began to tell them a story in which each child, called by his own name, had exciting adventures and performed thrilling deeds of valour. The children, when things got a bit tame, clamoured for savages and killing and lions to shoot. He provided these generously, as well as machine-guns and rifles, skulls smashed with battle-axes, Indians, wolves, and cannibals. Each child took a fine share in the action and inflicted and endured wounds and disablement, and excitement blazed high. No child slept, and Mr. Neill succeeded in his object, which was to make them interested and therefore happy. His note on the psychology of it all is extremely interesting, and may be quoted in part from *A Dominie's Five.*

"Why should healthy children find so much delight in killing? I had built up my school on the theory that the child is born good. How was it possible to reconcile with this theory the fact that five normal children found joy in sadistic deeds? If a child is born with a natural instinct to be good, that is to seek happiness, how can he want to handle a machine-gun? To answer in the old way that a child is a little savage is not satisfying. A child left to himself is not a savage, but a child is potentially a savage; when his desire for good is thwarted, he makes a complete turn-about and becomes cruel. . . . I differ with those modern educationists who say that the child must be surrounded with an environment of goodness, that is, that the child must be kept from hearing or seeing anything cruel or bad. These people refuse to give their children toy soldiers and guns; they aim at turning out pacifists. But what of the actual psychology of the child? I know positively that children will rather hear a story of scalping than

1925

story of scalping than of missionaries. The child wants to kill—let him kill in phantasy . . . .

one of missionaries. In spite of all efforts to keep the child pure, his unconscious will retains its sadism. My view is: The child wants to kill; I must try to satisfy this want. I shall let him kill in phantasy: he shall sublimate his killing. . . .

"Those who work with children become convinced that the Freudian psychology with its strong emphasis on sex and the Oedipus Complex is no sure basis for education. I can find no sex in the killing of cannibals, or the discovery of treasure. . . . An important aspect of the story is that relating to Stekel's great phrase, 'Pleasure without guilt.' . . . I am inclined to think that this is the guiding principle of every child. To kill savages and wolves in a story is to be sadistic without guilt. Helga wouldn't hurt a fly, yet her face used to shine at the description of a battle. When Geoffrey went to the circus he was really pained at the cruelty with which the horses were treated in the ring. But next day he bought a revolver and shot down every person in Hellerau. . . . Where the story did good was in this: each child felt that he or she was loved. 'Here is old Neill (father substitute) loving me so much that he makes me do brave deeds.' The ego desire for power and the desire for love were satisfied at the same time."

Without going further into the psychology of it, we can conclude that the ordinary child's love for a "clever murder" or for playing at Indians is quite healthy and useful.

And of course no child wants violence in books or play all the time. When he turns to other literature, what riches are at his disposal, beautifully gay, charmingly printed editions of all the classics for youth, stories, poems, even plays; and each year sees crowds and crowds of new books for children.

Never in any former age has the child

*Kidnapped, Treasure Island, The Three Musketeers*
—every boy owns some of these

been so commercialised and exploited in the shops, specially perhaps in the bookshops, as at the present moment. There is a constant and extraordinary effort to cater for a child's tastes, but the result is not always successful. Books for boys and girls are poured out in a stream; how few have any distinction, or any sort of real popularity. There are standard works, of course, that reappear in new dresses every year, and sell steadily. *Kidnapped, Treasure Island, The Three Musketeers,* Henty, Marryat, and the more recent Gunby Hadath and Hylton Cleaver—every boy owns some of these. And although it was announced somewhere not long ago that there was a slump in school stories for girls, these pour in a positive cataract from the publishers. Clever, brave, beautiful, popular, mysterious girls make terms terrible or memorable, or have thrilling holiday adventures with cyclones, grizzlies, snakes, or head mistresses. Nothing is too silly or too improbable for these tales, but they may have their uses in making the omnivorous girl reader finally turn from them to something better.

The children's department in any big bookshop is a bewildering but rather fascinating place to-day. Here is rubbish unimaginable, together with all the books that a parent with a literary conscience could wish his child to possess and read. All kinds of delightful books are bought and given to children, but between what the child is given by well-meaning relatives, and what he takes

*Continued overleaf*

1925

i heerd mum and dAD spekin won Nite and they sed i ot to hav a lot of munny wen i gro big enuf to gel marrid Dad sed He was worrid becos he did not no Whare the munny wos comin from. Eut mum sed if they rote to the Legal and General Assurance Society 10 Fleet Street. London and askt for a BABY GIRLS POLICY for my Wedding Day i wood hav lots of munny for my weddin and liv hapy erver after. So please send them wun.

✗ ✗ ✗ ✗
✗ ✗ ✗ ✗

mum and Dad wil be pleased cos they luv me ever so.

Sis wants wun two

*Legal & General Assurance Society Ltd., 10, Fleet Street, London, E.C.4.  Estd. 1836.  Funds £16,750,000.*

44

# What Does Your Child Read?

*Continued*

pleasure in reading, there is often a gulf fixed. "This is our very polite shelf," a small child said to me, pointing out a row of volumes in the schoolroom bookcase as clean and bright as the day they were bought. Polite in her sense meant just that. This particular family of children wouldn't read Van Loon's *History of Mankind*, or *Hereward the Wake*, or *Pilgrim's Progress*, or *King Solomon's Mines*, or potted editions of Dickens, or stories about the Empire, artists, operas, Greek heroes, or Scandinavian mythology. These were all in the "very polite" shelf, with many more. (Of course, when they are hard up they do dip languidly into them.) On the other shelves the Andrew Lang fairy books were all but torn to shreds, and other favourites that bore marks of hard usage were *The Wind in the Willows*, some E. Nesbit books, a Newbolt or two, a handful of Angela Brazil's schoolgirl heroines, *Alice* of course, *The Rose and the Ring*, some of Hilaire Belloc's beasts, and the *Lays of Ancient Rome*. Pirates, adventurers, and a few poets also found a place and did not seem to be in any too polite condition.

In the matter of poetry it may be doubted if children like it very much after they can read for themselves. The baby loves a jingle—"This little Pig went to Market" and "Ride a Cock Horse" for example, which accompany action—and all children love funny poetry, or rhyme that describes closely what they do themselves. Poetry *about* themselves and with the slightest suspicion of being addressed to an older audience, bewilders and bores the child. On the other hand, something to learn, or something to act, even when it appears to be above their comprehension, gives children keen pleasure; again their ego is finding expression, and they feel their own power. The child quoted above who loves a clever murder also has a genuine relish for Shakespeare. He can learn whole scenes with ease, and enjoys spouting long passages from the plays that he reads in school, and such plays of Shakespeare as he has seen acted, do not bore him for a single second. The elder who goes with him may yawn, but the end of the play finds the boy wishing it was all beginning over again.

The child who has few books or none at home, and who belongs to a free library, will often have a better appreciation and taste for literature than the child who has so many books that he doesn't know what

to do with them. It is interesting to note the books demanded in the children's department of any public library. Dickens is very popular here, so are nature stories, scientific stories of invention, and historical stories of heroes like Nelson and Florence Nightingale. Fairies, of course, go on for ever, rejected sometimes by the sternly practical child, but on the whole, and below ten years old, more popular than anything else. It is interesting to know that Mrs. Ewing's humorous and entirely delightful books are reprinted and sold year after year. Mrs. Molesworth, too, with less substance and less depth, finds a large public still, and after all no small child could well resist *Us*, or *The Cuckoo Clock*, or *The Carved Lions*. Lord Fauntleroy, that preposterous infant in golden curls and black velvet, still triumphs in the hearts of small maternal girls, cherished for his beauty and riches and romance, and no more "real" as compared with one's brothers than killing and skull-smashing are real in Mr. Neill's story. *The Little Princess* and *The Secret Garden*, Mrs. Burnett's other books for children, are even more popular than Fauntleroy. George Macdonald's fairy-books find favour, although he, like Kingsley, moralised too much. Children always like animal stories, which may be of two kinds, both equally acceptable. In one the animal is hunted, trapped, or overcome by heroic daring. In the other the animal is personified, and the child becomes his companion and learns his speech and shares his delightful life in burrow or cave or under the sea. Children enjoy this vicarious change of personality immensely, and to know the language of animals satisfies a deep and primitive desire. The less imaginative writers are content to give the animals the exact functions of men, while retaining their natural advantages of fin and wing, claws and paws, as they go about their business for and with man. This is what Mr. Hugh Lofting does in his "Dr. Dolittle" series, and children readily accept this convention too. Dr. Dolittle is quite serious and quite cheerful, and has qualities that appeal very much to the child's dramatic instinct. The child shares the adventures described, hence the real success of this type of book.

It would be easy and fascinating to stock a book-shelf with the best hundred books for children, from infancy to fourteen years, say. Shockers and Shakespeare would not be omitted.

1925

1925

## A Picnic Tea

### A Real Treat

MAISIE was on holiday this year when her birthday came round, so she was allowed to give a September picnic. It was great fun, helping to get ready for it. Ten children accepted, and they planned to go to a lovely wood by the sea. Mother let Maisie make some Elfin Biscuits for the picnic and they turned out to be so easily made, and were so delicious to eat, especially when just cooked, that I must tell you how to make some too.

### The Recipe

Put half a pound of flour into a clean basin and add a little salt. Rub in three-quarters of an ounce of butter, taking up tiny pieces in your fingers (which must be absolutely clean), and crumbling them into the flour, until you have used all the butter, and have in your basin a mixture like breadcrumbs. Moisten with hot milk to make a firm paste. Roll this out very thin on a floured board, cut it into small rounds, prick with a fork, and bake them light brown in a moderate oven.

### A Napkin Ring

Get a strip of stiff cardboard 6 inches long and 1 inch wide. Sew it up, so that it makes a round. Take some raffia of your favourite colour, and cover up the cardboard by wrapping raffia threads round and round it. Carefully finish off, when all is covered, by tucking the end of your thread securely through some of the strands of raffia. Tie a piece of ribbon to match into a bow at the side.

## Bathing Dolly

### By the Seaside

AT present, Mrs. Douglas, her eight-year-old daughter Margaret, and her baby girl, Natalie, are staying at the seaside. Every morning, when mother baths Natalie in a room overlooking the sands, Margaret is allowed to bath her dolly too. Natalie has rather a big rubber bath to be washed in, but Dolly Philippa is sponged in a little tin bath. Margaret is allowed to

use the bath thermometer that tests Natalie's hot water, and she is careful to get it just right, a hundred degrees Fahrenheit.

Margaret always washes her own hands before she begins, just as Mummy does. She wipes dolly's eyes with a tiny rag, and washes her face tenderly, with a face-cloth and no soap.

### The Bottom of the Sea

To leave the seaside after a lovely summer holiday is horrid; but there is always next summer to which to look forward. Have you ever thought, as you lay happily on the sunny beach and stared at the waves, about the very, very deepest sea? Do you know how far down light travels? A very small beam goes as far as about five thousand fathoms, which is about half a mile, so the bottom of the deep sea is perfectly dark, always. Think of the fishes down there, in thousands! Sponges, corals, sea-lilies, sea-spiders, and snails live also in the deep waters.

## Books

### Do You Know Them?

THERE are many Book People you lassies and laddies should know as well as your sisters and brothers. Here are the names of a few. These, if you do not know them, will show you have missed reading some of the jolliest children's books, and you had best set about getting them at once. Do you know the Bastables? Oswald, and the rest? (If not, get E. Nesbit's stories.) Do you know Polly Milton, country Polly who came to town in such old-fashioned clothes? (If not, get *An Old-fashioned Girl,* by Louisa Alcott.) Do you know Irene and Curdie, all you fairy lovers? (If not, George Macdonald's *The Princess and the Goblin* is the book for you.) Boys, do you know Thorhall and Glam? (If not, you should look for Baring-Gould's wonderful tale of Iceland called *Grettir the Outlaw.*)

### About Star-Folk

In *The Star People,* by Gaylord Johnson (Methuen), you will read how Peter, Betty, and Paul got their kind Uncle Henry to show them how to make drawings in sand of the great constellations in the sky. You'll love the book, and it will teach you a tremendous lot, and you'll want to look at the pictures over and over again. Do join the great world society of Star Gazers!

### Seed Time

September is seed time, and you will find it amusing and interesting to make out as long a list as you can get of fruits and seeds that you discover in your garden or on your holiday walks.

There is nothing more wonderful in all nature than the different contrivances of plants for holding seeds. Dry fruits that contain several seeds will split open, when ripe, to let the seeds scatter; dry fruits with only one seed, like the hazel, free that seed by the perishing of the seed wall. If you cut open the wallflower pod you will notice how beautifully it is arranged: two rows of seeds in two compartments.

Honesty has three sheaths of silver, and its black seeds are hidden between the sheaths. It is fun to strip the outside sheaths; collect the seed for sowing, and put the lovely clean middle leaf on its stalk in the nursery vase. An old-fashioned name for Honesty is " Moonpennies."

# *Like To Know*

### By
### Marjory Royce

## The Swing

*For the Village Green*

THE Committee of Children broke up.

"Now, you do understand, don't you, Toby?" said Maybell Morris.

Toby was only just eight. "You're planning to give a party," he said. "And we're going to charge the people money to come in, and we're going to take all the sixpences we get, and buy the village children a swing, because they haven't got one."

"Yes, Toby," said Maybell. "Now you must try to think of something to show at our Exhibition."

Toby's round blue eyes grew very serious. "Suppose I can't think of nuffink?" he said.

The boarding-school children of Ferny Nook Village went to different schools, but they all had a lovely time there. They lived in Ferny Nook only just for the holidays. But they had noticed that the Ferny Nook children, "the village kids," as they called them, hadn't half the jolly things *they* had at school, not even a swing. So Maybell Morris suggested they should get up a little show of some sort, to try to collect money enough to put up a swing in the village playground. They had decided on a Nature Exhibition, and everyone was to show something. Already Bertie Harris had thought of an Insect Zoo. Toby hadn't thought of anything, and it made him just a little bit miserable, especially as he had promised on his honour not to consult his parents about it.

*Toby's Problem*

Poor Toby! Whenever he went down the village street, he met one of the others getting ready.

Bertie Harris owned an old toy stable, with different stalls, and Toby met him capturing snails at the side of the meadow. The snails were each to have a tiny piece of sticking-paper on their backs with the name of a famous horse like "Manna." And on the afternoon they were to be shown as a joke, as horses.

Toby grew more and more afraid. What was *he* to do?

## What Toby Did

*The Story Continued*

IT was the day of the Exhibition. Already the others were putting things ready on the lawn. Just at twelve little Toby had his idea! He went to his kitchen, got two tumblers, and started out for Lilac Farm, and afterwards he visited Moonlight Farm.

*At the Bee House*

Then he came back, carrying two glasses of milk. Toby thought he would label them "Lilac Farm Milk" and "Moonlight Farm Milk." But, alas! he tripped over a stone, and the milk trickled down the street! Toby wept, but was raised from the ground by a jolly little village girl he knew.

"I haven't anything to show at the Exhibition, Maggie," he sobbed.

"Let *me* come," said the little girl. "Say I'm one that hasn't ever been on a swing once. Would that do?"

"I think it would," said Toby. So Maggie Ann stood by the Bee House with a label on her pinafore in Toby's writing, "Little Girl Who's *Never* Had a Swing." And people liked seeing her, and the children got so much money that they were able to buy and put up a really strong swing in the village school playground.

## Goldfish

*Cakes and Crackers*

GOLDFISH get so tame if you treat them properly that they will nibble ants' eggs out of your fingers. (Never give them breadcrumbs or other food.) I know three healthy goldfish, all over nineteen years of age, who have lived with the same family for years.

These fish, whose names are Shadrach, Meshach, and Abednego, give a children's party every year and swim round in their large, clear crystal bowl, which is placed in the centre of the table on a blue Japanese table-centre that looks like a tiny lake. All the cakes at the goldfish party are iced deep yellow, and the crackers are red and silver to match the hosts' scales. Little chocolate fish in silver paper jackets take the place of ordinary sweets and the guests enjoy red and yellow jellies made in fish-shaped moulds.

*Shadrach, Meshach, and Abednego*

If you want your goldfish to live for a very long time, like their cousins the carp, be sure to give them fresh water at least twice a day, if you keep them in a bowl, and be certain that the remains of ants' eggs given overnight are scoured away next morning. The simplest way to do this is to put a wire-mesh rosebowl cover on top of the goldfish bowl, then leave it standing beneath a tap of gently running cold water.

Never leave your fish in the sunshine, nor let their water be frozen over.

1925

# Christmas and the Child

## By Evelyn E. Kenwrick

*Decoration By Anne Rochester*

"IS it all finished and over?" anxiously asked a small child as she saw someone leaving early the delights of a small gathering—called by courtesy a party—and when reassured she returned with fresh zeal to the thrills and excitements of Oranges and Lemons and Ring o' Roses.

As I watched, I wondered anew at the ease with which the normal unspoiled child is amused and interested.

The inexhaustible joys of Christmas are not least on the anticipatory side of the Festival, and I have often tried to understand the point of view of the teacher who told me she did not encourage her children to discuss or work for Christmas till within a week of the Christmas holidays, for fear the "season should lose its freshness."

How did she do it? One can only imagine by preserving a very hush-hush atmosphere in the class, for everything in the children's home life, and in the atmosphere as they took their walks abroad, would speak of the delights to come. By the discussions of, and preparations for the cakes, mincemeat, and puddings, by the gaily decorated and festooned shops, pantomime posters, and so on, every sense is appealed to, and thought and desire are turned constantly to that great epoch by which the children measure time.

The Festivals of Saint Nicholas or Father Christmas or Santa Claus are among the earliest red-letter days of us all, though perhaps no one stands out in relief as the first in the pageant of Memory. Recalling the intimate personal delights of My Birthday, when one reigned supreme, we find it eclipsed by the joyous memories of Christmas Days when everyone participated in pleasures and presents.

Though all would agree that Christmas is pre-eminently the children's season, we can disclose to them this secret—that happiness is doubled as it is shared and that Christmas is a time for all to contribute to the common good and enjoyment.

The first really vivid impressions of Christmas are gained from Father Christmas's visits. Even Philippa, who was not quite two last Christmas, was deeply impressed as she watched with wondering eyes the hanging of her wee sock over the rail of her cot.

She became more intent and the blue of her eyes deepened as the story was told of Father Christmas coming down the chimney while she was asleep, to put a beautiful surprise in that sock. When she awoke at six o'clock next morning, she emerged from her warm nest and scrambled down to see if anything had come true, finding with great joy a new doll protruding from the sock, which kept her in ecstasy for the remainder of the day. The mystery and miracle of this experience have never been forgotten, and Philippa looks forward in faith to a repetition of the event as she *Continued*

# Christmas and the Child

is told that Father Christmas is coming again very soon.

For very tiny children Father Christmas's midnight visit with his gifts should constitute practically the whole of their excitement. Any interference with the regular routine of the day or variation of diet will certainly end in disaster, mental and digestive; for a disorganised programme is speedily avenged by nature, since temper and good health at this age depend largely on habit-making.

There are various opinions as to the desirability of preserving the myth of Father Christmas, and many parents, influenced by a school of modern thought which believes that a child "should not learn anything which will have to be unlearned later," would dispense with his visits and services.

When this notion was first propounded to Marion's mother, she thoughtfully enlightened Marion with no careful consideration first of her child's mental make-up. The news gave great distress as with tears the disillusioned child sobbed: "Why did you tell me? I would much rather have gone on believing, and now you have spoiled my pleasure!" and the mother felt that pang of unavailing pity for a lovely thing unintentionally wrecked.

Another mother also became impressed with the fact that eight-year-old Molly should be told the truth, and was very much taken aback at the cool reply: "Oh yes! I've known that for years, but you wouldn't tell me the truth when I asked you, so I have gone on pretending to believe because I thought you would be pleased!"

All theories are capable of several interpretations and should not be accepted and acted upon thus unthinkingly. They must be weighed up and tested—whether old or new—with special reference to the needs of each individual child. Marion's mother should have remembered the world of romance and make-believe in which her little daughter lives, and recognising that this is a gift not to be repressed but directed, should have striven to give it outlets in fields of creative and æsthetic activity. The time was not ripe for disillusionment, and her sensitive child's mind has received a shock which may cause irreparable harm, for she will be chary of confiding in the future in those whose sympathy and help she should be able to seek.

In the other case, the mother is also too readily responsive to outside opinion and adopts suggestions without due thought and reason. Last year Molly's charming innocence was a delight to her, and she parried all questions regarding the genuineness of Father Christmas. The child is now in a position to question her mother's statements, for she has discovered that she is not always reliable in her information. The seeds of scepticism and insincerity have probably more chance of finding root through adult ignorance and clumsy handling of child nature, than through learning things "which have to be unlearned in later life." The barriers of misunderstanding between a child and its elders need not be erected if we act on the principle that

confidence and frankness beget their like.

Parents who have gained knowledge as the result of thought and experience may see in Father Christmas and in all the celebrations of the time, forces which will work for good or ill in the child's mind and character, and exercise a permanent influence upon them. Ethel complains that her children are growing *blasé* and increasingly difficult to delight, though she tries each Christmas to gratify every wish and to keep the season by a long continuous round of pleasure. Everything is sacrificed to them and nothing is expected from them in the way of effort or self-denial as their contribution to the day's rejoicings, nor do they recognise how their mother has worn herself out to give them a good time.

How short-sighted is Ethel's mental vision and how superficial her conception of her children's minds and interests! Good-natured and well-meaning, she has never seen further than the pleasure-seeking quest with its motive of personal gain. The children never take part in the Christmas preparations beyond buying presents, and even that is done in the easiest way possible, for they choose what appeals to them as seen in the shops and their mother foots the bill. They can always tell other children at school what presents they are to have long before Christmas arrives. No eager attitude of expectancy here, their greatest enjoyment being not the good fortune which awaits them, but their undoubted superiority over their envious school-fellows! An anti-social spirit is being extensively cultivated and developed in these children—their aim is to outshine others, and some very strong influence will be needed in their lives if they are not to grow up with atrophied sympathies and an utter inability to weep with the sorrowful or rejoice with the glad.

Happily this is not a typical home. The majority of parents have realised that the true Christmas spirit of peace and good-will tends to deepen the spiritual, emotional, social, and mental nature. Christmas should be one of the most powerful influences in the children's lives, and much of that which is best in the spiritual and moral realms may be awakened through the experiences gained in its festivities, provided that there is a right understanding of the true needs of the child's soul.

John and Mary have a good working knowledge of their children's requirements, partly instinctive but largely due to a thoughtful, conscientious study of child nature. Their vision is directed beyond transitory pleasures; they know that the simple joys of the children's own choice and making are the main essentials for lasting gains.

In pursuance of this the children are deputed to initiate and carry through the Christmas programme. Thoughtful, helpful suggestions and sympathy can be obtained at all times, but the mother argues that it is impossible for her to undertake any other work than that connected with the extra domestic preparations. With this freedom the children launch out into various projects, family conferences are held, presents are discussed and a special

*Continued overleaf*

## Christmas and the Child
*Continued*

committee appointed to provide for the evening entertainment, which is the feature of the day.

At least one item in the programme is assigned to each child, and music practice and the memorising of recitations become a pleasure rather than a burden. Charades, in their arrangement and rehearsal, demand much work and effort, involving generosity and self-effacement as the cast is decided; and through all this work the criticisms and opinions of others are eagerly sought so that perfection may be attained.

All their free time possible is filled with the manufacture of dresses from old family clothes, the improvisation of stage properties; while the secret work of making many of the presents adds to the happy interest and makes the time all too short for the older children.

At last arrives the exciting day when they go to town to buy the presents (which cannot be made) with money saved during the year out of their very minute "fixed income," supplemented by a contribution from their father, whose own financial anxieties make him interestedly sympathetic as he hears the children discussing their problems.

Are there any such mathematical exercises in school arithmetic books as the self-imposed and numerous calculations these children have to make? And how differently they face their task, some with care and precision, others with a happy lack of method; their mother listening, contrasts the dispositions and tries to adjust the unevenness of undeveloped character by quiet suggestions.

In the case of the younger children, personal desires and ambitions govern the choice of presents. Four-year-old Daisy promises her mother a doll's tea-service, because "You will be able to let me play with it sometimes"; and tiny Peter cannot be prevented from buying Daddy a fish to swim in his bath! The older children are shocked and would like to expose these subterfuges, lecturing the little selfish mites meanwhile, but they are reminded that not so long ago they surprised their father with a box of soldiers for his birthday. This shows the big brothers and sisters that it is only a difference in outlook which is changed with increasing knowledge, and yet one more link is forged in the understanding between big and little ones, and Mary is deeply touched by the efforts of her big boys and girls to find presents which will more than compensate her for understanding the little ones' innocence.

The younger children, who have not yet learned that pooling funds is the most economical way of buying presents, cling to their purses and refuse to co-operate. They do not wish to profit by the more mature experience of the others; nevertheless, the lesson comes home practically when they find that a six-penny desire cannot be obtained with two-pence!

More joyous moments are still in store after the parcels are brought home by the little people—very tired mentally and physically—for the purchases have to be unwrapped, examined and admired, and carefully written notes enclosed before the gifts are once more restored to their wrappings.

This keeping and sharing of secrets helps to train the children to respect the confidence of others and is an upward step in the direction towards moral strength and right determination.

Only second in enjoyment to the great day itself is Christmas Eve, when final rehearsals are held, the house made gay with decorations, and presents handed over to the head of the family, who hangs them on the tree. All go to bed quite readily at an earlier hour than usual, feeling that perhaps it will bring the dawn of the longed-for day earlier if they do so.

And as we all know, it is literally long before dawn when not only John's and Mary's brood but many others venture from their cosy beds! Father Christmas need not take all the credit to himself and his generosity, for the great joy of the whole business is that the very ordinary new pennies, sweets, oranges, muscatels, etc., are found in a very uncommon place at a most delightfully extraordinary hour.

The celebrations thus begun continue on the same lines; commonplace experiences are imbued with a feeling of adventure and romance because of the unusual aspect they assume—even the short church service is said and felt to be different from all other services and produces a glow altogether in harmony with the day and season. Christmas dinner, though of vast importance, takes a secondary place, for by far the best is yet to be. The revels, it has been decided, shall continue in a large, disused attic which has been specially decorated for the occasion.

John demurred when this arrangement was first propounded—there seemed to him no sense in leaving the pretty, comfortable rooms downstairs for the low empty room with its slanting ceiling and old-fashioned grate. Mary, however, sensed the romantic appeal of the unusual, and reminding her spouse that it was the children's day, cheerfully gave herself up to discomforts, and John followed suit, knowing how sound was her instinct in such matters.

In these novel surroundings the presents are distributed, charades and recitations repeated for the thousandth time and enjoyed as if they had been precious novelties. Finally, willing feet run up and down stairs, fetching the fruit, sandwiches, crackers, jellies, etc., which make a Christmas supper of rare enjoyment, eaten as it is in picnic fashion on the floor.

The musical items of the programme have perforce to be left till the return to the drawing-room and "civilised comforts," as John remarked *sotto voce,* and these with carols complete the day's enjoyments for the younger ones, who loudly lament as they climb the stairs again—but bedwards—that "it will be so long before another Christmas."

The older children complete the bliss of the day by staying up late, comparing presents and dipping into their books as they agree that it is the best Christmas they have ever had, in which John and Mary happily agree.

In their review the children enumerate the various experiences to which they attribute its success. The parents, listening, dwell not so much on the performances or presents; they see in these simple family enjoyments further experiences which will contribute to the all-round development of their bodies, minds, and souls. Sympathy, love, and devotion have been awakened and stirred into activity by individual and co-operative enterprises, and the work achieved through effort and self-sacrifice has brought with it satisfaction, for "desire accomplished is sweet to the soul."

1925

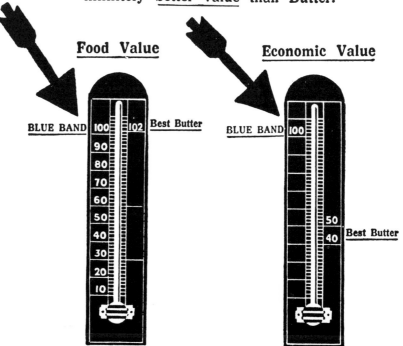

1926

Illustration by J. H. Dowd

*With eyes front on the future, the modern tendency is to concentrate on
the importance of the Child, somewhat at the expense of its Parents.
When is the cult of the latter to be revived? asks this writer*

PARENTS are apt to complain in
these days of the low esteem in
which they are held as a class.
Steep indeed has been the descent,
rapid and cruel the deflation, which
their pride has sustained in the last century or so—so steep, so rapid, that we
almost need to be reminded of the
veneration which they once commanded.
Notoriously, this veneration was until
recent times universal, though it found
expression in a great diversity of ways.
Within living memory, children have
called their fathers " Sir." In ancient
Thrace, according to Herodotus, they
did them honour by eating them. Nor
was this tribute, equivocal as it might
seem, ever misunderstood by the persons
consumed, who, as the historian hastens
to add, " count nothing more blessed
than to be entombed in their offspring."

And if the manner of honouring
parents has varied from time to time,
so also has the motive. Sometimes, no
doubt, such honour has been paid as

a genuine concession to merit, real or
imagined, in the ancestor. Sometimes
(to judge from the very frank language
of the fifth commandment) as a mere
specific for longevity. Much ancestor-
worship among the Greeks was a mere
form of insurance against failure of
crops or cattle-disease, with which the
ancestor was certain to plague his de-
faulting children if the appropriate rites
were withheld. Still, under whatever
forms and for whatever reasons, parents
have had a long and majestic innings.

Consider, for instance, the Roman
father. How sharp a struggle it cost
Roman children to acquire the right,
which seems to our notions elementary,
not to be pawned more than three times
by their father. This change, wrought
by the Law of the Twelve Tables, was
thought at the time a perilous innovation—a concession, as it were, to the
Reds of the nursery. Yet even when
shorn of his unlimited despotism, the
Roman father must remain an object
of sneaking envy to many modern

parents with a teeming nursery and
empty pockets.

The modern parent would probably
not dare, in this humane age, to exercise
his full powers. Yet he may, if he
reads these lines, secretly toy with the
speculation whether his children would
be thought a first-rate security and how
much he might hope to raise on them.
And besides, even if the act were unthink-
able, how potent might not be the mere
threat : " Will you obey me this minute,
darling, or do you wish to be pawned ? "
Can one doubt that some such formula,
uttered quite quietly, would produce a
sort of Locarno spirit in the home?
The crime of parricide, for which the
Roman lawgiver made quaintly elaborate
provision, has, one must confess, somewhat gone out of fashion. The modern
child does not waste powder and shot
on its parents. But any lingering attraction which it may possess would
surely evaporate if the offender knew,
as the Roman child did, that he would
be tied in a sack, with a cock, an ape,

# *A R E N T S*

*By* Lady Violet

Bonham-Carter

and a goat, and tossed into the Tiber.

In Rome, as in some other places, the lion's share of filial reverence fell to the father, the mother receiving next to none. Nor was this distinction peculiar to the mind of the ancients. We see its operation even in Shakespeare. Hamlet's mother, it must be allowed, was no paragon. But neither was his father. He had, no doubt, genuine martial qualities, and was probably at his best when " smiting the sledded Polacks on the ice." But he was not always engaged in this austere and chilly pastime, and in the intervals would seem to have been less reputably employed.

I do not refer here to his slovenly and insanitary habit of spending every afternoon asleep in his orchard, instead of attending to his royal duties, although this in itself goes some way to account for the rotten state of Denmark, and was the direct occasion of his death. I refer to those " foul crimes, done in my days of nature," on which he dwells

with such sepulchral insistence, and even, I cannot but think, with a sort of ghostly gusto. For he complains less of being murdered than of being " cut off " as he puts it, " even in the blossoms of my sins." It is surely not fanciful to read into this phrase something more than a natural irritation at not having time to get " houseled "— some suggestion of regret that he had not had time to sin rather longer.

Assuredly, he was no Hyperion. Yet, towards these two parents, not unevenly matched in turpitude, what is the attitude of their son? He administers to his mother the most gruelling curtain-lecture in literature : but bestows on his father nothing but reverential eulogy. The man, it seems, may steal a horse : the woman cannot look over the stable door. What a text for the woman suffragists, if they could only have devoted a few quiet hours to the study of our national poet !

In the centuries since Shakespeare the balance has been somewhat redressed.

A profound slump in fathers and a mild boom in mothers has resulted in their occupying the same, and that a low place, in the public regard. The Pre-Raphaelite movement and the efforts of poets like Coventry Patmore gave mothers a faint fillip. The insufferable fathers in Fielding and other eighteenth-century novelists first caused the paternal market to sag. It collapsed under such works as Samuel Butler's *Way of All Flesh* and Sir Edmund Gosse's *Father and Son*. Butler was not too kind to mothers, but fathers were to him like a red rag to a bull. Several generations of young men are portrayed in his pages who might, as celibates, have remained quite tolerable. But on the threshold of their careers they are poisoned by paternity. Tarred with its inky brush, they abruptly degenerate into charlatans, bullies, hypocrites and cheats. Such was the acid delicacy of his satire that the type of father he assailed has practically been driven out of circulation. Butler permanently *Continued overleaf*

**1926**

# Give them St. Ivel for tea to-night

*They'll be home soon, hungrier than ever for their tea now the days are chilly. Why not make them one of the delicious things in the St. Ivel book. It'll be a treat for them, and for you, too.*

NOW that it begins to get dark early and it's jolly to light a fire in the evening, it's time to think of new ways of serving St. Ivel. For St. Ivel's a friendly cheese. Everyone in the family likes it. Some like it best just plain with biscuits and butter, some prefer it cooked. St. Ivel cooks beautifully, never losing its smooth creaminess, and it's just as digestible whether you eat it hot or cold. The children love it, and the phosphate lactic cultures in it are doubly good for them now that the sunny days are gone. The good country things in it— rich new milk and smooth curds—bring a breath of Somerset farms to your table all the year round.

If you want to find all sorts of delicious ways of serving St. Ivel, send a card now to St. Ivel, Ltd., 56 Newton Road, Yeovil, Somerset, for their little book— 'St. Ivel Cheese Recipes.'

*You'll score a real success with these St. Ivel Cheese muffins— they really do melt in the mouth.*

## Parents

*(Continued)*

depressed the shares of fathers. Correspondingly those of the children rose, not without some assistance from the poets.

Wordsworth did fathers no good when he proclaimed that the child was father to the man, and the better philosopher of the two; and that the longer we live, on the whole the worse we become. Children were quick to profit by the ideas which this malicious bard and his school put into their heads. They are no longer impressed with the favour which their parents were supposed to have done them in bringing them into the world. It was not unnatural that they should be so impressed when the simplest notions of heaven prevailed. Getting born into this world was then regarded by everyone as a pre-condition of attaining bliss in the next, and was therefore thought a good thing on balance, however disagreeable at the moment. Such arguments are wasted on the agnostic in the modern cot, who, seeing life steadily and seeing it whole, often decides that its discomforts exceed its blessings, and is little inclined to be beholden to the authors of his being.

One consequence of this is that parents, unable to cut any figure in their old *rôle* of wise and grave persons, have frankly resigned this task to their children, and given themselves over to an exaggerated juvenility. A sense of their own worthlessness has driven them forth from their own firesides; some few of them into colleges for adult education, the mere existence of which would have been thought an outrage by their ancestors; others (more numerous these last) into sexagenarian dancing-classes in which they soon learn to outdo the nerveless and sophisticated caperings of their offspring. A sort of second adolescence, an Indian spring, descends on this type of parent. As he walks (I use the masculine for brevity only) he rises on the ball of the foot. Knowing he is a mere butterfly and can never be anything better, he jazzes along the primrose slope before the indulgent eyes of his brood, to the skirl of ukeleles and the popping of champagne corks, secure in the knowledge that if the temple of learning is closed to him, the *Palais de Danse* is, and remains, open.

Parents of this last type are unlikely to be numbered among readers of this periodical. Its name repels the idea. Yet let not its readers imagine that by refusing the cheaper consolations which the situation affords, they have escaped from the situation itself. The logic of the New Child is harsh and faulty. It claims that a monopoly of vision and virtue resides in the young, and denies their existence in its parents. Be it so, but in that case let children realise that you cannot get blood from a stone. As it is, they are quick to lay at the door of the parent any defects in their own upbringing. On their own view parents are incapable of doing anything better, and an abominable upbringing should be reckoned like bad weather, among the inevitable mischances for which no one is to blame.

As it is, the parent has responsibility, but no power; and is expected to combine the parts of mentor and butt. His advice is sought, but disregarded; his jokes listened to, but deplored. And the sting of his plight lies in this, that he has learnt to share the low opinion in which his qualities are held. He has lost the sense of pontifical infallibility which buoyed up his predecessors and nerved them to their impossible task. He hopes he has acquired greater breadth of view, but suspects it is mainly greater vagueness, and knows it will be construed as such by his children.

Yet it is inherent in the nature of children, that he must do something about them. They cannot simply be allowed to rip. Something, however meagre, he must tell them, "of man, of nature, and of human life." He, who lacks instruction, must go through the form of imparting it. He, who lacks character, must affect to shape theirs. An involuntary jurisdiction over their every act is thrust upon him by the inexorable nurse or governess. He, who in his own eyes as well as theirs, stands on his trial, must in the forum of the schoolroom play the part of constable, judge, and sheriff's officer. Convicted himself, he must conceal the arrows of the convict under a mockery of ermine.

Hs is thus placed in a hopelessly false position, from which at the moment I see little prospect of escape. If children were consistent, he could impress on them that it is no use coming to parents for what ex-hypothesi they do not possess. If children were far-sighted, he could remind them that they will most of them be parents themselves some day: and that unless they wish to foul the nest in which their riper years will be spent, they should extol the status of parenthood instead of vilifying it. But children are not consistent nor far-sighted.

---

## Practical Demonstrations

Fully qualified members of the Institute staff are available to give lectures and practical demonstrations on any domestic subject at private houses, Women's Institutes, schools, and institutions of all kinds. Application, giving full particulars, should be made to The Director, Good Housekeeping Institute, 49 Wellington Street, Strand, W.C.2

---

The time is therefore ripe for desperate expedients. I think an appeal should be made to the poets to "write up" parents. Changes in the prevailing note of poetry are so rapid that this is, I think, perfectly feasible, and the first step to be taken. If some bold lyrist of the Sitwell School could be persuaded that the cult of the parent was sufficiently farcical—no difficult task surely—parents might easily become the rage. People would tumble over each other to avoid the young. Their society and pretensions would not be tolerated for an instant. They would be regarded as thundering bores. Blackleg hostesses who had young persons to their parties, would see their photographs disappear from the Society papers. Those who gave Christmas Trees would be cut. A swingeing majority of Darbys and Joans would be regarded as essential to make any dinner party go.

1926

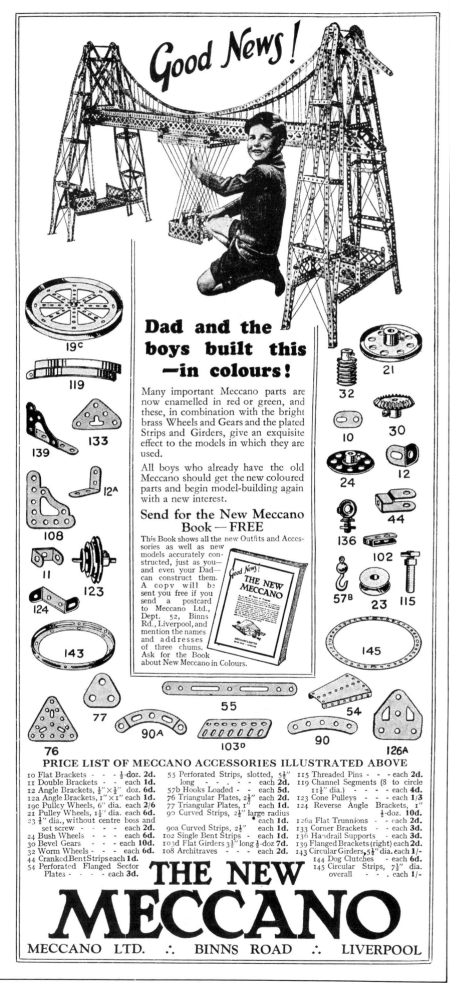

1926

# Things You'll

Decorations by
Elizabeth Montgomery

## Playing Ninepins

*On the Lawn*

IF you have six ninepins, set three at one end of the lawn and three at the other; if no ninepins, find some empty vinegar or lime-juice bottles. The game is played by two people and a judge.

At a signal from the judge, one child starts from one end of the lawn and the other from the opposite end. Each has to fetch the ninepins opposite to him, separately, and the one who reaches the point he started from first, after his three, swift, breathless journeys, is winner. If more than two play, they should be timed, and the one who is the quickest wins. Each ninepin must be made to stand up; it must not be thrown down.

*Books for a Boy*

Here is a little list of books that I am sure you will enjoy very much: *Prester John*, by John Buchan; Dickens's *Tale of Two Cities*; *The Last of the Mohicans*, by James Fenimore Cooper; *The Invisible Man*, by H. G. Wells; *Uncle Tom's Cabin*, by Mrs. Beecher Stowe; *Fifth Form at St. Dominic's*, by Reed; *The Abbot*, by Scott; *St. Paul the Hero*, by Glover.

*Making the String Box*

You ought to make a string box for Mother. Visit Cook, and get from her a large, clean empty tin with a round top, the lid of which presses on. Then take your lid, place it on something flat, and punch or bore a neat hole through the centre.

This hole is for the string to come through, when you pull at the ball inside. Now comes the joy of painting your tin. You must do it from the tubes in your oil-paint box.

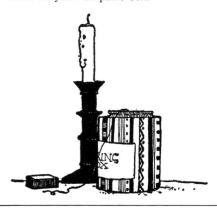

## Signcraft

*For Country Rambles*

IT is great fun to play at Red Indians when you are out these long sunny days. You must learn the trail signs for " danger," " peace," " wait here," " I have gone home," etc. You can have an imaginary war if you like, with ambushes and other exciting happenings.

With a stick on the ground trace a circle, with a small circle inside. This means, " I have gone home."

*A Country Walk*

A London boy was lucky enough to be taken for a whole day into Buckinghamshire the other week. Just before he went, he asked his mother what he should specially look out for on the walk. Mother put her hands on Charles's shoulders, and whispered these things in his ear:

" Blue sky, white and silver clouds, deep green grass, blaze of golden buttercups, red and white campion, ragged robin, cows, sheep, the cuckoo, if you can catch a glimpse of him. Tell me, Charles," she added, " if you hear the nightingale; and see if you can find any tiny forget-me-nots. Do bring me back some young beech leaves for my vases."

Charles loved the walk, but best of all he liked the pond. He lay down on the grass quite near, and had his lunch of tongue sandwiches. The water was full of black tadpoles; and he saw newts, the trumpet-snail, a dragon-fly, and best of all, the water-spider.

## The Donkey

*A School Tale*

IF you had looked in Mrs. Green-Edwards's field on the first of May, you would have seen a donkey standing among the buttercups and daisies. She had a rough brown coat, and melting long grey eyes full of cleverness and understanding, *most* beautiful ears and a noble tail. Altogether she was a great darling.

" But I want to see the world," she sighed. " It is so long since I got any exercise, and went along the pleasant country roads. I want to draw a cart, and take somebody about, who will like me and talk to me. It is dreadfully dull living in this field! "

In the big red house rich Mrs. Green-Edwards was yawning. This lady often forgot things; and she had forgotten that she wanted to sell the donkey she had bought in a foolish moment. Just imagine, Jinny had been living in a green meadow for a whole year doing nothing. She was too fat, and very much bored!

*Mr. Speedy's Plan*

Now, that very May morning, in a big white house standing in the New Forest five miles away, a whole classroom full of small boys was thinking about donkeys. The master of the school, Mr. Speedy, had been telling them that there was to be a school donkey just as soon as ever they could find one; a donkey to pull about the littlest ones when they went for a picnic, a donkey to take Mrs. Speedy to and fro from the village, a donkey with a cart into which the whole school would pile bracken from the Forest. Oh, how they were going to enjoy that donkey! The boys were very keen. If only they could find one!

All the time, five miles away, Jinny sighed, and tossed her head about, and longed for something to happen, and in the big red house rich Mrs. Green-Edwards was dozing, dozing.

Now, the *lucky* first of May was the birthday of Jones Major, and he had been invited to bicycle over to see his aunt.

So down the road he went, past forest land and ponds fringed with May flowers, and sandy places, on and on; and by and by, at the end of his journey, whom should he see but Jinny, the prettiest donkey in Hampshire, leaning sadly over a fence.

# Like To Know

### By
### Marjory Royce

## Pretty Jinny

*Meets Basil Jones*

JONES MAJOR leapt off his bicycle, ran up to Jinny, and stroked her very carefully and respectfully on her lovely long nose. Jinny was very delighted, and allowed him to stroke, for nobody had spoken to her for *so* long! And Jones Major was a rosy-cheeked, smiling lad.

"I must give you a birthday present, my dear Basil," said Jones's aunt half an hour later, as she cut the pink-and-white birthday cake. "A really good one, as I always believe in giving an *extra* good present when a boy is twelve."

Jones tried to pick up courage. Would he seem very greedy?

"I would love that donkey," he said shyly. And he explained about Jinny.

"I do believe Mrs. Green-Edwards would let her go," said Aunt Betty; and after tea they called on the sleepy lady, and she woke up with a start, and gave a glad "yes," and for two pounds and the certainty of a good home, Jinny was sold!

Jones Major left his bicycle and rode Jinny back to school in triumph.

*The Little Red Cart*

The first thing he saw was a beautiful red donkey-cart outside the school; but *no* donkey! A crowd of boys stood round, and when Jones came along, friendly Jinny was so pleased by the sight of the children, that she actually trotted up to them at the pace of five miles an hour!

"Oh, Basil," cried Mrs. Speedy, "we've had this cart offered us and have bought it; but there's no donkey. You don't mean to say that you've got one? How perfect!"

"Jinny is my birthday present," said Basil, halting his pet, patting her, and dismounting. "She's for the use of the school. Shall I harness her up at once, Mrs. Speedy?"

"Oh, at *once*, please," exclaimed everybody. "*What* a beauty!"

And there and then Jinny was joyfully harnessed to the little red cart, and in no time Jones Major was taking Mrs. Speedy and Jones Minor, his brother, for a spanking little drive.

I told you that May-Day was lucky!

## The Merry Month

*Dancing Round the Maypole*

MAY'S birthday falls on the first of this beautiful month. She is just five and lives in the prettiest of the Surrey villages, where they set up a great maypole with fluttering ribbons on the green on May Day. May has been learning a special dance for it.

*The Dolly's Times*

Find a big sheet of lined paper, and rule it into four divisions. Blot the lines down and across carefully. At the top, print the date, and the title. *The Doll's Times,* or *The Nursery News,* or *Dolly's Journal* would be good titles.

*Good News.*—Cousin Celia is coming and bringing a new head for Clara.

*Pretty Good News.*—Two doll's cakes I baked were said to be eatable by Mother.

*Bad News.*—I spilled ink over Dinah's best red silk coat.

*Pretty Bad News.*—I can't find Sailor Boy. Did I leave him at the Vicarage?

In the paper say how the dolls are doing at their singing lesson, report their marks, and you can give animal news as well, if you like. Advertisements can go on the back, and have a serial story running every week. Viola is writing a thrilling detective tale.

## Spring Flowers & Sweets

*Chocolate Custard*

CHOCCY custard is just the sweet to eat on a warm May Day. You use the ordinary powdered custard, and when it is nearly cooked, stir through it an ounce of cocoa moistened with milk. Prunella, a little girl I know (who ought, I suppose, only to eat prunes), tells me that she puts this into a tiny custard glass, and eats it with cocoa-nut sprinkled on top, quite cold.

*A Flowery Cone*

When Aunt Audrey came to stay the other day, she was perfectly delighted to find as a greeting a most unusual-looking bowl of spring flowers standing on a satinwood table in her room.

Her niece Jennifer had been out in the woods, and had brought in a fragrant load of cowslips, primroses, anemones, violets, little sprays of the beautiful crab blossom, tall fresh bluebells, and graceful beaked parsley. She had arranged the flowers in a china bowl with a round glass flower-holder.

*The Victorian Posy*

The bowl was completely filled. In the central holes stood the tallest blossoms—the crab; round it the just less tall wild hyacinths; next came tallish cowslips all the way round. All the colours were mixed at the end; there were no spaces: every flower touched another. Of course all the stalks were in water.

1927

# "Muvvers and *Farvers*"

"I *never* let her have too many sweeties."

"Umph! P'raps she needs more nushment. Do you give her lots of milk?"

"Oh, doctor! she *hates* it."

"Dat's dreadful! Well, see how she likes milk and Instant Postum. I specs you've got some in the house."

"Of tourse!"

"Well, you try it. My muvver— I mean a lady I know—*always* gives it to her children. They just luv it."

Instant Postum, made with hot milk, ranks in a child's mind with cake and other toothsome delights. Mothers like their children to have it because it is so good for them—the nourishment of milk and the delicious purity of Instant Postum. Instant Postum is just wheat, bran, and a little sugar-cane molasses converted into tiny sparkling granules that dissolve instantly in boiling water or hot milk to make a drink as innocent as childhood itself.

"I'LL be muvver, Joan, and you be Auntie Pat, and *you'd* better be farver, Peter... No—o! I fink I'll have Tommy for my farver ... you ... can be ... the doctor ..."

Mothers and fathers—the game of which children never tire.

And, if you go on quietly with your sewing, you'll probably get some illuminating side-lights upon your own system of child-welfare.

Listen to the consultation.

"I *weally* don't know what can be the matter wiv her, doctor. She goes to bed early, sleeps wiv her windows *wide* open. And

### Give it a month's trial

You can't expect to discover how much better Instant Postum is for your youngsters than other hot drinks unless you give it a fair trial; can you? So we suggest that you give it them, not once or twice, not even "now and again for a treat," but steadily, for, say, a month. That will give you a real chance to prove how much good it does them when drunk regularly. In order to start you on this test, we will send you the first week's supply—free.

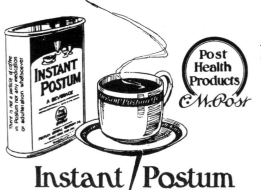

Post Health Products *C. M. Post*

Instant ! Postum

**FREE!**————*Post the Coupon to-day*

Most good grocers sell Instant Postum—45-cup tin 1/7; 90-cup tin 2/8. (These prices do not apply to Northern Ireland or to the Irish Free State.)   Instant Postum is one of the Post Health Products, which include Post Toasties (Double-thick Indian Corn Flakes), Post's Bran Flakes and Grape-Nuts

1927

# The Children's Room

By *HARRY LEE*                    *Illustrated by Lucile P. Marsh*

This is the room where the children played.
Here are the toys : the pensive bear ;
The elephant ; the dog-eared books ;
Jack-in-the-box with crinkly hair ;
Grenadier in his scarlet coat ;
A broken top ; the train that swayed
With such brave clatter around the room—
The happy room where the children played !

This is the room where the tales were told—
Told at dusk when the stars looked down.
Hop-o'-my-Thumb set forth from here,
Dick and the Cat for London Town :

The vine that shadows the window yet
Was the Bean-stalk ; here lay the pot of gold
For this was the end of the Rainbow Trail—
The magic room where the tales were told !

This is the room where the children slept—
Men now, strong in the world of men ;
Home they come with boys of their own,
Home to Mother and off again !
But though they go they are with her still—
With her as children—and she has kept
As a holy place—a place of her own—
The little room where the children slept !

1927

*Friction frequently arises when children form intimacies which the parents resent;*

# Youth in Rebellion

Decoration by Clara Elsene Peck

IN youth we are all idealists, although idealism is often disguised as cynicism. It is difficult for the middle-aged, who have forgotten their youth, to understand that cynicism in young people is over-compensation for ideals which are unrealised or disappointed. Youth seeks perfection, independence and love. Boys and girls rebel against the prohibitions of their elders. They believe them to be false and hypocritical. They see hate and bitterness reigning in the world which was meant for love and harmony.

Every normal boy and girl wants to love and be loved, and they realise that many of us who are middle-aged have forgotten that human beings are born to happiness and harmony. They see the older generation unhappy, irrational and irresponsible; the tragic victims of their uncontrolled emotions. And they demand freedom, they say, to live according to their own standards, not the false standards of older people.

The conflict between the generations is often intense over the right to friendship and love outside the home. A son or daughter reaching out for love, forms an intimacy which the parents resent. Their reasons may be trivial, based on false values. "This young person," they say, "is not of our world, in

our set or class, and you must choose your friends from the children of our friends." The young people naturally rebel and there is discord in the home. Friendship and love are strong sentiments and opposition intensifies the feeling for the friend or lover who is disparaged.

The most superficial student of human nature realises the importance of the emotional factor in life. No one of us is rational, especially when stirred by emotion. Some feel more deeply than others. They are ardent, with a vivid, emotional nature, and such people suffer intensely when crossed in friendship and love. The most bitter family quarrels centre round the emotional love life, and parents may estrange for years the love of a child by the harsh demand that their grown boy or girl should give up a friend or a lover of whom they disapprove. If the parents were rational and responsible people instead of grown-up children, they would never *oppose.* They would leave the love emotion to fade if it was weak and unworthy as they believed, and they would provide new interests, the opportunity of new, better, and worthier friendships for the children. Through every disagreement they would be cool and friendly, ready to help if their ad-

# LO

*In the fourth article of this vitally the complexities of emotion which Love. Their constructively help since it represents the friendly between the older and*

vice was asked, fair and just in what they said of the companions of their children.

The day has passed when fathers could have their way by uncontrolled outbursts of temper or mothers prevail through their tears. Most of us know that if the right sentiments are cultivated in childhood, young people can, later in life, be left to choose their friends. It is hard sometimes for the parents who see their son or daughter caring deeply for someone they think unworthy, but most of us have to learn that the strength of love depends far less on the worth of the person loved than upon the quality of the emotions, the temperament of the lover. Love is a more powerful passion than egoism. When young people fall in love the

Clara Elsene Peck

*objecting: "These young folk are not of our world, in our set or class . . ."*

# By Dr. Elizabeth Sloan Chesser and

# Lady (Neville) Pearson

# VE

*interesting series, the authors probe are summarised in the term— ful advice is particularly valuable halfway house of partnership the growing generation*

primitive emotions are concentrated on the lover and love dominates the mind so that caution and common sense are non-existent. The lover is often indifferent to other aspects of life, incapable of work or interest in others. When love is at this fever point and the love affair is broken, there is a dangerous damming back of emotions which may affect the mind very seriously. It is possible to die of a broken heart, but more usually the emotion is sublimated in work or service, in religion or love of some other person. People of strong feeling and deep nature may never be able to love again, because their power of intense love is exhausted.

When we are very young the emotions are more superficial, as a rule,

and early adolescence is the period of easily broken flirtations, of affectionate friendships between boys and girls, which serve a good purpose. There are people who say ugly things of the friendships between modern girls and boys. They suggest that girls of to-day are immodest, eager for sex experience, careless and shameless in their code. But is it true? In every generation there are various types. Eighteenth-century literature does not give us an impression of women's chastity; the Victorians concealed many an escapade beneath the cloak of hypocrisy. Ugliness and vulgarity exist in every age. Youth to-day has fewer repressions. Young people talk more freely and they are sometimes noisy, silly, pretentious. The absence of chaperons gives opportunity to the lawless of both sexes, but sensualists, young and old, will always evade restrictions somehow.

Idleness in every age makes for sensuality. Girls as well as boys require regular occupation in adolescence. Hard work compels self-discipline and is the basis of morality. We must face the facts of life and love. Every normal individual must love something, to give order and unity and beauty to life. Self-love is the first and lowest form of

love, normal in childhood when the egoistic and self-regarding emotions and sentiments are strong; pride and vanity, avarice and greed. As life develops, external loves should have their place in life; love of parents and of brothers and sisters, of friends; love of games, art, beauty and work. With such concrete love, there should arise in the normally developing personality the more abstract love of moral sentiments. What Shand calls " respect for conscience " makes human beings " conscious-stricken," miserable, when they fail in conduct to come up to their ideals. In youth there is often a sudden development of love of moral sentiment, and the new generation has evolved farther than any before, because there is less prejudice, hate and intolerance of other people's religion and other countries, for example, among people to-day, compared with the era of our parents.

The new generation realises that love is the greatest thing in life, but some of them forget that it is not the only thing. The best and kindest, most loving and most sympathetic boys and girls are those who are in greatest danger from love.

1927

"My Nightcap"

# OXO *for Winter nights*

The best tonic in the world is a good night's sleep after a cup of hot Oxo. In this climate you <u>must</u> have Oxo. Cold wet days, frosty nights, and sudden changes of weather call for <u>extra</u> nourishment—the nourishment of Beef which Oxo gives.

# Get the OXO Habit

Hot Oxo removes that tired feeling, quiets the nerves, and puts new strength into you. Tens of thousands of people make Oxo—or Oxo and milk—their daily "nightcap." Many who dislike milk take it readily when a little Oxo is mixed with it.

*It's <u>Beef</u> that counts*

Some 500,000 cattle, including what are probably the largest herds of pure bred Herefords in the world, assure a constant supply of prime beef for the preparation of Oxo.

**Oxo on hot Buttered Toast**

When you want something really good, add a little Oxo to the butter before spreading it on the toast. The savoury taste of Oxo makes it a delicious dish. Children love it.

# A WONDERFUL NEW BOOK ON DRESSING CHILDREN —FREE!

1927

## LET PEOPLE SAY—'HOW BEAUTIFULLY YOU ALWAYS DRESS THEM!'

Deep down in her heart every mother wants her children always to do her credit. Wherever they go—out walking, at parties, or at school your children are *you!* And it is by your children's clothes that people judge your cleverness and good taste. Study the pages of the Duro Book of Children's Dress. You will find in them such help and inspiration as you have never had before!

## Read these chapter headings from the children's Duro Book

*Introduction*

*Dressing Little Boys*

*Dressing Little Girls*

*The Quaint and Pretty Child* ·

*Dressing them for School*

*Dressing them for the Holidays*

*Duro Fancy Dress*

*Embroidery for children's clothes*

*Furnishing the Nursery*

*Duro pattern service*

*Write for your copy to-day:* Sit down this very afternoon and write to Burgess, Ledward & Co. Ltd. (Dept. 2), 22 Dickinson St., Manchester (the makers of Duro Fabrics) for your *free* copy of the Children's Duro Book. And see how a little fascinating work can make your children's clothes a pride and joy to you!

1927

# SCHOOL

*Parents and others entrusted with the responsibility of*

*series of articles in which the writer discusses modern educa-*

*of the choice of schools. She will deal in turn with primary,*

PROFESSOR COMPAGNAC has compared the educator to a man moving from one point to another of a ship travelling through rough waters. "The point from which he meant to start has changed its place before he can even set out, and his point of arrival will not change less, if indeed he ever can be said to reach it. The romantic terror of his devious course might serve to indicate the troubles of a man who tries to prepare a child whom he cannot catch for a world which he cannot overtake."

Perhaps no more accurate description could be applied to the rapid changes which are taking place in those highly-organised institutions of to-day—British preparatory schools. Kipling wrote that "there are nine and sixty ways of constructing tribal lays; and every single one of them is right;" we might

say that there are now, seemingly, nine and sixty ways of child-education, and in every single one of them we may find something not only right, but of high value to the present generation, even if much may be found to be but ephemeral and unstable—the froth, as it were, on the surface of the educational ferment.

To young parents who are looking forward to the first term for their small boy or girl, preparatory schools appear to be in a state of chaos. From

numerous quarters, far and near, at home and abroad, there has swept into our scholastic institutions a great unrest and upheaval. The conflicting reports, discussions and controversies of the teaching world in the Press, the ever-increasing variety of schools recommended and advertised, the multitudinous array of subjects in the school curricula, and the many new teaching movements and methods, may well be confusing and bewildering to parents who are endeavouring to study and

1927

# DAYS

### By
### *Marian Bethell*

*securing the best education for children will welcome this new*

*tional problems, with special emphasis on the important subject*

*preparatory and public schools, and, finally, the universities*

understand the mighty problem of modern education.

As the Principal of the Cheltenham Ladies' College writes: " These are indeed days in which all who are responsible for the training of the young need much sympathy towards others, much courage for themselves . . . *Never was there a time when parents and teachers alike needed a greater vision,* a wider understanding of the place which self-expression as related to self-sacrifice must take in life

—if life it is to be. It is an age in which the joys of self-expression are offering themselves in lavish manner, and the danger is that the search after much that may be beautiful, attractive and satisfying for the moment may obscure the sense of values which lies behind the real purpose of life—the fashioning within oneself of a character, a self which shall be of eternal value."

In these words is expressed the key-note of the whole matter. Every one of the new educational movements has

arisen to meet a demand, and is adapted not only to action in accordance with our new knowledge of the child-mind and the depths in the child-nature revealed by the New Psychology, but also to the period through which we are now passing. Now, as always, in every age, new methods come naturally into being to meet the demand of each new movement, and to secure its aim.

A full inquiry into the educational advance of to-day reveals undoubtedly the fact that principles have never been recognised so clearly, or so generally and successfully carried to practical fruition as now. Opposing contradictory attitudes there may be between the disciples of the pioneers of the various movements, but on the whole, the upholders of the new education are fast approaching a high standard of unity; and all agree that education should not only prepare *Continued overleaf*

65

# Do **YOU** know the Grape-Nuts secret?

1927

# Those Robinson youngsters at No. 23..

You'd think they were going to a picnic. They both carry satchels —Billy swings a cricket bat rather dangerously. Two pairs of rosy cheeks—all aglow with happiness and health. They are "those Robinson youngsters," going to school.

It's Mrs. Robinson knows the secret,—that it is breakfast time which makes all the difference to kiddies. *She knows the Grape-Nuts secret.*

Grape-Nuts? Yes. It contains those vital energy-giving elements in an easily digested form, which growing children *must* have if they are to be strong, energetic and healthful.

**Post Health Products**

*CN Post*

**GRAPE-NUTS**
supplies the body with:

Energy-producing dextrins, maltose, and other carbohydrates.

The essential vitamin-B, the appetite builder.

Iron, to enrich the blood.

Protein for muscle and body-building.

Phosphorus to strengthen the bones and teeth.

*Grape-Nuts is one of the Post Health Products, which include also Post Toasties, Postum and Post's Bran Flakes.*

Eaten with milk or cream, Grape-Nuts has a rich nutty flavour— different from anything else. It is a crisp food—a food you will enjoy chewing. Chewing promotes good teeth and tends to prevent cavities and tooth ache. Get a package from your grocer *to-day*.

# Grape=Nuts
## *for Breakfast*

# School Days

*(Continued)*

a child for adult life by the development of character and right feeling, by the building-up of a highly-controlled emotional nature in a sound, healthy body, but also give rein to the *development of his innate interests,* and the latent gifts and talents, which rise spontaneously within him.

For this, after all is said, is the true meaning of the word "education" —"a release of power from within"— that latent power which exists in every child, for the growth of which parents and teachers are working to-day in greater unison and co-operation than ever before. The vital connection, too, between the child's home and social life, and his school life and discipline, is being widely realised. If the teachers of to-day dare not neglect the study of the new methods, neither may parents ignore or neglect the study of the new movements; or the great work which is being carried on, so patiently and perseveringly, in such a quiet and unostentatious manner, within the walls of our best schools and colleges.

"Amidst all this mass of new knowledge what, then, shall we study?" cry the parents. "We would co-operate, we want to take a more active and direct share in the education of our children; and to do our best to help them to obtain life more abundantly."

What should be the scope and aim of their education?

Should we teach them *to take the cash and let the credit go;* or to work with a single eye for the good of their country and their fellow-men, never troubling about competition.

Should our small sons learn French and German, rather than Greek or Latin?

What should be the subjects included in the curriculum of a preparatory school?

Should children of eight or nine years of age study Science as the basis of knowledge?

Should home work be abolished?

Should punishment be abolished?

Are we right in allowing self-government?

Should hand work or head work take first place?

Are large or small schools the best?

Are co-educational schools beneficial?

Has any one method of education been found to triumph as universally the best?

What is meant by The Dalton Plan, The Heuristic Method, The Eurythmic System, and The Reform Methods in Latin and Mathematics?

At what age should our children enter a primary, preparatory, or public school?

How shall we choose the schools which will best develop their gifts and individuality in preparation for a future career?

These are some of the questions which parents to-day are asking, a few of which we will now proceed to discuss. We would like to mention first, however, that all details included in these discussions of movements and methods, and all descriptions and accounts of schools, are written *entirely free from any idea of advertisement,* but with the sole aim and hope of proving of real assistance and of practical interest to parents, puzzled by the infinite complications of present educational problems.

Parents with wide vision, who look forward into the future, foresee—though, perhaps, only as yet, as through a glass, darkly—the day when education will become a process which changes in accordance with the growth of the child, and the development of his consciousness.

Many are realising, however, that more important than all the training of primary, preparatory, public school or university training is the influence of the early home life, for the parent during the first years of a child's life is the greatest educator.

Through the strides made in psychological discovery and our increased knowledge of human nature, we know that gifts or curses of so-called heredity and ancestry are more often than not worked into the child's opening consciousness by suggestion from the parent-mind. We now know that a child inherits *tendencies* only—tendencies for good or ill according to the gifts or failings of the parents, who realising these facts, watch over the child's growing consciousness from babyhood, and surround him with controlled, guarded thoughts of physical, mental, and spiritual strength.

During the first six years of a child's life undesirable hereditary tendencies can thus be entirely eradicated; and parents can send their son or daughter forth into the school-world equipped with an armour which will grow stronger as the years pass.

## Duresco'ed walls will keep their summer brightness all through the dark days

Because Duresco colours are fast, sun does not fade them. Exposure to sea air or even to chemical fumes leaves Duresco unaffected. The tints you chose in early summer time will hold the same warmth and colour when summer is forgotten.

That is only one reason why you should choose Duresco for decoration inside and out. Other reasons are—Duresco is a preservative, too; it is washable and therefore sanitary; it endures, and more than fifty of its tints are fast on new plaster; above all it is inexpensive. *Ask your Decorator.*

*Choose your colours. There are over 60 in the Duresco Tint Book. Your Decorator, who has known Duresco since he was a boy, can give you a copy, or we will send you one direct.*

Manufacturers:
Silicate Paint Co.
(J. B. Orr & Co. Ltd.)
Charlton,
London, S.E.

# DURESCO

## THE KING OF WATER PAINTS FOR INTERIORS & EXTERIORS

1927

# *Things You'll Like to Know*

### Carry's Visit

"WELL, I'm sure it's very good of you to have Caroline to stay," said Caroline's Aunt with a weary sigh. "She's so terribly untidy."

"I like having her," murmured kind Mrs. Hayes, with whom Caroline was going to stay a fortnight. But she couldn't help seeing that Caroline's hair was like tossed hay, and that her nails had a black rim as if in deepest mourning.

"You are to share Dewdrop's room, dear," said Mrs. Hayes.

"And I hope you'll keep it tidy," said Dewdrop in rather a bullying voice.

Dewdrop's shingled head, her trim long legs, her well-creased jumper suits, all were perfect. And her room was perfect. A hundred and three china animals were ranged on the top of her chest of drawers, and she dusted them *all* daily.

Caroline flung down her suitcase on the bed, and looked round. She looked at the old oak beams that ran across the attic ceiling, and at the wide window seat which showed such a very thick wall.

"Tell me about this darling house, Dewdrop."

"I don't know anything much about it," said Dewdrop. But her mother came in, in time to hear the question and said, "The house was built right away back in 1702. A wonderful little old lady is said to have lived here called Dame Broome. She made herb medicines and cured sick people for miles round; also wines, they say, all kinds—ginger, lemon, rhubarb, dandelion, cowslip, and buttercup. And sweets. That beautifully round bay of ours downstairs was her little shop window. Can't you just imagine her arranging her stores?"

*Dame Broome kept a shop and sold herb medicines to the village*

*Illustrations by*

### Behind the Fireplace

"Oh, how I shall love staying here," said Caroline. "Have you any books about her?"

"She does come into an old book I have," said Mrs. Hayes.

"Oh, let me see it at once!" And Caroline bounded to the door.

"Hadn't you better brush your hair before lunch?" drawled Dewdrop.

"What does it matter?" cried Caroline. But stayed to do it.

"What an awful child she is," said Dewdrop to her mother that evening. "She looks like a little rag-bag, and loses everything."

"I know; and she must try to get over that. But she may *find* things as well as lose them, you know."

And Caroline did. Routing behind the marvellous old fireplace in the cottage sitting-room, on hands and knees, grubbing among the rubble, she found a wonderful little pair of old-fashioned spectacles with a *very* high arch to the nose.

"I believe they belonged to Dame Broome!" she shouted. "So she's *true*."

"And, Caroline, I believe they *did*. They are so ancient and they are made for a very little old body," said Mrs. Hayes.

"And, oh, how well I can seem to see her now!" said Caroline ecstatically. "Looking over the top of the rims in her bunching, green flowered print gown. I shall make up a story about her."

Dewdrop, who seldom found anything (proper people don't, you know), began rather to like Caroline from that very hour. People who find things are always worth knowing.

And when the first Christmas fancy dress party came on, both girls wished to go as Dame Broome, but Dewdrop gave it up, feeling that Caroline really knew more about her.

QUEENS OF ENGLAND

*Elizabeth Montgomery*

# By Marjory Royce

1927

*A History Rhyme*

Names of the Queens of
England,
How beautiful they are,
There's Mary of Modena,
Berengaria of Navarre,

Avisa, too, of Gloucester,
Eleanor of Guienne,
I think the Kings of Eng-
land
Were all poetic men.

For Philippa of Hainault,
Eleanor of Castille,
And fair Anne of Bo-
hemia
Sound charming, don't
you feel?

But later Queens of Eng-
land
Make just such lovely
dames,
*The Times* gives the an-
nouncement
But seldom prints the
names.

Babe Pamela of Padstow,
Babe Rosemary of Rye,
And tiny Anne of Ash-
ford,
In cradles sweetly lie.

Elizabeth of Eltham
And Joan of Jesmondene,
Each shall grow bonny,
fearless, fine
And be an English Queen.

## A Tumbler Trick

Take a match, light it, drop it into the tumbler, put your hand over the tumbler. Wonderful to relate you will find the tumbler presses tightly to your hand. This is because when you put your hand on top of the glass the match goes out, the air contracts when cool, making a partial vacuum, and the outer air pressure clings tightly and holds the glass fast to your palm.

## What's an Abalone?

While you are quietly falling asleep, just think of some of the funny things that are happening all over the world. Do you know that men in rubber suits, lead-soled shoes and real iron hats, divers in fact, are walking about on the bottom of the sea at Monterey Bay on the Californian Coast. They are unfastening the plate-like shells of the abalone fish from the rocks. The abalone tastes good, they make him into steaks and his beautiful shell is used for jewellery, knife handles and souvenir spoons.

## Stars in Dim Blue

In this month of blue mists and grey skies do not forget to wake early sometimes during the first fortnight to have a peep at Mercury shining in the East-South-East. Search, too, for brilliant Jupiter as the sky grows dark.

*Jupiter shines brightly as the twilight falls*

## Butterscotch

Put one pound of Demerara sugar into a saucepan, with a teacupful of water. Boil till a little dropped into cold water immediately becomes hard and brittle. Add 2 oz. of fresh butter, and boil four or five minutes longer. Pour on to a buttered dish, and cut into oblong pieces.

## An Easy Apron

You can make the prettiest apron for yourself or Mummy with a yard of Russian crash. Buttonhole it round the bottom and sides with bright wools, make a gay pattern along the bottom in blues and yellows, turn in the top corners to make the bib, have shoulder straps of blue braid.

## Breakfast in Stuart Days

If you had lived long ago, in Stuart days in London, you might have sat on a little green stool in a parlour hung with grey linsey-woolsey and gilt leather, and you might have had for breakfast, cold meat, small beer, and oat-cake. A wooden platter and a pewter mug!

1927

*Youth in Rebellion—*

# Reactions *in* the School *and* University

## *By Dr. Elizabeth Sloan Chesser and Lady (Neville) Pearson*

Illustrated by
Clara Elsene Peck

*These articles are written with a view
Sympathetic understanding and know-
bringing that*

THE study of psychology is raising new problems of education. The mothers of modern schoolboys are many of them critical about school methods as never before: they are dissatisfied with the type of education that has been considered perfect by previous generations. Some of them declare that school changes their children, their sons especially, out of all recognition, and not for the better.

School reactions are interesting but not easy for the mother to understand. Small boys of nine and ten years may suffer intensely when they leave for the strange, cold, critical, and often cruel world of school. The very sensitive child is often terribly unhappy when he first goes to school, and parents may well ask whether this unhappiness is essential to a boy's development? Perhaps we send our boys to school too early, perhaps the best education is at day schools, if mothers were better educated in the psychology of the child, so that sentimentality and spoiling were eliminated from home life. Many doctors realise that neurasthenia and other psychoneuroses associated with fear complexes, originate at school through an inability of the child to adjust himself to school environment.

In this country amongst the well-to-do, children, boys at any rate, are usually sent to boarding schools. The original intention was presumably to remove boys from feminine influence and to rear them in a hardier masculine environment. Why have we adopted the same method with girls? In the great public schools for girls there are, we must admit, certain advantages of companionship and facilities for education, but where home life is happy and harmonious, there is a great deal to be said for day schools, which provide a first-class education and the opportunity for games and team work.

The advantage of day schools is the closer community of family life. The association with parents, brothers and sisters ought, somehow, to be maintained through childhood and youth. This association appears normal from the psychological point of view. Girls and boys who live in an ideal home have every chance of adjusting themselves to reality, of growing up amidst normal social relationships, and so they retain more of their own personality. In the great boarding-schools the young people are encouraged to conform to a pattern or type.

The separation of boys and girls in large schools entirely under the influence and reactions of one sex is unnatural. These form little artificial worlds in which it is impossible to maintain a sense of proportion. During the school terms the boys and girls live a life cut off from the real world and from adult

interests. The boy who becomes captain of his cricket eleven is apt to feel in the school that his achievement is stupendous. If he could go home on the same evening and listen to a scientist describing a recent discovery, or an explorer speaking of buried civilisations in different parts of the world, his achievement would dwindle to its proper significance.

On the other hand, there is a gulf between the interests and needs of the adolescent and the adult, and the boarding school may provide a better and happier environment in many ways than the average home of a small family. It is also the first step in the process of breaking away from parental influence and control, and although it may be said that school is an exchange from one form of authority to another, it involves the child in a progressively widening field of activities and responsibilities.

The normal boy and girl love school life as much as home life, and often think it far more important. They replace many of their home standards and values by those of the school, and it is therefore of importance that parents should exercise care in the choice of schools, according to the type of the child. Few parents realise their power

*to helping both parents and young people to solve many problems during the difficult years of adolescence.
ledge of each other's work is the only way towards bridging the gulf between middle age and youth and
reconciliation and friendship which will add to the sum of humour and happiness in the world*

of ensuring good education, and healthy environment at school. In this connection, The Parents National Educational Union, 26 Victoria Street, S.W., and the Parents Association, 56 Manchester Street, W.1, provide opportunities for parents to study these problems and make demands for reform.

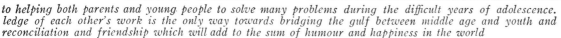

So far, parents have with amazing credulity and trust handed over their children to schoolmasters to be fed, clothed and taught as they considered fit. The mother is asked for no record of the early home life, and in her turn asks no details of the future school life. Both from a psychological and physiological point of view such lack of co-operation between parents and teacher is devastating. The young mothers of the present and the future can hardly be asked to work hard at rearing children by the light of scientific and psychological knowledge, if their work is to be completely disregarded and even marred in later school life.

The ideal schools of the future will have a doctor, who is also a trained psychologist, living on the premises. Thorough medical examination for both boys and girls will be frequent in order to avoid harmful physical strain from athletics, and the doctor will give advice on such subjects as baths, diet, clothing, and the mental capacity of normal and subnormal pupils. Education and present methods of teaching are bound to undergo big changes during the next few years. We all agree that the present methods are wasteful and inadequate, and that with the increasing demand for efficiency and the growing competition in wage-earning, education becomes a more and more vital problem to the parents of to-day.

During the preparatory school years, from eight to twelve years, the normal boy or girl is healthy, active and well controlled. There is a fairly general stability of mental and physical characteristics; children of this age are on the whole well looked after in schools, but the onset of adolescence disturbs the mental, moral and physical constitution. The resulting changes have far-reaching effects, yet at this critical phase of life very inadequate attention is given by teachers and parents to psychological and emotional development.

The years between eight and twelve are those most suitable for acquiring necessary facts. The early years of adolescence call for imaginative and inspiring work which absorbs the interest and attention. We should provide adolescents with outlines of the history of civilisation, inspiring biographies, and cultivate the imaginative attitude towards science, the æsthetic approach to literature and art. Towards the later period of adolescence, from eighteen years onwards, the mind becomes capable of interest in and application to details. Outlines, and the relationship of one subject to another, are essential before the details can be attacked intelligently, or with any lasting value to the mind.

Teachers persuade themselves too easily of the fact that children are naturally inattentive and lazy, and unwilling to learn. We are beginning to realise that the fault is in the teaching and not in the children. If we study the young child and the infant we cannot fail to appreciate the natural desire to learn and the natural aptitude for concentration when interest is stimulated. The fact that the average child loses these early qualities during school life, and learns to regard work not with joy and delight, but as a weariness, a duty, something to be shirked, is a condemnation of our educational system.

# For Embroidering Children's Clothes
## Clark's "Anchor" Coton à Broder

1928

*Also :*
*"Anchor"*
*Stranded Cotton*
*"Anchor" Flox for*
*bold designs*
*"Anchor" Velveno*
*for crochet hats*
*"Anchor" Filosheen*
*for mending*
*"Scintilla" & "Estella"*
*for knitting & fringing*

For embroidery that will wear and wear—that can be boiled, rubbed, wrung out and still come up gay and fresh as the day it was new—use Clark's "Anchor" Coton a Broder. It is a cotton thread with a delightfully glossy finish. It is made in an amazing range of exquisite shades, guaranteed fast.

Use Coton à Broder to give charm to children's clothes, lingerie, tub frocks, table linen. Obtainable in skeins in various "grists" or grades of thickness.

Remember always that whatever your requirements for needlework—embroidery thread, every kind of fancy sewing or crochet cotton, artificial silk—you make sure of getting the best possible article if you look for the famous names of Clark and Coats.

## Clark's
*Threads Embroideries Cottons*

*Made in Gt. Britain*
*Clark & Co. Ltd. and J. & P. Coats Ltd. Paisley*

C 91

72

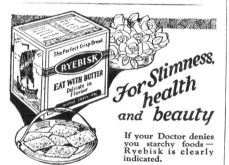

*Films hold endless possibilities as a factor in educating the child. The time has come, this writer suggests, for exploiting these possibilities to the uttermost by inaugurating*

# Children's Cinemas

### By L. M. Grant

**1928**

"OF course that comes of allowing children to go to cinemas!" How often does one hear a remark of this sort! The misdemeanours of our boys and girls are only too readily traced to the pernicious influence of the films. The modern child is too sophisticated; he is occasionally morbid and even criminal in his thoughts and actions; and many people try to persuade us that our picture-palaces are directly responsible for this moral deterioration.

It was therefore really refreshing to have a conversation with a clever woman who held the opposite opinion. Miss Beatrice Forbes-Robertson, a niece of the great actor, spoke to me with enthusiasm about the cinema. She maintained that many a child who now went to see cow-boy films, would have been taken in the days before the existence of the cinema to see badly acted melodrama in a tenth-rate music-hall. She dwelt on the educational value of the film, how it helped a child to visualise places and historical incidents in a way in which they could never be imagined from mere reading.

Teachers realise to the full what good work the cinema is doing for their pupils; that it is helping them in a pictorial, and therefore interesting way, to grasp what was once beyond their comprehension. Children are too fond of reading mechanically. They have a habit of concentrating on the plot and of skipping the descriptions. The films counteract this weakness, and the young readers are enabled to understand the beautiful word-pictures of our best writers. The young would rather see things than hear about them.

It is because of the undoubted good that the cinema is doing, that the public would like to feel that this new method of education is doing no harm at all. We cannot deny that there are innumerable pictures that are interesting for adults but which ought never to be seen by school-children. It is a shame to bring the sordid things of life into the beautiful little world of childhood: on the other hand, it is a pity to let the younger generation miss that which naturally appeals to them and is at the same time instructive. Pictures, whether in books or on films, belong essentially to the children.

A good solution of the problem would be cinemas for children. There they could revel in the delights and wonders of Nature; they could take an interest in the events of the day; and they could be shown how various articles are made. I have heard numbers of school-children discuss intelligently the various educational films that they have seen.

The well written novels which appeal to a child should be dramatised and shown. One should remember that the young mind turns automatically to adventures and humorous situations.

Let us provide for the younger children the old fairy tales, animal stories like *Monarch the Great Bear, The Call of the Wild, White Fang and Red Fox*; and some of the old classics like *Alice in Wonderland, Gulliver's Travels* and *Robinson Crusoe*.

The lower-form boy likes the tales of Henty, Ballantyne, Talbot Baines Reed and Stables, and the lower-form girl those of L. M. Alcott, Angela Brazil and Charlotte Yonge.

For the older children there is a fund from which we can take our choice. I suggest *Tom Brown's Schooldays, Treasure Island, Kidnapped, Westward Ho!, King Solomon's Mines, The Black Arrow, The Scarlet Pimpernel, A Christmas Carol, A Tale of Two Cities, Kenilworth, Ivanhoe, The Talisman, Four Feathers, Lorna Doone, The Lost World*—but the list becomes too long.

The whole point is, that these films would cater for the adventure-loving child and would do him no harm. How comforting, moreover, would it be for parents to know that their sons and daughters were being entertained only by the humours of Captain Good in *King Solomon's Mines*, by the adventures of Malone in *The Lost World*, or by the stirring fights of the Round House in *Kidnapped*!

Unfortunately, promoters feel that a children's cinema would not be a profitable investment. This would probably be true in relation to small towns, but surely the experiment might be tried in London and in the bigger centres. Both the secondary and elementary schools would co-operate in helping to foster a healthy interest in an educational venture of this sort.

Another suggestion is that the cinemas should give children's performances two or three times a week, or the first week in every month.

Pictures are the child's prerogative.

*Illustration by Marcus Adams*

# The *Child* and *Books*

## By H. J. Fells, B.A.

**G**IVE a young child a book and he may surprise you with his actions. He may merely turn over the leaves, he may look for the pictures, he may monotonously and constantly open and shut the book, or he may carry it about as a burden. These are all typical of different attitudes of mind, but there is one childish characteristic which can always be appealed to and which will cause him to respect the book. Children endow inanimate things with their own feelings. They can be made to feel sorry for a torn book. They are not primarily sorry for having injured it, which they so frequently do. They are sorry for giving it trouble and pain. It is better to appeal to this characteristic than to let the worst be done with an indestructible book. Your armour-plated rag book may defy his destructive energies, but he will probably take his revenge by tearing every other he lays his hands on.

It is generally agreed that little attention should be given to reading before the third year of school life, while some would not have a child learn to read under ten years of age. Learning to read is almost purely a mechanical product of drill and incessant practice. The less appeal is made to conscious-

*Children read because their receptive powers are naturally far in advance of their creative ones. They read out of curiosity and with a desire to imitate*

ness the better. Stuttering, by the way, is largely due to reading aloud under abnormal conditions. It occurs particularly at the seventh year or the period of second dentition. It is also the time when the control of the articulatory muscles passes from a lower to a higher brain centre.

The child's tendency to keep place and to follow his reading with the aid of the finger is helpful, and both reading aloud and lip reading have their place in the early stages of the art. Neither of these aids, however, should be continued longer than is absolutely necessary since they defer, and may indeed prevent, reliance on vision alone. This is absolutely essential for great rapidity. People vary tremendously in this respect, but there are certain important occupations in life where this ability is essential to success. There are some talented folk who can get the gist of

a page of print as quickly as an accountant can scan a column of figures.

The most natural place for the child to learn to read is the home, and most talented men and women will agree that their love of reading was acquired through parental attention in this matter. In these days the excuse of no time is frequent, but there is a recorded instance of a conscientious parent listening to the reading efforts of his young heir whilst engaged in the pressing business of the morning shave. The more easily a child gets over its reading drill, the more time can be devoted in school to the less mechanical studies.

The relation between the eye and its object is of interest in the matter of reading. We read in eyefuls and with jerks, and the child eye has a shorter span than the adult's. Print for the young should, therefore, be in short lines, and if the page is large, in double columns. As to the arrangement of print for reading, there are a number of interesting queries. It has been asked whether there is any particular advantage in reading from left to right. Some languages are written from right to left. Then again, why should the print not alternate, since the eye in the normal way *Continued overleaf*

1928

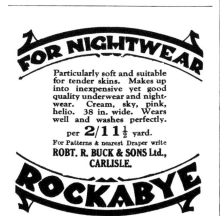
# The Child and Books

*(Continued)*

1928

has always to go back empty. With some oriental tongues one reads down the page, and one might ask whether there might be any advantages in being able to read up and down.

There was no considered catering for a child's reading taste earlier than the beginning of last century. The first step was not peculiarly appropriate, for those writers who took up the task felt that their chief purpose was to clothe moral instruction in a dress of choice words suitably strung on a tenuous story thread. They were domestic dramas showing the value of truth and honesty and becoming behaviour.

The supply has now a scientific basis to proceed on for it is determined by interest. It is an interest of a catholic kind, for it is of the widest appeal. This is so since no book is good for a child which a grown-up cannot enjoy, and is expressed in the paradox that if an author would write for youth he must not write for youth.

Mythical stories are of intense interest to young children. Myth was the groping of the primitive mind after truth. It was the basis of religion, philosophy, science, art, history and poetry. The young soul nourishing its latent faculties on this diet is developing in the right way.

After learning to read with facility it is, of course, fiction which is devoured with the greatest avidity. Later, girls begin to develop a taste for poetry, while boys incline to history and historical fiction. Boys show a greater individuality in the choice of books. Nothing pleases a boy more than to be able to say that he has read a book which none of his friends or classmates have heard about. Girls rely much more on recommendations, and prefer stories about children and domestic animals. Growing boys do not care about style in the slightest. They want a hero and plenty of action. The so-called "blood" is so popular with boys on this account. Parental displeasure will hardly keep them from this refreshing oasis.

The dangers of this appetite arise only when it persists beyond the age at which a change of taste should normally arise. If this occurs the imagination runs wild, and the impractical antics of the hero are regarded as enticingly possible. The younger reader is sanely conscious that he is bewitched by flights of fancy, but if he does not grow out of the liking the safeguard is apt to disappear.

Children's books need to be rich in interest, true to Nature, exquisite in art, and abundant in every quality that replies to a child's keen and fresh perceptions. The innate ability of the young to see through shams and inconsistency puts a writer on his mettle and so it should parents, for any discord in their character is more apparent to their own children than it is to any of their equals in age. As a rule young readers prefer direct to indirect speech, since they appreciate the personal appeal. Any descriptions need to be full of colour, over- rather than under-stated, riotous rather than monotonous. They require very clear and frequently repeated details as to time and place, and their appreciation of humour is direct and not suggestive—they need funny incidents.

Children read because their receptive powers are naturally far in advance of their creative ones. They read out of curiosity and with a desire to imitate, and because they can see what they wish for themselves, and are probably denied, granted to others.

The curiosity of the young needs no stressing. Their earliest desires are mainly concerned with the important question of food. They exhibit the instinct of self-preservation in its most primitive form. They are delighted with stories about youngsters who have much to eat, who are regaled with Gargantuan feasts. Possibly satiated by these stories, they turn for a change to stories in which the young hero has nothing to eat and is badly treated.

As the child is natural in himself and has a right to be in as normal a relation to Nature as is possible in these days of city life, he should be given animal and bird books. Such books need much illustration, and should be true to fact, and have a lively style. Care needs to be exercised in the choice of all picture books, since child monstrosities with goggly eyes and gaping mouths are more an artistic nightmare than an artistic reproduction of Nature. Books should never get between the child and Nature—they should merely add something essential to the knowledge which he has acquired at first hand.

The reading hunger or craze begins in the early 'teens, and too few parents realise that this is the one opportunity to attempt a cultivation of good tastes. The craze has its dangers if persisted in long after adolescence, and fixed reading habits should be acquired at sixteen. The trait is not so much a proof of a thirst for knowledge as of a desire to have the feelings stirred. The age is the age of self-assertion, when too great a concentration on an idealised life spurs boys to actions sometimes foolish though considered magnificent, and drives girls to reverie with dreams of comfort and luxuries.

If there is any criticism of school books for reading, it is that too great a stress in choice is laid on form and style, with a marked tendency to footnotes explanatory of peculiarities in grammar, syntax or style. This is putting critical appreciation the possession of a matured mind, before the sympathetic appreciation which every child can possess.

The finest school reader ever written was the result of years of work by German scholars who ransacked the whole of their literature and produced no aimless anthology, but nearly 4,000 pages in ten volumes of carefully graded reading, to nourish each stage in the mental growth of childhood and youth.

---

## *When Ordering Advertised Goods*

or writing for particulars of them, please make a point of supplying your full postal address. If this is omitted, as sometimes happens, the transaction is at a deadlock

1929

### Vital Facts about Food

You can never be sure of the purity and wholesomeness of your food when it is kept in a merely cool temperature. For, at any temperature over 50° bacteria can multiply 400 times as fast as in temperatures below that degree. Statistics prove that on 330 days of the average year your larder's temperature is above 50°, *i.e.*, on 330 days bacteria are free to multiply in your food, and destroy its *food value.* The basic reason why you need Frigidaire is that its temperature is always below 50°, and consequently your food is always safe.

# How will she grow up?

IN ten, fifteen years' time, will she have the beauty, the vitality, that come from faultless health?

With growing children so much depends on food and its quality. Do you realise, for example, that a joint of beef may contribute to one family nourishment and strength—to another, nothing at all beyond a satisfaction of the appetite?

There will be no *apparent* difference in these joints when served, but—the one has been kept in proper conditions such as Frigidaire provides, the other has been left in an ordinary meat-safe, exposed to warmth and damp. In a few hours bacterial growth has commenced—in a few more, the nutritive value of that joint, the vitamins, the body-building, strength-building goodness, has been irretrievably destroyed.

Every mother of a growing family should read

and know these "Vital Facts about Food" given above—and then send the coupon to see how inexpensively the goodness of her children's food may be guaranteed at all times.

London Showrooms :—
Frigidaire House, Chapter St., Vauxhall Bridge Road, S.W.1, and Imperial House, Kingsway, W.C.2.

Branches at :—
Birmingham, Manchester, Leeds, Brighton, Glasgow and Edinburgh.

# Frigidaire
## *Automatic* Electrical *Refrigeration*

FRIGIDAIRE LIMITED (*Incorporated in Canada*),
Dept. A-68.
Frigidaire House, Chapter Street, Vauxhall Bridge Road, S.W.1.

Please send me, without obligation, complete information about Frigidaire.

Name .....................................................................

Address..................................................................

...............................................................................

No. in Family.......................................................

## The New Way in

# Nursery Education

## By Marian Bethell

1929

*What may now be called the Old Education seeks to develop and cultivate intellect without studying interest or curiosity: in the New Education the interest of the child is made of first importance and is developed so as to lead to the awakening of the mind*

"HOW wonderful to be born in 1928! These children of To-day and To-morrow . . . They will play about with Chemistry and Physics instead of leaden soldiers and Teddy Bears. Their fairy-tales will include the wonders of Natural Science. They will be awakened very quickly to the great adventure of Knowledge, instead of having it thrust upon them as a dull, damned thing. They will learn mostly what they like, and not what they hate. How good to be a schoolboy in 1940, if such things may be!"

(SIR PHILIP GIBBS).

Since Dr. Montessori first opened the eyes of the world to the needs of auto-education, and gave her great gift to her generation, many educationists, receiving inspiration from her clear and scientific idea as to the training of little children, have set out on the quest for new methods. "Individual work" is the keynote of them all—or that which might be termed "self-learning."

The discovery of the need of the early sense-training of the child by apparatus and by environment is still spreading fast through every part of the educational body of to-day, and the results, important and far-reaching, are as yet unpredictable. But it is undeniably leading to early creative activity according to individual talent in the child, in a greatly increased degree, and in older boys and girls to an almost unprecedented development of originality and gifted individuality.

In all parts of the world is this idea of the child's part in his own education exerting a wide influence on educational thought and practice. The Old Education, as it may now be termed, seeks to develop and cultivate intellect without studying interest or curiosity. In the United States, the underlying principle of the New Education is based upon the philosophy of John Dewey. In Dewey's Laboratory Schools the interest of the child is made of first importance; and is developed so as to lead

to the awakening of the mind. For it is found that such interest, if truly aroused, leads to spontaneous effort, a need for action, an appetite for knowledge, and increases the spirit of inquiry and wonder. (Laboratory

## READ

### "I Meet Lady Astor"

By Sewell Stokes

### "Youth & A Second Blooming"

By Mrs. Belloc Lowndes

### "The American Woman"

by St. John Ervine

### *in July*

## Good Housekeeping

Schools, it may be noted, is the name given to private schools in which experiments are carried on. Many of the methods found to work successfully are afterwards adopted by the State schools. The private schools thus may be looked upon as "laboratories" for the testing of new educational methods.)

Under Dewey's famous Project Method, an object of research is chosen, and the children left to find out all they can about it from their environment, thus developing initiative and co-operation. Naturally, a child does not enjoy being given things to do. He likes finding things to do for himself. His interest must be aroused before his

intellect. American children are specially encouraged to possess the spirit of curiosity, and to wonder about things; the aim being to develop powers of self-education and self-learning. Each child progresses at his own rate: and he is never allowed to be defeated or discouraged by tasks beyond his powers.

Based on the same method of Free Work is the Lincoln School, New York. The great difference between the Free Work methods and the auto-didactic systems such as the Montessori, is that in the former the objects of real life are used as educators, instead of formal apparatus, as in the latter.

The chief aim of the Lincoln School is to give a child the kind of education which will fit his life needs, in the belief that the best life in the present is the best preparation for a future career. In the curriculum, new possibilities, experiments and activities are constantly making progress. Every new experience is selected with the idea of it being in some way related to the child's everyday needs, of answering some of his questions, of leading him to ask more questions, of making him more alert to his environment, or of stimulating his imagination.

The curriculum has had many tests in the light of the requirements of modern life. Such activities as the making of play villages out of packing cases, the construction of boats and bridges, trucks and trains, the study and care of pet animals, are constantly practised. The making of toy boats of different types has led to great interest in history, geography, science, industrial and practical creations. Geography plays are planned. Toy boats go backwards and forwards from New York to Europe, bringing stores for the shops. Each child learns to measure the material for his boats, to make maps, to buy and sell in the classroom at wholesale price, making a profit. This is but a small branch of the many practical activities carried on by the *Continued overleaf*

1929

# The New Way in Nursery Education

*(Continued )*

children at the Lincoln School.

Under the same heading of Free Work may be placed the Decroly Method. Dr. Decroly, Physician and Educator, and a Professor of Child Psychology at the University of Brussels, is the Founder and Director of *l'Ecole pour la Vie par la Vie,* Brussels. In his studies of child psychology he interested himself greatly in the development of backward and dull children. Like Dr. Montessori, his work in this direction was so successful that gradually he applied his now famous method to normal children; and to-day it is used not only in his own private school in Brussels, but also in many schools in England and other countries. The method takes the things of every day in a child's environment, the things in which a child takes his greatest interest, and from that point leads on by easy steps to ordinary school subjects. The foundation of the method is that children should be educated for Life by Life.

" *Let the child prepare for Life by living. Organise the environment to afford adequate stimuli for the tendencies favourable to development,*" is the now famous Decroly slogan. For the past sixteen years, Dr. Decroly has been developing and perfecting his school plan. To give an idea of the method in as brief a manner as possible the following points may be noted.

(1) The school should be placed in an environment affording the children daily experiences with the phenomena of nature, and with manifestations of the life led by living creatures in general, and by man in particular.

(2) The ideal schoolroom should be on the lines of a small studio or laboratory, with tables, running water, apparatus for artificial heat and light (gas and electricity) and counters and shelves for exhibits.

(3) The teacher should be active and bright, and possessed of creative and inventive ability; should be trained in methods of animal and plant life, and in observation of children: and able to keep order without special effort.

(4) The morning hours should be given preference for work in the three R's, lessons in these taking the form of games. Lessons in observation, drawing, singing, and active games should follow. The afternoons should be devoted to creative work, and a foreign language.

(5) On certain mornings excursions should be arranged for the children to follow nature study, visit works of art, museums, railway stations, and other places of interest and instruction.

(6) The interest of the children should be stimulated by the constant variety of such activities. A list of these should include their collections, pictures, books, and readings; the making of charts, of pieces of apparatus, of boxes and envelopes for classifying purposes: the repairing of articles in use, when broken or worn; care of the nature study collections; the writing of little essays and stories.

Thus, such a curriculum gives the child knowledge of himself, his needs, and his environment. He early learns to perceive, to think, to act, and express. The activities that the school should provide, Dr. Decroly classifies as

Observation,
Association,
Concrete expression,
Abstract expression.

The lessons in observation are planned to habituate the child to note each morning any events that may have occurred in the schoolroom since the day before, such as the growth and development of plants, seeds, flowers, the changes that result from meteorological conditions, the classifying of objects of nature study carried home after country walks: the habits of pet animals, tadpoles, silkworms, rabbits, goldfish, etc.

The lessons under the heading of association appeal to the imagination, and aim to arouse curiosity, in the first place by pictures and stories, and by the description of distant countries. Nature study, the fauna and flora of all parts of the world, as well as at the bottom of the sea, plays a big part. Geography, the study of other lands and other nations, is entered into. The history of countries follows: and the commencement of a knowledge of industry is gained by stories, or object lessons, illustrating the making of objects in everyday use.

The activities which come under the heading of Expression are of two kinds —concrete, including manual work, such as plasticine, painting, drawing, woodwork, raffia-work, etc.: and abstract, those concerned with reading, writing, spelling, numbering, original composition, and conversation. The children create their own museums, and collect and classify animal, vegetable and mineral specimens to be placed in their respective cabinets. The older children are encouraged to keep big note-books, illustrated by drawings and paintings, or by cut-out pictures, and specimens.

Such is the Decroly Method in outline, carried out during the first four or five years of the child's educational life.

The Reading Method is considered by many, however, to be the most important feature in the new school plan. It is on a psychological basis. Dr. Decroly found that when a child is learning to read, he does so by a visual process; that is, he associates the written or printed word with an object. The child is first acquainted with things, then with sentences; words come last; and finally, the word is separated into letters. By this method, children of six years old have learned to read in six weeks, but Dr. Decroly thinks it best for children to observe and experience for the first year of learning, and to defer the study of reading until the second year.

The method is somewhat as follows:— the names of various objects in the schoolrooms are written on labels, and placed on the objects. A command is given orally, and then written on a label in large characters. The child hears and understands the command, and studies the look of the writing. Afterwards, a box of labels is given to him, and he is able to pick them out and understand their meaning. He can identify the commands or the names of the objects, with those written on the cards. Later on, he learns to copy these words and sentences in his note-book, and illustrate them by drawings: and he is encouraged to express his ideas by drawing as much as by writing. In a later stage, familiar words are grouped together to make a story, longer words are broken up into syllables, and when the child can identify any syllable at sight as part of some word he knows, he is given his first reading book.

Under the Auto-didactic System, many methods have been evolved. Among the pioneers of the new way in nursery educa-

1929

# Mother !

## Banish those coughs and colds once and for all!

The Ministry of Health report has exposed the weakness in our children's health. It is the after-effects of early rickets, often unobserved in baby days, that later lead to coughs, colds and frequent ailments. What can a mother do for the best?

Just rely on SCOTT'S Emulsion. This household favourite stops a cold and breaks up a cough. More than that, it removes all trace of rickets. It builds the body, hardens the bones and maintains the powers of resistance. There can be little risk of a long and serious illness once SCOTT'S Emulsion has restored virile strength. There are certainly fewer coughs and colds when parents insist on this proved lung tonic.

### Every other child is handicapped by RICKETS

**What the Ministry of Health Report reveals.**

A doctor examined un-selected children all over the country He found 48.7% showed signs of R i c k e t s — the terrible deforming disease of childhood. Thousands are crippled by it. *Hundreds of thousands suffer in general health from its effects.*

Yet Rickets can be cured. The 44% of cod liver oil contained in SCOTT'S Emulsion is the richest natural source of the anti-rachitic vitamins. The bone-building hypo-phosphites make strong bones. SCOTT'S Emulsion is the one *proved* weapon against Rickets, and all child-hood ailments.

# SCOTT'S EMULSION
## of Pure Cod Liver Oil

*The sign of safety.*

Recommended by doctors in cases of

| | | | | |
|---|---|---|---|---|
| **COUGHS, COLDS** | **BRONCHITIS** | **WASTING** | **DEBILITY** | **ANÆMIA** |
| **CONSUMPTION** | **INFLUENZA** | **MEASLES** | **RICKETS** | **TEETHING** |

# The New Way in Nursery Education
### *Continued*

tion in England, Miss Jessie Mackinder takes a foremost place. She tells us that she was inspired by Dr. Montessori, but realising the difficulties in the way caused by the misunderstandings of the child's mind by many parents, and also by the high cost of the apparatus, she determined to create her own method. She writes that "a teacher's duty is to fit the child to take his place in the world as it may be when he is grown up," and that she should arrange the child's environment so that he may choose his work; also that she should continually enlarge this environment so that the child's range of choice is continually increased and his means of expressing his creative instinct improved. No difficulty should be removed, but all difficulties should be graded and presented one at a time, so that in each child is implanted a love of encountering difficulties and a habit of sticking at them until they are overcome. This determination to succeed is one of the characteristics of children educated on such lines.

Miss Mackinder gives as the *four* essentials to success with her method: (1) a happy teacher, (2) a carefully graded scheme of work, (3) a system of recording each child's progress, (4) the maintenance of the child's enthusiasm in his work.

She finds that children of about five years of age can teach themselves the sounds of letters by means of pictures illustrating these sounds. The children can then train themselves by using other pictures and words; and by means of self-explanatory phonogram placards they can discover the sounds of thirty-six double symbols. When they have learned twenty-four sounds they begin word-building. Cards bearing pictures of various objects have the names of the objects attached on a string, and the children find great amusement in picking out the name to place over the picture. They are trained from the beginning to refer to indicators on the wall, these indicators both for words and numbers being formed by a series of most delightful picture friezes, a variety of which can be obtained with the Mackinder apparatus.

Children taught by this method are eager and enthusiastic, and love their lessons. No coercion is used: and they are allowed freedom of choice in the ordering of their work.

In a recent address by Dr. Crichton-Miller on "*The Child's Reaction to Freedom and Discipline,*" he said that one of the greatest things that Dr. Montessori had taught this age was the spiritual depth of the word freedom: and that we have to realise that we must aim at some sort of freedom in which self-control replaces disciplinary control.

The leaders of the many methods of the new way in nursery teaching all find that freedom in lesson time is removing disciplinary troubles, and that the children who have freedom reveal themselves, and are far more responsive in every way than those taught by the old methods. As Miss Mackinder writes: "When we are wise, we shall realise that we cannot train children to respect authority, in any form, unless they are capable of self-control, and capable of seeing that the greatest freedom for individuals is obtained when all of them make the other man's well-being as important as their own."

# 'CELANESE' FABRICS
## for children's frocks

1929

JOAN'S a chubby little lady with a mop of golden curls —'Celanese' Taffeta for her, all frills and furbelows, in a heavenly shade of blue. Mary's dark and rather dreamy . . . . 'Celanese' Georgette, please, white and fluttery. The twins are just too lovely for words— pink and brown and sturdy— smocks of 'Celanese' Crepe-de-Chine for them, one red, one daffodil yellow. Every one of these lovely little garments will wash time and again without losing a shade of its charming colour. 'Celanese' is the ideal wear for children.

## 'CELANESE' *Fabrics*

### *Specially suitable for Children's Frocks:*

'Celanese' Taffeta, 38/40 ins., 6/11 yard.
'Celanese' Foulard, 36 ins., 5/11 yard.
'Celanese' Marocain, 38/40 ins., 8/11 yd.

'Celanese' Surah, 38/40 ins., 6/11 yard.
'Celanese' Voile, 38/40 ins., 3/11 yard.
'Celanese' Georgette, 38/40 ins., 6/11 yd.

*These are only a few of the fascinating Fabrics from the 'Celanese' Range. Ask to see Children's Frocks, ready to wear . . . . look for the 'Celanese' Label.*

SOLE MANUFACTURERS: BRITISH CELANESE LIMITED, CELANESE HOUSE, HANOVER SQUARE, LONDON, W.1

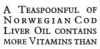

FABRITIUS, OSLO

*There was a little girl who wore a little curl,*
*Right in the middle of her forehead;*
*When she was good, she was very, very good,*
*And when she was bad, she was horrid.*

**1929**

The habitually bad-tempered child, the difficult girl, the naughty boy — are you yourself not to blame for their bad behaviour? Are you certain that they are not suffering from malnutrition, or that their distressing conduct is not simply Nature's danger-signal against what may in effect be chronic underfeeding?

See your Doctor about it. He will probably recommend more vitamins. Get them bottled — in the form of Norwegian Cod Liver Oil, the most economical source of Vitamins A and D, without which healthy childhood is impossible.

A TEASPOONFUL OF NORWEGIAN COD LIVER OIL CONTAINS MORE VITAMINS THAN ALL THE BUTTER AND MILK ANY INDIVIDUAL CAN EAT AND DRINK IN A DAY

# NORWEGIAN COD LIVER OIL

National Committee for Promoting the Consumption of Norwegian Cod Liver Oil, Bergen, Norway.

1929

# My Room

### By
### Gladys A. Cope

There's no locked door to **my** room,
I could not shut them out,
Those dirty little people,
They're noisy, and they shout,
They're very rough and clumsy,
But to me they're simply fine.
　　They've never to knock,
　　With a little torn frock,
On the door of this room of mine.

When somebody's lost a button,
Or somebody's bumped his nose,
Or somebody's broken a boot-lace,
He bundles along, and he knows
He'll find the door wide open,
He'll make his own bee-line,
　　Up the stairs,
　　With his little affairs,
Into this room of mine.

The chairs are more " comfy " in my room,
Than any the nursery contains,
There are wonderful reels and scissors and things,
To fascinate busy young brains !
The machine that is always so busy
With wheels that glitter and shine—
　　It hums and sings
　　As it hems the things
In this interesting room of mine.

But think of the time when they'll all go to school.
I shall sit here, the door open wide,
Then no one will interrupt me,
No one will chatter and slide,
Over the polished linoleum,
To spoil its beautiful shine,
　　Then how I shall long
　　For their chatter and song
In this sewing room of mine.

*Decoration*
*by*
*Mower*
*White*

MOWER WHITE

1929

# Sit by the Window

Use the window-seat in the depths of winter as you did in summer.

Remember your experience during the last cold spell. It was probably that of thousands who depended solely upon the open coal fire for the heating of living-rooms— a roasted face and a frozen back.

Now is the time to ensure clean, healthy heating during the cold months.

"Unity" Tubular Electric Skirting Heaters can be fixed to the skirting boards beneath the windows.

Switch them **on** or **off** as required and control them automatically to keep the room at any required temperature.

## Tubular Electric Skirting Heaters

*Write to-day for "Heating the Home," a beautifully illustrated folder.*

**Young, Osmond & Young Ltd**
**47 Victoria Street, S.W.1**

*The "Unity" System is used for electrically heating churches, cinemas, theatres, workshops, factories, offices, etc. Full particulars will be given on application to all interested.*

# The Problem of School Bills

## Discussed and illustrated with actual accounts from leading schools

### By MARJORY ROYCE

1929

THE expenses of good boarding schools for boys and girls, the difficulty of obtaining skilled domestic help within the home—these, on inquiry, I find to be the great problems before the professional classes to-day. (I had guessed it already.)

I have been at great pains to obtain some actual school bills to set before parents who have children of their own growing up to boarding school age.* A prospectus of any school, however comprehensive, can hardly cover the ground. It is thought that some actual accounts copied down might be of real service to mother and father. Never has the desire for a first-class education for their children been keener in the minds of all thoughtful parents than to-day, never have the fees been higher, never have the schools been more efficient, never has it been more difficult to meet the bills both for equipment and learning.

Here is the formidable list of outfits required for College, House, Swimming and Games at Cheltenham Ladies' College, with figures opposite the items as a mother of a pupil there to-day has filled in. Some of these details do not apply to all houses. The prices stated are those actually spent by one mother, and cannot all be standardised.

### I. COLLEGE OUTFIT

|  | £ | s. | d. |
|---|---|---|---|
| 1 navy blue regulation dress (for everyday) | 2 | 5 | 6 |
| 1 navy blue regulation tailored coat | 2 | 17 | 9 |
| 1 navy blue regulation blanket coat | 4 | 19 | 6 |
| 6 regulation Schappe silk blouses | 5 | 12 | 6 |
| 2 black hair ribbons, 2½ in. wide | | 2 | 0 |
| 2 regulation white woollen jerseys | 1 | 4 | 6 |
| 1 regulation navy blue hat (winter terms only) | | 7 | 6 |
| 1 regulation grey felt hat (summer terms only) | | 7 | 6 |
| 1 pair gymnasium shoes (black) | | 5 | 0 |
| 1 shoe bag | | 2 | 6 |
| 1 comb; to keep at College | | | 6 |
| 1 regulation navy blue waterproof | 2 | 2 | 6 |
| 1 pair indoor shoes, for College only | | 10 | 6 |

### II. HOUSE OUTFIT (Boarders only)

|  | £ | s. | d. |
|---|---|---|---|
| 1 regulation navy blue dress (for best) | 2 | 5 | 6 |
| 1 regulation best tie | | 2 | 6 |
| 1 regulation tussore frock with knickers to match (summer terms only) | 2 | 5 | 6 |
| 2 to 3 coloured afternoon frocks (warm, for winter) | | 6 | (about) |
| 1 simple white afternoon frock, with long sleeves | | 2 | (about) |
| 1 regulation panama hat—Sunday (summer only) | | 15 | 6 |
| 1 regulation black velour hat—Sunday (winter terms only) | | 15 | 6 |
| 1 regulation navy woollen scarf | | 7 | 6 |
| 1 dressing gown (warm) | 1 | 0 | 0 |
| 1 dressing jacket | | 10 | 0 |
| 2 pairs walking shoes (black) | 2 | 5 | 0 |
| 1 pair indoor shoes | | 10 | 0 |
| 1 pair evening shoes | | 15 | 0 |
| 1 pair shoes without heels (for dancing classes) | | 15 | 0 |
| 1 pair bedroom slippers | | 5 | 0 |
| 1 pair goloshes | | 5 | 0 |
| 2 to 3 pairs of gloves (dark, plain, not gauntlets) | | 15 | 0 |
| 4 nightdresses or pyjamas | 2 | 0 | 0 |
| 4 combinations (essential in winter) | 2 | 15 | 0 |
| 4 vests (optional) | 1 | 0 | 0 |
| 4 slip bodices | 1 | 0 | 0 |
| 1 pair white woollen knickers (for cold nights under white frocks) | | 5 | 0 |
| 2 pairs white knickers, for wear with white frock | | 10 | 0 |
| 2 princess petticoats (white) | 1 | 0 | 0 |
| 4 pairs linings | 1 | 0 | 0 |
| 3 pairs regulation navy woollen knickers | 1 | 7 | 0 |
| 3 pairs cotton knickers, for hot weather (optional) | 1 | 1 | 6 |
| 6 pairs stockings (black) | 1 | 4 | 0 |
| 2 pairs thinner stockings (black), for dancing | | 10 | 0 |
| 2 pairs Liberty or other boneless stays (not elastic) | | 15 | 0 |
| 24 or 36 handkerchiefs | | 10 | 0 |
| 1 shoe bag | | 2 | 6 |
| 1 umbrella | | 10 | 0 |
| 2 clothes bags | | 5 | 0 |
| 1 nightdress case | | 5 | 0 |
| 1 brush and comb bag | | 2 | 6 |
| 1 clothes brush | | 2 | 6 |
| 1 suit-case (large enough for half-term week-end) | | 10 | 0 |
| 1 dark jersey (navy preferred, to wear in house or garden) | | 10 | 6 |
| 1 fitted work basket | | 5 | 0 |
| 1 fitted writing-case | 1 | 0 | 0 |
| A supply of name tabs in full | | 5 | 0 |

(* *This article, having gone to press some months before publication, cannot be strictly up-to-date in every particular, but gives a reliable idea of conditions as a whole.*)

# Nursery heating *must* be healthy!

1929

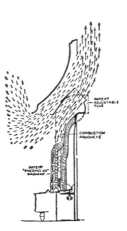

The
Davis "Antony"
Gas Grate.

(Armoured Finish).

*Diagram showing
action of patent
"Injector-Ventilator."*

If there is one room in the house where heat *must* be healthy it is the nursery. Wise mothers are installing Radiation Gas Grates because they know that with them there can be no draughts and no stuffiness—just a radiant, healthy warmth and pure, fresh air in the room. Ask to see Radiation Gas Grates at your Gas Showrooms. Note the "Injector-Ventilator"—the patent device which causes the air in the room to be changed *completely* many times an hour, whilst maintaining comfortable warmth without draughts. Radiation Gas Grates are made in a variety of styles and "finishes" to suit every decorative scheme.

# Radiation
## GAS GRATES

SEE THE NAME "RADIATION" ON THE FRONT OF THE GAS GRATE.

# The Problem of School Bills

### III. SWIMMING OUTFIT (*Summer only*)

| | £ | s. | d. |
|---|---|---|---|
| 1 rubber cap (regulation) | | 2 | 6 |
| 1 bathing dress (regulation) | | 9 | 6 |

### IV. GAMES OUTFIT

| | £ | s. | d. |
|---|---|---|---|
| 1 field tie | | 2 | 6 |
| 1 regulation blue serge tunic | 1 | 5 | 6 |
| 2 or 3 regulation games tops: | | | |
|    3 flannel | 1 | 7 | 0 |
|    3 cotton | | 15 | 6 |
| 1 pair black hockey boots (winter terms) | 1 | 0 | 0 |
| 1 pair black lacrosse boots (winter terms) | | 10 | 6 |
| 1 pair white canvas shoes | | 5 | 6 |
| 1 regulation sports coat (summer terms) | | 15 | 0 |
| 1 white thick sweater; polo collar | | 15 | 0 |
| | £68 | 13 | 9 |

Here is the actual bill for a girl's term, printed as received from the parent. The items add usefully to our general information. Each girl must, of course, vary.

### THE CHELTENHAM LADIES' COLLEGE

| | £ | s. | d. |
|---|---|---|---|
| To Fees for Regular Course in advance: | | | |
| Tuition | 12 | 12 | 0 |
| Board, £31 10s; Laundry, £1 10s. | 33 | 0 | 0 |
| Sanatorium | | 12 | 6 |
| Stationery | | 12 | 0 |
| Nomination | | | |

*To Fees for Extras:*

| | £ | s. | d. |
|---|---|---|---|
| Books and drawing materials | 1 | 13 | 11 |
| Music | | 2 | 0 |
| Piano | 3 | 13 | 6 |
| Sight reading | | — | |
| Harmony | | — | |
| Theory | | — | |
| Singing | | — | |
| Elocution | | — | |
| Violin | | — | |
| Orchestra | | — | |
| Organ | | — | |
| Art work | | — | |
| Needlework | | — | |
| Dancing | | — | |
| Riding | | — | |
| Medical inspection | | 7 | 6 |
| Remedial exercises | | — | |
| Playing field | | 10 | 0 |
| Total | £53 | 3 | 5 |

*Bill on Blue Paper:*

| | £ | s. | d. |
|---|---|---|---|
| Pocket money | | 12 | 0 |
| Share of cabs, trams, 'buses | | 3 | 0 |
| Taxis | | 1 | 2 |
| Historical lecture | | | 6 |
| Concerts: | | | |
|   String quartette | | 1 | 2 |
|   Tickets | | 13 | 0 |
| Entertainments: | | | |
|   Ben Hur | | 2 | 2 |

| | £ | s. | d. |
|---|---|---|---|
| Play | | 1 | 6 |
|      ,, | | 1 | 7 |
| *Excursions:* | | | |
|   House expedition: Bude | | 2 | 3 |
|   Lillybrook and tea | | 2 | 3 |
|   Half term expedition to | | | |
|     Bath | | 6 | 9 |
|   Entrance Roman Baths | | | 6 |
| Telegrams and telephones | | — | |
| Breakages | | | 6 |
| Mending | | — | |
| Chemist | | 7 | 6 |
| House medicines | | | |
| Extra washing | | — | |
| Hairdresser | | 11 | 6 |
| Doctor | | — | |
| Carriage of books to College | | 3 | 6 |
| Games | | — | |
| Swimming | | — | |
| House library | | — | |
| Dress | | 12 | 0 |
| Shoemaker | | 3 | 0 |
| Porterage, advanced luggage | | 2 | 0 |
| Miscellaneous | | — | |
| Share of tips on expeditions | | 1 | 0 |
| Half term lunch at Bath | | 3 | 0 |
| | 4 | 10 | 7 |
| Less deposit paid | 3 | 0 | 0 |
| | 1 | 10 | 7 |
| Plus deposit due | 3 | 0 | 0 |
| | £4 | 10 | 7 |

Now follow the actual figures of one term's bill, taken from a parent's account book for a daughter of twelve years old, at another great school—Roedean.

### ROEDEAN SCHOOL, SUSSEX

| | £ | s. | d. |
|---|---|---|---|
| For one term's fees in advance | 60 | 0 | 0 |
| For one term's piano lessons in advance | 3 | 13 | 6 |
| Art lessons in advance | 2 | 2 | 0 |
| Violin lessons | | — | |
| Fencing | | — | |
| Elocution lessons | | — | |
| Solo singing | | — | |
| Remedial exercises | | — | |
| Stationery | | 10 | 0 |

| *House disbursements:* | s. | d. |
|---|---|---|
| Mending | 1 | 6 |
| Mending shoes | 1 | 0 |
| Extra laundry | 2 | 6 |
| Extra fruit | 3 | 9 |

1929

1929

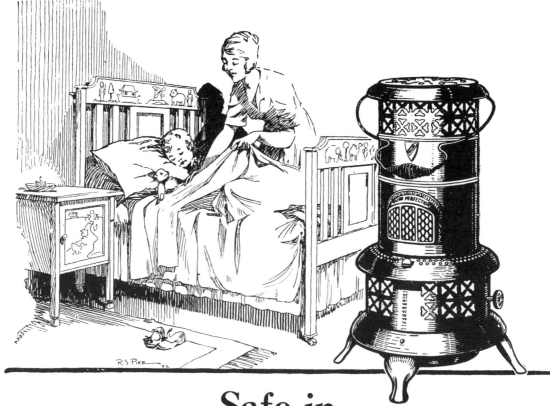

# Safe in Blanket Bay

When the day's romp is over—and tired little eyes are closed in the perfect slumber of healthy childhood—then is the time to keep the room warm and comfy with a regular healthy temperature just sufficient to take all the dampness and chill out of the evening air.

The best way of all is with a "Valor-Perfection"—the clean, smokeless and odourless heater. Now Oil is cheaper the "Valor-Perfection" is more economical to use than ever.

*Look for the Valor Shield, without which none is genuine.*

# VALOR-PERFECTION
## Oil Heaters

### OIL STORAGE

SOLD BY ALL IRONMONGERS AND STORES

| SMALL BLACK 26/6 | LARGE BLACK 32/6 |

**OIL CABINETS**
50 Gal. Capacity - 50/-
30 Gal. Capacity - 45/-
**OIL DRUMS**
10 Gal. Capacity - 12/-
5 Gal. Capacity - 8/6

VALOR PERFECTION OIL CABINET

VALOR PERFECTION OIL DRUM

Distributed Wholesale by
**ANGLO-AMERICAN OIL CO., LTD.**

Descriptive Pamphlet Free from
(108) Stove & Heater Dept., Queen Anne's Gate, London, S.W.1

ANGLOCO

*Always use*
# ROYAL DAYLIGHT OIL

D.A. 500.

# The Problem of School Bills

**1929**

| (Roedean School—*continued*) | s. | d. | £ | s. | d. |
|---|---|---|---|---|---|
| Hairdresser | 6 | 9 | | | |
| Chemist | 4 | 0 | | | |
| School outfit | — | | | | |
| *Sundries:* | | | | | |
| Bus for Empire Day picnic | 7 | 5 | | | |
| Eclipsia | 1 | 6 | | | |
| | | | 1 | 8 | 5 |
| School Magazine | 2 | 0 | | | |
| Taxi | 2 | 9 | | | |
| Piano music | 6 | 6 | | | |
| Songs | | 6 | | | |
| Carpentry a/c. | 5 | 0 | | | |
| Sewing a/c. | 4 | 0 | | | |
| Studio a/c. | 5 | 0 | | | |
| | | | 1 | 6 | 0 |
| | | | £69 | 7 | 8 |

### Printed Books and Sundries

| | s. | d. | | | s. | d. |
|---|---|---|---|---|---|---|
| Scripture: | | | Mathematics: | | | |
| Atlas | 1 | 0 | Algebra | | 1 | 2 |
| English: | | | Sundries: | | | |
| *Henry V* | 1 | 4 | Geometry box | | 2 | 3 |
| *Ivanhoe* | 2 | 0 | | | 7 | 9 |

### Clothes List, Roedean

| | | | | |
|---|---|---|---|---|
| Blue serge coat and skirt | 1 | Canvas shoes, black | 1 |
| Thick white shirt blouses | 2 | Games shoes with indiarubber soles | 1 |
| Thick school djibbahs | 2 | Walking shoes or boots | 1 |
| Thick school djibbah blouses | 3 | House shoes | 1 |
| Thin school djibbah (optional for summer terms only) | 1 | Bedroom slippers | 1 |
| | | Overalls | 2 |
| Thin djibbah blouses for summer terms only | 3 | Overcoat | 1 |
| | | Blazer | 1 |
| Afternoon djibbah | 1 | White sweater | 1 |
| Afternoon djibbah blouses | 2 | Black stockings | 4 |
| Cloak | 1 | Tan stockings | 4 |
| Black velours hat (for two winter terms) | 1 | Combinations | 4 |
| | | Nightgown or pyjamas | 4 |
| Petticoat bodices | 2 | Nightgown bag | 1 |
| Knickers, blue | 2 | Large linen bags | 2 |
| Linings | 6 | Small linen bags | 2 |
| Handkerchiefs | 24 | Sponge and flannel | 1 |
| Dressing gown | 1 | Work bag | 1 |
| Dressing jacket | 1 | Gymnastic tunic | 1 |
| Brush and comb sets | 2 | | |
| Panama hat (for summer terms) | 1 | *Summer Term only:* | |
| Boneless stays | 2 | Linen hat | 1 |
| Felt hat | 1 | Dark blue bathing dress | 1 |
| Gymnasium shoes, white | 1 | Tennis shoes | 1 |

The sixty-pound fee is for those pupils entering under the age of fifteen. Pupils entering afterwards pay sixty-five pounds. These fees cover tuition in all school subjects, including Swedish dancing, gymnastics, dancing; also board, laundry, seat in church, school entertainments, use of swimming bath, use of sanatorium for cases considered suitable by the School Authorities, and the services of the School Medical Officer during term time.

Wycombe Abbey, also of great prestige and renown, is a magnificent school run on most intelligent lines. I am told by a parent that it states its inclusive fee at two hundred a year; this includes laundry, but not sanatorium. The outfit-list may be of interest, the idea underlying it being that clothes may be kept as simple and as reasonable as possible. New girls need not necessarily have new clothes and the list is sent out early in order that parents may avoid unnecessary expense by preparing beforehand. Four nightgowns or pyjamas, four camisoles, four pairs woollen combinations, a dressing-gown and jacket are suggested.

### Regulation Garments provided at the School

| | |
|---|---|
| Hat | Ties |
| Cloak | Dark blue mackintosh |
| Gymnastic suit—**tunic** | Mackintosh cap |
| Knickers with linings | **Tan stockings** (if required) |
| Overblouses | Goloshes |
| Dark blue cardigan | 1 pair plain evening shoes |
| Shoes (gymnastic and playground) | **and** 1 pair black house shoes |
| Overall | |

### Garments to be brought from Home

| | |
|---|---|
| 1 long dark blue coat | 2 plain white silk overblouses for Sunday or special wear |
| 1 dark blue coat and skirt | 1 white cardigan for evening wear |
| 1 dark blue school skirt | Stockings—six black and two tan, or eight pairs of black |
| 1 white dress for concerts (thin woollen material or silk, no colour in trimming, long sleeves) | 2 pairs of silk stockings, black or brown, for special evening wear (if desired) |
| 2 dresses for afternoon and evening wear | 2 pairs walking shoes |

1929

*"Always Fit"*

Get that manly youngster of yours a **St.Margaret** Jersey —and he will begin to take a pride in his clothes. And even if he does not it matters little.

**St.Margaret** Jerseys are made for hard, rough wear—the kind of hard life they usually get with high-spirited youth inside them. Your Retailer will be able to show you a fine selection of styles and prices—all the finest value for money that 120 years' experience can produce. At the same time ask to see **St.Margaret** Children's Socks and Stockings.

# St.Margaret

*"See how they Wear"* JERSEYS

*Any Draper or Outfitter can obtain St. Margaret productions for you direct from the makers, N. Corah & Sons, Ltd., St. Margaret's Works, Leicester.*

HOSIERY · UNDERWEAR · JERSEYS

# The Problem of School Bills

2 white petticoats
3 large and 2 small linen bags
2 nightdress cases
2 brush and comb bags
2 hairbrushes and combs
1 clothes brush
1 table napkin ring
1 small despatch box to lock up (in which the purse and every article of value must be kept)
1 flat music case
1 work basket
1 handbag or suit càse
An eiderdown or rug (if desired)

*For Summer Term only:*
  3 cotton and washing silk blouses

1929

No silk or crêpe de Chine underwear is allowed at school. Only low square heels are allowed on indoor and outdoor shoes; curved heels sloping inwards are strictly forbidden. The afternoon dresses may be made of fine serge, marocain, wool crêpe, or velveteen, and should be as simple as possible. All should have pockets: and sleeves below the elbow.

A mother adds, "After the first term, the clothes' bill is large on account of all the regulation garments to be bought at school, but they last all their school career. In winter, dark blue velour hats are worn with house ribbon; in summer, panamas. They never wear hats in the grounds unless there is a baking sun, when they wear cheap, rush garden hats with house ribbon. It is a very neat uniform. Extras covering all school things come to thirty pounds, roughly, per annum. Certainly not more, except at the end of the first term."

It will be noticed that all these schools—Wycombe, Roedean, and Cheltenham—go in for the (to the mother) tiresome, soilable, white blouse top. It is well known that the dark blue, apparently almost universally preferred by school mistresses, shows every mark, inkstain, and grease spot. Girls usually loathe black stockings, but perhaps they are usually enjoined for discipline.

Sherborne School for Girls is more fortunate, perhaps, in its choice of green coats and skirts rather than blue, and tan stockings. I have been given the following figures of education and clothing at this deservedly famous school by a parent of a girl there at the moment.

| | | £ | s. | d. | | £ | s. | d. |
|---|---|---|---|---|---|---|---|---|
| 1925. | Board and tuition | 115 | 3 | 1 | Clothing | 60 | 14 | 8 |
| 1926. | „ „ „ | 179 | 6 | 5 | „ | 46 | 15 | 0 |
| 1927. | „ „ „ | 183 | 3 | 3 | „ | 55 | 12 | 5 |

Parents ambitious to send their girls to the leading schools should draw in their expenses at once, and save against the time when school age is reached. Girls often have to do without an expensive education because their brothers have to be considered first, and the money soon goes. The poor professional parents of *boys* have all through the ages clenched their teeth and managed somehow.

The expenses of a boys' Public School vary. Of Rugby, a mother writes:

"I have looked up the old amounts of bills for over four years and find the term's bills varied from about £75 or rather less to £80, the last is exceptional, the average is £76. They increase chiefly as a boy goes up the school. The bare fees are £67 a term. The rest is games, subscriptions, books, cleaning of clothes, extra laundry, and such things; nothing unreasonable, I think. We allowed Peter two pounds a term pocket money; we were specially asked not to give him more, and he also had a shilling a week at school, which went into the bill."

CLOTHES LIST. RUGBY

3 pairs pyjamas
3 flannel shirts
3 pants
3 vests
6 pairs socks
6 or 8 collars
12 handkerchiefs
2 black coats and waistcoats
3 pairs dark trousers
3 black ties
1 sweater
1 overcoat
3 pairs black shoes

1 pair indoor shoes
1 hand bag
1 dressing gown and bedroom slippers
1 mackintosh

*Winter:*
Football clothes, provided at school

*Summer:*
For cricket:
  3 white flannel shirts
  3 pairs white flannel trousers
  1 pair cricket shoes

A bill from Sherborne is also supplied by a father. The boys like to wear dark blue suits; they are allowed these or very dark grey, and a merciful change to grey flannels in the summer. The clothes list is simple compared to that of the girls.

SHERBORNE SCHOOL

| | £ | s. | d. | | £ | s. | d. |
|---|---|---|---|---|---|---|---|
| Terminal School Fee | 55 | 0 | 0 | Cash advanced | | 2 | 10 |
| *Extras:* | | | | Stationery and note books | | 5 | 7 |
| Private tuition | — | | | Parcels and porterage, etc.. | | 1 | 0 |
| Advanced drawing | — | | | Extra milk, etc. | | — | |
| Instrumental music | — | | | Matron's account | | 2 | 0 |
| Workshop | — | | | Damages | | — | |
| Musical Society | — | | | Haircutter | | 1 | 6 |
| Boxing lessons | | 2 | 6 | | | | |
| Swimming lessons | — | | | | 56 | 8 | 5 |
| O.S.S. fee | — | | | *Tradesmen's bills* | 14 | 7 | 8 |
| *Boarding House Expenses:* | | | | | | | |
| Study, fire, and light allowance | | 13 | 0 | | £70 | 16 | 1 |
| School Certificate fee | — | | | | | | |

It was pleasant recently to hear the Headmaster of Lancing, in a lecture, praise the present-day schoolboy as a "good serious type, out to serve his country rather than to make large sums of money." Boys like this are worth the tremendous sacrifices which often their parents have to make to send them to the school of their ambitions. As for the girl of to-day at a great public school—what happier person could be found?

# *Things You'll*

Illustrations by

Elizabeth Montgomery

## *The Fairy Party*

"ASK him, ask him," cried the Fairy Duke, as he lay in his roseleaf cradle while outside the Owl hooted softly in the great walnut-tree avenue that runs down from the Princess Gossamer's palace. "*Ask* that pretty bird to stay with me! For my birthday to-morrow, Mummy."

"Yes, let's," said the Fairy Princess, his mother, and laughed merrily.

"Where would he sleep, Mother?"

"Oh, in the Daffodil Chamber. It is all lined with golden petals, and they would set off his grey feathers beautifully. I'll send a note by a messenger to ask him."

But to the Fairy that was sent flying up into the walnut tree, the Owl made no reply. He read the note right through, with his blinking deep brown eyes.

By five minutes to three o'clock the next day the whole palace was agog with excitement to see whether Mr. Owl would come or not. He was the only bird that had never been bidden to the revels of the Fairy Duke! Fairy heads popped out of every window, and the Fairy Duke cried sorrowfully:

"He's not answered, and he's not coming!"

"I don't think, darling, that he'd have liked it much. He probably hates dancing and games," his mother said, patting the Fairy Duke's little sunbeam head.

But lo! and behold as the crystal clock of the palace chimed three-thirty there slowly winged in sight the Owl, himself, *come to stay,* carrying a small suitcase in his beak!

They welcomed him by turning out the fairy band. It had been waiting behind the palace gates in case he came. "One, two, *three,*" sang out the fairy bandmaster, and out came the fairy heralds, blowing long trumpets.

Mr. Owl flew straight to the balcony, deposited his luggage, and bowed before the Fairy Princess.

"It was delightful of your Royal Highness to ask me," he said. "It will make a great change for me. My only trouble is," and he yawned—

The little Fairy Duke was already beginning to stroke his guest's feathers. "What is your trouble, you Most Lovely One?" he said.

"I'm not used to keep awake in the afternoon," answered the Owl very politely.

"Can nobody do anything?" called out the Fairy Princess sadly.

"Oh, but we can all go to bed *now,*" cried the Lord High Gnome Chamberlain, quickly advancing to the front. "Go to bed *now* and get up at eleven, and have a night party!"

"What do you say to that?" cried the Fairy Duke. "Clap, all of you, if you like it."

And all the fairies hanging out of the windows clapped hard.

"To bed then, everybody!" cried the fairy heralds, and began to play a soft lullaby.

*The spring flowers are the dain-a posy and see how many*

And the Princess and the Duke escorted the visitor to his bedroom, and the Owl looked round and said he had never slept in such a pretty yellow room in his life. He was used to a green one. He shut his eyes.

At eleven o'clock exactly the Cuckoos came rushing out of their little doors in their clocks, to cry, "Cuckoo, get up, get *up,*" and everything was at once joyous. Fairy bakers were seen in the courtyard of the palace carrying trays of coffee ices. The court conjurer drove up in his pink glass coach.

The Owl had brushed his feathers most beautifully, and at the party he flew here and there and everywhere among the guests, holding out a small claw and shaking hands. And the best part of it all was that when they had feasted he taught them some new Owl Games that you and I and they had never heard of, games like "Pouncey-poo" and "Feathery Flick" and "Silentswish," the greatest fun in the world!

# Like to Know

## By Marjory Royce

*tiest and sweetest of all. Gather different sorts you can find*

### Daffodil Time

This is the month in which to look for the daffodil in all its loveliness in the wood. There is something sweeter about the little wild one than those grand golden beauties we get in the garden. Perhaps its bright yellow crown attracts the insects to it by day, and the night moths in the twilight may be guided to it by its pale petals.

Peep under any yew tree if you pass it now and notice the tiny blossoms, for it is in flower in March. Why not collect wild flowers this spring? Get as many as you possibly can and ask the wisest botanist you know in the neighbourhood to help you name them.

### Singing Games

Before a party buy Kerr's *Guild of Play Book* (Kerr, Glasgow, 1s. 6d.). In it there are many singing games—" There stands a Lady on the Mountain," and " Three times round went the very Gallant Ship " and others.

### The French Fairy Shops Here

*I met in Ludlow Market a Fairy like a
    dream,*
*The little thing was a'carrying Pansies
    and Cream,*
*I'd thought that Fairies were not true
    (things are not what they seem),*
*When I saw her with a basket of
    Pansies and Cream!*
*I stammered to the Fairy, " Come walk
    beside the Teme,*
*I've always longed to know you, we'll
    play beside the stream."*
*So past the yellow farmhouse, beneath
    the morning beam,*
*We walked, I and the Fairy, with the
    Pansies and the Cream,*
*Such pretty French she taught me, and
    poems by the ream,*
*Until she had to leave me, because she
    lives in Nîmes,*
*And she skipped across the Channel
    with her Pansies and her Cream!*

### March Chatter

Why not plant some mustard and cress? The cress will take much longer to grow than the mustard so let it go in first. Don't dig deep holes but just scatter the seeds broadcast on the earth, take a spade and pat them gently in, and then give them some water. You may cover them up with a sack and take it off when the shoots begin to appear.

### Belgian Wisdom

We were playing the old game of proverbs the other evening when a Belgian girl came in and taught us three famous Belgian proverbs. They were: " Life is a spoonful of sour and a spoonful of sweet." " You must run between the raindrops as they do in Bruges." " Where can one be better than in mother's kitchen? "

### Pictures on Postcards

To make your own schoolroom frieze yourself is rather fun. At the National Portrait Gallery in London, after seeing the pictures of Kings and Queens for yourself, you can buy their portraits reproduced on postcards. You can stick them in groups on to strips of brown paper or coloured paper and pin round your wall. Van Dyck's Queen Henrietta Maria is one of the prettiest.

### Windy March

What book can I recommend to you this windy, blowy month but the old-fashioned, ever-new *Little Women* about the beloved March family?

### This Month's Animal

It is the March Hare, isn't it? Mr. Hare has a longer body, longer hind legs, longer ears than Bunny, and has black tips to those ears. It is a most extraordinary thing to find a hare sleeping, he is always on the alert. He has his food at dusk when it is safest, and he sits a good deal in his " form," a slight hollow in the grass, just listening.

1930

*Jolly times with the 'Pianola' Piano*

# THE POPULARITY OF THE
# 'PIANOLA' PIANO

The secret of the great increase in popularity of the 'Pianola' Piano is that it affords entertainment that no other musical instrument can provide, the pleasure of actually making music as well as listening to music.

## And you really do play it.

For instance, on every 'Pianola' Piano you will find a simple device known as the Metrostyle, which shows you how each piece of music should be played. Even those who know nothing about music can use this guide to play exactly as if they were playing by hand. And this is but one of the interesting features of the 'Pianola' Piano.

Even the little ones are not forgotten, for there are some splendid new Rolls called the Children's Playtime Series, with stories and pictures and everything that appeals to youngsters.

Remember that the 'Pianola' Piano is invariably a fine piano for playing by hand, and the advantages of the 'Pianola' action are, therefore, additional.

*Come to Aeolian Hall and try a 'Pianola' Piano for yourself,*
or write for Catalogue E.2

# THE AEOLIAN COMPANY *Ltd.*
## Aeolian Hall · 131-137, New Bond St., London, W.1

# By HELENA NORMANTON

## *What* Shall *I do* *with* That Boy ?

Is your son a dreamer or a man of action ? Does he follow the crowd or strike out for himself ? This writer offers suggestions to parents on the problem of making the most of a boy's individual abilities in a career that allows scope for them

1930

SO many fathers and mothers have been writing to me recently about the choice of a career for a son that I hasten to assure them all of the following two facts. One is, that to my own everlasting regret, I have no sons or daughters. Secondly, if I had had, I feel perfectly assured that I should have made the usual parental mess of things. To which I might also advise contemptuous reference to my own contempt for advice (given or received) in a recent issue of this periodical.

Having made this graceful preliminary bow, may it be suggested that the perplexed parent might well consider how all geniuses must have had unsympathetic parents who persisted, in the teeth of all the experience of the race, in pushing their offspring into whatever career was most embittering and unsuitable for them? Think of young Keats, apprenticed to an apothecary; of Shakespeare to a butcher—or was it a bacon factory ? Dickens, again, washing blacking-bottles, or Disraeli and Arnold Bennett as solicitors' clerks.

Nothing embitters and enrages a young genius more than a job of useful work. If he hates the necessary labour of this workaday world with a sufficient degree of intensity, he may be more or less relied upon to leave imperishable literature describing his stark horror of prosaic tasks. I have deep suspicions about this whole affair. Dickens never shone, in my opinion, less than in those vitriolic passages he wrote about his parents' " wickedness " in letting him work in the blacking factory. Why not? They were all terribly hard up, and young Dickens had more to be proud of in earning a few shillings and to that extent relieving the family exchequer than if he had sat at home scribbling. Also, he learnt life there.

However, there it is. If you wish your young to shine in the writing world, push them hard down into an ordinary job. They will escape, if the urge be sufficient; and you yourself will obtain the usual marbly niche in your son's autobiography as the usual parent. Parallel considerations apply to an artistic career—dramatic, musical, painting and the like. An unsympathetic parent is a *sine qua non*. If parents are too fondly gushing, reliance for encouragement must be placed upon a crushing outside Eminent Authority. A distant, far-back kinsman of my own was encouraged by his parents to paint, and they actually sent a specimen of work to Ruskin. " Tell the young lad to put it in the fire ! " fulminated the great one. Did he? Of course not. He vowed he would live to exhibit in the Royal Academy. Did he? He did. Many times. Serve the Royal Academy right. And Ruskin too. Treated politely the lad might have become a Master Plumber or something really lucrative and decent.

Artistic careers apart, study the boy. Say to yourself: Money or monotony? The lone hand or the team-worker? Then play your cards accordingly. For the gaining of large amounts of money, one must turn away from the steady and safe ambits and consider such careers as replace in these times buccaneering in the good old days of yore. Pirates needed sinfulness, dash, resource, exact information of trade-routes and departures of richly laden vessels, courage, tenacity and a strong desire for bullion. The qualities involved to-day in the origination and promotion of large enterprises do not seem to me to be markedly different.

Well, if your son is of the adventurous, carve-out-a-career type, all you have to do is let him get on with it.

But qualities do not develop to such high intensity very often. Perhaps it is as well for the world that every boy who wants to see it a bit does not necessarily desire to paint more of its map red. Where a parent can help in such a case as when a boy is determined to go to sea, is to amass from all the reputable sources he can all the available information, so that the schoolboy shall be able fairly to choose between the Royal Navy, the Merchant Service, and other seagoing careers such as those of wireless operator, purser, and so on.

A boy's uncles and his father's grown-up friends are often of great use and influence. Manuals of facts, such as Sir Charles Wakefield's book on boys' careers, will often supply useful information about costs of different kinds of training; but for all that, the minute a lad begins to express a desire to become a particular sort of worker, *then* is the time for parents to count the cost. If money be unobtainable in sufficient quantity, it is far kinder to say so when a boy is twelve than when he is seventeen and has been telling all his schoolfriends that he is going to take up medicine or law. The young are abnormally sensitive about parental lack of money, which they often seem to consider as a sort of moral disgrace. Of all most cruel things, what can be harder than to half-train a young fellow for some profession, and then remove him for lack of funds to complete his course? Only one thing perhaps, and that is to complete it at a sacrifice to the education of other brothers and sisters.

Where a boy has an exceptionally steady and honourable character, it may be a successful experiment in some families for the eldest to skim off the cream of the family's educational fund in the trust that he will help the younger ones from his own early earnings. I am bound to say that I have seen this scheme work out far better in " mid-middle " and lower middle than in higher grades of social life. There are probably reasons for this, but they escape me.

Parents have a peculiarly difficult task these days in budgeting for their boys' and girls' trainings, because it may now so often happen that a girl has the qualities for the more costly career—the boy not. Here I do not suggest just a *Continued overleaf.*

# Treasure Cot

## *The only Store entirely devoted to Mothers', Babies' & Children's needs*

**1930**

TREASURE Cot is a complete store entirely devoted to the needs of the expectant mother, the many requirements for the birth of baby and clothes for children up to 12 years of age. In the department for Children's Clothes there is now a delightful selection in the newest spring styles. Dainty garments for baby's early years and smart little suits, coats or dresses for older children. Mothers and expectant mothers should do all their children's shopping at Treasure Cot.

**PRACTICAL COTTON WASHING FROCK**, No. 1268, in small spot pattern. Colours, red, blue, green and other shades. Knickers to match. 24″ **15/9**
26″ **16/3**. 28″ **18/-**.

**DAINTY FLOWERED LAWN SMOCK**, No. 7300. Sleeveless, with white collar, and armholes bound with white. Knickers to match. Colours, blue mixture, pink and other shades. 16″ **17/9**
18″ **18/9**. 20″ **19/9**.

**GIRL'S SPRING COAT**, No. 058, in repp, the collar and cuffs are finished with tiny picot frills. Colours, pink, sky and all white. 16″ **48/9**
18″ **50/-**.

**NATURAL LEGHORN STRAW BONNET**, No. 5221, trimmed satin ribbon. The brim is underlined with georgette to match coat. All sizes, **30/-**.

**LITTLE BOY'S TUSSORE COAT**, No. 951, fastening up at neck with double pleat at back. 16″ **37/6**
18″ **39/9**.
In natural tussore, 35/6 and 37/6.

**STITCHED PADDY HAT**, No. 5209 to match. All sizes, **9/6**

**DAINTY SPOT MUSLIN FROCK.** Smocked and appliqued with contrasting colour. 16″ **24/-**
18″ **24/6**.
Also in other colours.

**GIRL'S SMART COAT**, No. 935, in natural colour tussore, with cuffs and collar of green crêpe de Chine. 16″ **33/9**
18″ **35/9**.
**BONNET TO MATCH**, No. 5166. **13/9**

**WHITE HAIRCORD SMOCK**, No. 4380, and knickers to match. Smocking in blue, red, pink, green, lemon and other shades. 16″ **9/6**
18″ **10/6**. 20″ **11/6**.

**ALL GOODS SENT POST FREE**

# Treasure Cot Co. LTD.

Telephone: Regent 2104 (3 lines)
*Specialists in Everything for Mother, Babies & Children*
**(Dept. D.Z.10) 103 OXFORD ST., LONDON, W.1**
Nearly opposite Bourne and Hollingsworth's

*Flynn's*

# What Shall I Do With That Boy?

*(Continued)*

mere academic egalitarian feminism. Consider the nature of both boy and girl very carefully and what return each is likely to make to the community and to the family before spending large sums. If the girl is all for self and the boy for others, tip the balance against the girl, for she will look after Number One anyhow; and *vice versa*. If the girl's career is one which marriage will abruptly end as with an iron curtain—e.g. teaching or Civil Service—do not make too much of it. It is more productive to spend upon medical training, for no one can stop a woman practising medicine because she marries. So that, as between the claims of girl and boy, balance all factors before allocation.

Consult carefully those who have in hand the formal scholastic education of your son and two things will surprise you —what they know about him, and what they do not. The headmaster can tell you, and so can the form-master, that the lad is a good team-worker or indifferent to the classics, that he is a born leader or an enthusiastic follower. They cannot tell you that his deep passion for entomology is a legacy from great-uncle Tom, or that his fondness for collecting boxes and receptacles is just his grandmother all over again. Pay, however, the deepest attention to what your son's educators can tell you, for they have the advantage over you in not being partially blinded by affection and limited as to comparisons. Particularly usefully can you check by the light of their information mere imitative fads which boys pick up from each other. I remember a case where, after a magnificently inspiring set of lectures on Archæology, half the boys in a particular Sixth Form wanted for a time to become excavators. One father received the wisest possible advice from a brilliant but sympathetic headmaster as to the defects in his own son which would have made him quite useless at such work, and the young fellow was promptly headed in another direction, whereat he afterwards made good.

A wise thing to do is to ascertain by medical examination whether a boy comes up to the physical standards wanted for certain callings. A colour-blind boy cannot become an engine driver nor a short-sighted one a sailor. It is best to know these things quite early on—treatment may mitigate, and on the other hand, early bendings of the twig are easier straightened out

again where physically necessary.

But all these things, to my mind, are minor considerations compared with a paramount one—what is the broad classification of the boy's temperament and talents? Does he play for safety and can he work in and with a crowd; or is he markedly an individualist? Is he like the wild dog who hunts in packs, or the tiger lone in his kill and his life? No more acute misery can be caused than by bottling up talents in the pressure of a crowd too close around one. Great powers fret and waste thus; whilst mediocrity causes no friction and monopolises promotion. Originality and independent thinking are an absolute curse in some occupations. They arouse jealousy in colleagues, suspicion in superiors, and provoke criticism and ultimate failure in most of those careers where people have to produce standardised work by hordes and battalions. On the other hand the crowd mind is equally a curse to us all in positions where fecundity of idea is desirable—as witness the dramatic and film world of to-day, cluttered up with people of the lowest common measure of originality.

Do not force a boy of independent type into the great public services of Education, Civil Service, Army, Navy (I would not say Air Force here), or municipal services. People there are going to be liked because they are "safe"; "sound"; conventional and so on. Tell an original lad he may make a howling success or a horrible failure of his life, but anyway he need not be quite miserable if he avoids the grooves of life. Shepherd your safety-firsters into the regularly-paid occupations and leave them to get their thrills in life by their emotional relationships and such vicarious mental escapes as the theatre and the adventure-story.

Talk freely to your sons and try to take them to many places where they will see the world's work carried on. Teachers cannot do much of this. Consider your sons' careers from their early days and put your own brains and observations to work to help them. Hope for the best and prepare for the worst. Let your sons fare forth gallantly and do not deter them from going to the ends of the earth. Remember they are scions of an imperial race which has done great things in the past and must accomplish even greater in the future. Let them be Vikings, not specimens of Virginia Creeper.

1930

# *Dainty Summer Dresses for*

## Embroidery by Anne Orr

**H**AVE you not often seen pictures of lovely French clothes for children and wished you could get them for your own youngsters? The secret of the charm of these French clothes is the fine hand-work which is put into them. Sometimes it is only tiny little tucks finely sewn by hand; sometimes it is fine embroidery, beautifully done. Clothes of this type may be easily made at home by a mother who has patience and a little skill with her needle. The cost of making them is very low indeed, as they can often be made from a remnant which you have on hand or which can be bought for very little.

The little frocks illustrated have simple lines and use tiny tucks and hand-work for ornamentation. All are made from colourful cotton or linen fabrics which are charming for children for any time of day all the year round, but are specially suitable for the coming three or four months when we expect plenty of sunshine. In addition, they launder perfectly and are therefore greatly appreciated both by the little girl and by her mother.

The brother and sister suits at the top of the page are knitted by hand with a nursery figure for decoration. Just now, when there is a vogue for dressing

292

291

294

293

*For cool days little knitted suits are just the thing. Design A-1900, above, can be obtained in pamphlet form for a 1½d. stamp. The boy's jersey has a dog knitted in it, the girl's a kitten. The knickers fasten round the waist with a draw-string and skirt has shoulder straps. The square necks button on the shoulders on both sides. Ribbing across the shoulders, round the hems of the jerseys and knickers and round the cuffs, helps the garments to keep their shape*

**HOW TO**

All Hot-Iron patterns, phlets for embroidery are where otherwise stated. 1s. 2d. post free, with the Nos. 296 and 299, which knickers and are 2s. 4d. to match all the other each post free. Patterns ding to the descriptions between each size. Send postal-order or cheque to tern Service, 153 Queen ing in block letters your of pattern or embroidery

*Blue gingham with white smocked frills makes the attractive frock, No. 291, in sizes 4 to 10 years, left of the two above. The collar, cuffs and pocket are decorated with frills smocked in pastel colours, worked from Hot-Iron Pattern No. A-1904. The sleeveless handkerchief-linen party dress, No. 292, is adorable for sizes 2 to 6 years. The centre part is of a pastel colour, joined to a white hem and yoke with faggoting. The appliqué design is in Hot-Iron Pattern No. A-1902*

*The simplicity and good taste of the party frock at the right, No. 293, make it suitable for any formal occasion. It is of white crêpe de Chine, for sizes 4 to 10 years. A wide yoke is smocked in red and blue, while the cuffs and front panel are cross-stitched in the same colours. A hot-iron pattern for the smocking and chart for the cross-stitch are in Design No. A-1903. The everyday dress, No. 294, for sizes 4 to 10 years, is made of lavender linen with touches of white, and is cross-stitched in a butterfly motif from printed pamphlet No. A-1901*

1930

# Small Girls of all Ages

## Patterns by Caroline Gray

1930

children alike, there is nothing more serviceable or smarter for the younger generation than these knitted suits which are so easily made.

The other dresses shown on the opposite page range from two to ten years. Two are party dresses, and two are daytime frocks. The little sleeveless frock in the centre is decorated with coloured appliqués in the shape of fruit and leaves. Beside it is a gingham frock with crisp white frills for an older child. Below is a white crêpe de Chine frock, smocked and cross-stitched in red and blue. A lavender linen dress with a cross-stitched yoke is beside it.

An ensemble, a party dress, and a daytime frock are shown on this page for both the very small girl and her slightly older sister. At the top is a simple little party frock. The ensemble beside it is made of linen or piqué combined with printed cotton. Below in the centre is a play frock of coloured lawn with an interesting tucked yoke effect. Next is a frock of corn-coloured handkerchief linen which has a touch of simple embroidery and is appropriate for parties. A piqué ensemble and a cotton print dress are shown below. The dress of the ensemble is sleeveless and the coat is unlined. The printed play frock has crisp frills.

### ORDER

charts and printed pam-
1s. 2d. post free, except
All cutting patterns are
exception of the ensembles
comprise frock, coat and
each post free. Knickers
dresses can be had for 6d.
are in different sizes accor-
given, rising 2 years
correct amount in stamps,
Good Housekeeping Pat-
Victoria Street, E.C.4, giv-
name, address, number
design and size of pattern

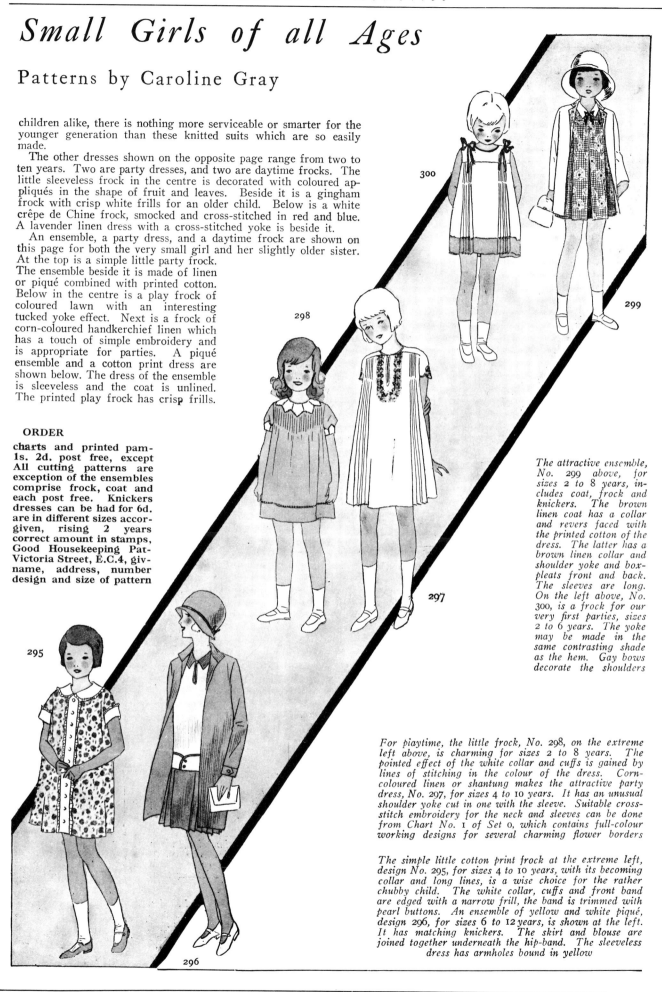

*The attractive ensemble, No. 299 above, for sizes 2 to 8 years, includes coat, frock and knickers. The brown linen coat has a collar and revers faced with the printed cotton of the dress. The latter has a brown linen collar and shoulder yoke and box-pleats front and back. The sleeves are long. On the left above, No. 300, is a frock for our very first parties, sizes 2 to 6 years. The yoke may be made in the same contrasting shade as the hem. Gay bows decorate the shoulders*

*For playtime, the little frock, No. 298, on the extreme left above, is charming for sizes 2 to 8 years. The pointed effect of the white collar and cuffs is gained by lines of stitching in the colour of the dress. Corn-coloured linen or shantung makes the attractive party dress, No. 297, for sizes 4 to 10 years. It has an unusual shoulder yoke cut in one with the sleeve. Suitable cross-stitch embroidery for the neck and sleeves can be done from Chart No. 1 of Set 0, which contains full-colour working designs for several charming flower borders*

*The simple little cotton print frock at the extreme left, design No. 295, for sizes 4 to 10 years, with its becoming collar and long lines, is a wise choice for the rather chubby child. The white collar, cuffs and front band are edged with a narrow frill, the band is trimmed with pearl buttons. An ensemble of yellow and white piqué, design 296, for sizes 6 to 12 years, is shown at the left. It has matching knickers. The skirt and blouse are joined together underneath the hip-band. The sleeveless dress has armholes bound in yellow*

## The Story of
# The Gardener
## and the
# WHITE ELEPHANTS

### And how they defied the Rabbit
### Whom None Dare Disobey

THERE was once a gardener, who had to look after such a big garden that he had to get up at one in the morning and didn't get to bed till twelve at night. In fact, he only got one hour's sleep each night. And working so hard made him get thin and old and rheumaticky and lame long before he should.

One day he planted out a beautiful bed of sweet peas: but when he came in the morning something had been and eaten them up.

"Slugs!" said the gardener: and when he planted out a fresh bed he made slug-traps out of orange peel and set them among the sweet peas. But when he came in the morning the sweet peas were all eaten up, but the slug traps weren't touched.

"Then it isn't slugs," he said: "I wonder what it is. There is only one thing to do: to-night I must miss my only hour of sleep and sit up and watch."

So at twelve o'clock he went and sat by the sweet pea bed to watch. And he got sleepier and sleepier, till at last when it was just a quarter to one he couldn't keep awake and fell fast asleep:

Illustrations by
Elsie Harding

and when he woke up all his sweet peas had been eaten again.

So the next night he went to watch again, and this time took with him his fountain pen: and each time he was just going to fall asleep he gave himself a jab with the nib, and woke himself up again. And at five to one, what should he see but a very old rabbit, so old that its fur was all coming off, and its whiskers were white, and it hobbled as much as he did. But although it was so old, in a twinkling of an eye it had gobbled up all his sweet peas, and was hobbling away. Then the gardener got up and tried to chase it: but though the rabbit limped he limped too, and though they both went so slowly, he couldn't quite catch it: but they hobbled and hobbled till they reached the rose garden: and when they

*On the third night the gardener chased the rabbit, but it was still ahead of him when they got to the rose-garden*

got there the rabbit nibbled a rose leaf, and no sooner did it do that than all of a sudden it became a gay rabbit again and galloped away at ever such a pace while the poor old gardener was left rubbing his eyes.

"Well, well," he said: "well, well, well!"

So the third night he went to watch again, and again he kept awake by jabbing himself with his fountain pen, and again the rabbit came, old now as it had been before it ate the rose leaf. It gobbled up the little sweet pea seedlings, and the gardener chased it: but though he went as fast as he could it was still ahead of him when they got to the rose garden. Then the rabbit nibbled a rose leaf and quick as lightning it was galloping away. But this time the gardener ate a rose leaf too, and in a moment he was turned into a strong young man and began to chase the rabbit again. This time the rabbit couldn't get quite away, but it was still ahead when it reached its hole.

The rabbit dived into the hole, and the gardener dived in after it, and the rabbit burrowed and the gardener burrowed, but still he couldn't quite catch it

*The gardener (who by this time had become a young man again) struck a match and saw a herd of great white elephants within the pit*

nor could the rabbit quite get away—no, not though it dug like mad. Then all of a sudden, the rabbit dug its way through into a great black pit, and the gardener following close behind suddenly found himself falling head over heels. But he didn't have very far to fall: only when he sat up the rabbit was nowhere to be seen.

It was quite dark, but all the same he could just make out some huge white shapes. So he struck a match to see what it was and found he was among twenty or thirty white elephants, all sleeping on the ground. Then one of them woke up, and asked him who he was, and what he was doing.

"I came in chasing that rabbit," said the gardener. The white elephant looked most shocked.

## *Told to the Children by* Richard Hughes

*Author of* "*A High Wind in Jamaica*"

"What!" he said, "you were chasing our terrible Lord and Master, the Rabbit Whom None Dare Disobey?"

"Indeed I was," said the gardener: "but do you mean to say all you great white elephants are the slaves of one silly old rabbit?"

"Of course we are," said the white elephant.

"And you do what he tells you?" asked the gardener.

"Of course we do," said the white elephant.

"But supposing you didn't?" said the gardener. "What would happen?"

"I don't know," said the elephant: "no one has ever dared to try."

"Then try!" said the gardener: "Nothing *Continued overleaf*

## The Gardener and the White Elephants

*(Continued)*

will happen! Do something disobedient and see!"

"But what is there disobedient we can do?" said the white elephant.

"Is there a way out of this cave?" asked the gardener.

"Yes there is," said the elephant: "but the terrible rabbit has told us not to go out."

"Then come out!" said the gardener. "Show me the way, and we will all go out together."

So the first white elephant woke up the others and explained the idea to them. Then they all began to go up the tunnel that led out of the cave together. But they hadn't gone far when they found the rabbit blocking their way.

"Go back!" said the rabbit, and all the elephants were ready to turn round and do what they were told. But the gardener called out, "I'm not afraid of you! You're only a silly old rabbit!"

"Oh, I am, am I!" said the rabbit in a most wicked voice: and before their very eyes he began to swell and grow, and his teeth grew sharp as a tiger's, and his eyes flashed fire. Then he sprang at the first elephant with a savage growl, and plunged his teeth in its trunk.

"That's what comes of disobeying *me*!" he said.

But the gardener was not afraid, and big and fierce although the rabbit had become he sprang at it and seized it by the throat, and then began the most terrible fight between the gardener and the rabbit. Sometimes the gardener got the best and held the rabbit down on the ground, and sometimes the rabbit got the best and tried to bite the gardener's throat. But at last the gardener won, and managed to strangle the rabbit till it was quite dead; and then the other white elephants marched on up the tunnel till they reached the open air.

"Now will you be my white elephants?" asked the gardener.

"We will, of course, we will," sang the white elephants all together.

Now that he had all these white elephants the gardener, of course, was rich, and didn't have to work in the garden any more. Instead, he had a small but comfortable house for himself, and a perfectly enormous stable for all the white elephants: and there they lived happily together for ever after: and this was the strange thing, that though when the rabbit had eaten the rose leaf it had only made him young for one night, when the gardener ate his it made him young for ever, so that he never grew old again at all.

1930

ROWE                                                                                    FAIRYLAND

## NURSERY FOLK FOLLOW          GROWN-UP STYLES

*The little boy who longs for a "real" suit will like the raglan cut of the beige tweed overcoat with its flap pockets. A small peaked cap goes excellently with it*

*His companion with the rake is dressed for school in navy blue trousers and grey flannel jacket. His trousers are straight and short, a secret of the young Parisian's smartness*

*Above, right: a school coat of brown and beige tweed, cut on boyish lines, with heavy stitched edges and patch pockets. The jaunty hat is of beige felt, turned off the face*

*The older girl's frock of green crepella finished in points has white piqué collar. Also of white piqué is the baby's bonnet, cut in scallops and worn with one of the new fancy piqués*

FAIRYLAND

# By Jessica COSGRAVE

1931

# The Control

NOT without misgiving do I write the words at the head of this article, for no one can live among young people to-day and not be occasionally frightened, no matter how ingrained one's optimism, by the apparent hardness one so constantly sees. Better, perhaps, the tears and "vapours" of our Victorian grandmothers with their often genuine tenderness and softness of heart, than the steely exterior of these practical young people who show no emotion at all, at either their own vicissitudes or those of their nearest and dearest. Most of us have seen the shell broken through, and have realised with a burst of gratitude that it covers much the same kind of heart as beat in the young people of former generations, though the manners of the period certainly seem to do all in their power to hide this fact. If the thesis of this article is a correct one, these deceptive manners in themselves have their dangers.

No one wants to control emotion completely and to become hard and unfeeling in order to spare oneself pain, but there are certain emotions, such as fear, anger and grief, which cannot possibly be allowed to swamp our souls without some effort to channel and curb them. Women, especially, tend to be too much a prey to the emotions, and to wear themselves out by them, even when they are not turned towards self but are sympathetic in their nature.

James, the famous psychologist, has given us a wonderful hint for a rule of action in his theory, which he shared with several French psychologists, of "Motion and Emotion." This theory states that when we are confronted with a strong stimulus—such as, for example, a terrifying sight—our hearts beat wildly, our skins roughen, our hair rises on end, and *therefore* and *after* this has taken place, we feel a sensation of fear. Of course the popular belief is that all of these physical symptoms take place *because* we are afraid—not that we are afraid because they take place. It may be difficult for us to follow him all the way, and that is not necessary. James gives a hint that the casual relation may not be wholly one-sided, and that is enough. Certainly, when we examine it, we find that the physical symptoms are of more importance than we had thought. Imagine for a moment, an angry person, yourself or anyone else, without a single physical evidence of anger; no clenched fists, no rigidity of muscle, no suffusion of blood, no frown or scowl. Immediately you think of a person who may have an intellectual conviction that something wrong or unjust has occurred, but not an angry person. All good old-fashioned child-raising—and what a lot of it there was!—is, of course, founded upon good psychology, and the old admonition, "When angry, count ten, or one hundred" is an illustration of this. You necessarily relax during the counting, and when you come back to take up your anger, it has cooled!

The same rule applies to fear. "Whistling to keep one's courage up" is an age-old device. Everything about whistling throws the body into the posture of gaiety and care-free ease, and fear finds lodgment difficult.

When we first apply the rule to grief, many of us think that it does not fit, for we are all familiar with the shallow

*Parents must keep watch if they are to of their children into*

Illustration by

An article on the child-
mind that every mother
should read and remember

# of Emotion

1931

mourner who grieves aloud and soon recovers, and the quiet, self-contained bereaved one, who alarms his friends because there is no outlet for the grief which is none the less deep and sincere. This is only an apparent contradiction. It is quite true that wailing and tears seem to relieve grief, but this is just because they form a relaxation from the tension within. Test the muscles of the quiet, self-contained mourner, and you will find them strained to the utmost. If not, the grief has already become simply sorrow, which is intellectual in its nature, and although with a sensitive person this sorrow must remain for some time after a shock, nature is always at work with the healing power of time, and each week will find an improvement. Not so if the tension keeps up. Each week the body finds it more difficult to carry the burden, each week the mind falls deeper into despair, and a complete collapse is sure to follow.

This analysis has not been made for purely intellectual interest. It is of the most absorbing practical importance to every mother. These three destructive emotions, fear, anger, and grief, are the cause of most of the world's woes. If individuals can learn to control them, nations may do so also, and we may make an end of international hatreds and wars, even although rivalries, through the workings of the instincts of self-interest, may persist.

Every one knows how difficult it is to work directly upon the emotions themselves. To say, " I ought not to be angry, I am not to be afraid," does literally no good at all. One recognises that one ought not to be, but is, just the same. But to work upon the physical expression is quite another matter. That is something practical to do, and it is one's own fault if one does not learn how to do it.

The power to relax comes first of all. Any mother who has not learned this lesson is really remiss in her duty, and cannot possibly give her children the same care and thought that she could if she knew how to renew and conserve her strength in this way.

Whenever difficulties and annoyances press in upon you until it seems as though you could not endure any more, you should get away by yourself for a few moments and lie down flat on your back, relaxing every muscle and thinking of the joyous and happy things in your life and in the world around you. Unless there is actual physical danger to the children, this pause will help far more in most cases than the immediate presence of a tired, cross, exhausted mother. Then one must control the tone of the voice; practice hearing the tone yourself, and notice whenever an edge creeps into it. Nothing upsets a whole household like the wrong tone of voice. Both father and mother should understand this, and watch themselves for it. It is natural, but absurd, that we should so frequently justify ourselves in being angry or superior or bored or cross, just because we control these emotions everywhere but in our voices. Really the voice is the greatest tell-tale of all, and we might as well show what we feel frankly and get it out of the system, as let the tone indicate it.

*over their own emotions*

*direct those*

*healthy ways of expression*

C l a r a    E l s e n e    P e c k

# Parents I

I AM well aware that boiling constitutes a confession of failure. We do not torture the man we can persuade. The lute of Orpheus was a handier instrument for big-game hunting than the rifle, and the order for " Something lingering with boiling oil in it " is the expedient of despair. It is costly; it is messy; it has to be defended by complicated processes of mental justification which leave the torturer almost as uncomfortable as the tortured, whereas the victory of moral suasion leaves the victor crowned with self-approval. If reasonable argument availed, the rack, faggot and thumbscrew never need have been invented.

But reasonable argument does not avail among mankind. I used to think it did. I believed in the Power of Education, and thought that the Right Type of Moral Appeal could conquer the world. I acted up to my belief so well that for five years I was a teacher, instructing adolescent girls in the rudiments of history, English literature and translation from the French, in the wild hope that Mr. H. G. Wells was right when he wrote, " Give me the Schools, and I will give you the Millennium." I had the schools; at least, the schools had me. I sat up at nights correcting exercise books and wondering whether Joan deserved that conduct mark, and teaching myself the lessons to teach my class next day. But the Millennium has not yet arrived. Perhaps I was a bad teacher.

There was one lesson, however, which I taught successfully in those days; I taught myself the limitations of reasonable argument. I discovered that condition of hopeless defeat in which only physical violence seems to offer any comfort. Oddly enough, it was never a pupil whom I wished to boil. The people who made me understand the Imperial Russian landowner's use of the lash and knout, were the parents. For you can argue with children; you can amuse and persuade and even, if you are very competent, coerce them. I have, indeed, upon occasions, and making due allowances for original and derivative sin, known of successful appeals to their better nature. But there is nothing to be done with parents. Headmis-

tresses, of course, can do a little. They have authority; they interview mothers at set appointments in imposing offices; even fathers have been known to respect their opinion. But the humbler members of the staff can do nothing with parents. They can only sit and rage in silence and dream of the good old days when power was power, and the cauldron supplemented private conversation.

Even since I left school, the people whom I have most wanted to boil have been Parents. For Parents, whatever one's own status, are in a privileged position. What right has anyone else to interfere with Barbara's education? Who dare come between a mother and her child? Even the cinemas say that " Mother knows best," and who would dare to contradict the cinemas? No one. No one has any right to speak; and where there is no right, might is the only weapon.

I first became aware of this desire to murder complete strangers when I was teaching at a girl's private school in the South of England. It was an expensive school, where the pupils were mainly daughters of well-to-do middle-class people. The majority left to " finish " in France or Switzerland, and then go home to a life of bridge, golf, dancing, and a little mild philanthropy in the form of Girl Guides, or Women's Clubs as a preparation for the serious social responsibility of marriage into another leisured, prosperous home, with more bridge, more golf, and perhaps one or two children to be reared in order that they also might be finished in Paris and play a little golf and run a Guide Company and marry and produce yet another family. The head-mistress and a few members of the staff used sometimes to attempt to steer some of the girls into more socially useful and expert occupations, but home influence usually defeated school encouragement, and home influence was almost always unfavourable to professional training.

I remember that when I read a year or two ago Lady Rhondda's challenging essay on " Leisured Women," there rang through my head echoes of old conversations. I remembered the pride in one lady's voice as she declared, " But dear Lois will never *have* to work. Why *should* she struggle with all those examinations? " I remembered the plaintive self-righteousness of the plea, " But I'm sure I've spared Zoë quite long enough. I think I've been very noble letting her have that extra year at school. I left when I was just seventeen myself. And now I want her at home. A mother likes to see a little of her daughter before she leaves home for good." I knew that " leaving home

*Decoration by*

*Edgar Spencely*

# should like to BOIL

## By

## WINIFRED

## HOLTBY

### who, writing from experience as a teacher, will probably convince you that "Mothers are a Mistake"—at any rate in schools

suspected that her mother was not enthusiastic about her career, we said good-bye to Gwenda fully believing that she was leaving us for one year in Paris, to polish up her French, and that then she was going to take her entrance examination for Oxford or Cambridge.

Eighteen months later Gwenda appeared at an Old Girls' gathering. She had not begun to coach for her examinations; but she had learned to drive a car, and had bought quantities of new clothes. She had learned how to wear them too, in Paris, and she looked very handsome, distinguished—and discontented. We asked her whether she was not going to try for Somerville, and she told us that she had given up all that childish nonsense. We asked her if she was happy, and she said that she was having a good time. We asked her what she intended to do and she said that she supposed she would go on having a good time—or of course. . . . She meant, of course, she might marry, and even then she probably supposed the good time might continue.

But that was some years ago, and when I last heard of her, Gwenda had not yet married. At first she used to be rather rude to the nice young men who proposed to her, because they seemed so dull and unintellectual; now the young men are rather shy of her, for, dash it all, Gwenda's jolly nice looking and clever and all that, but she's rather sharp-tongued, and not as young as she was, and not the kind of girl likely to make a man comfortable. As for the good time, it probably goes on; but Gwenda's mother sometimes wonders what she has done to have a daughter unlike other people, an odd silent daughter, who finds everything rather a bore, and is not amused by continual dances and parties, and who seems to grow more difficult every year.

Now the truth about Gwenda's mother was that she could not bear to see her daughter carried away by interests which she could not share. It hurt her vanity to think that the life which was good enough for her was not good enough for Gwenda. She wanted the girl to remain in a world of which her mother was mistress. In the world of scholarship and the life of a University, the mother would have been lost. Her daughter, she felt, would grow away from her. She would lose her far more inevitably than if she merely married and went to live in another charming house, sharing with her mother the experiences of a hostess and housekeeper. So day after *Continued overleaf*

for good" had one implication only in the eyes of Zoë's mother; and to suggest that, after all, Zoë, a plain, dumpy, conscientious creature, the soul of neatness, loyalty and exactitude, born to be the Perfect Secretary, might not marry, was to cast a doubt upon her mother's efficiency in the great duty of her Life, to act as matrimonial agent for her daughter.

But I reached boiling point with the case of Gwenda. Gwenda happened to be really good at my own subjects, and

the joy of a collector swooping down upon a genuine antique is as nothing to the joy of a teacher swooping down upon the discovery of a really bright pupil. Gwenda was the born scholar, fastidious, inquisitive, eager, and methodical. We wanted her to go to college, to study English or history, and then to write or teach or research as her inclination and opportunities dictated. And Gwenda wanted to go. She was not a demonstrative girl, but she knew what she wanted, and though we

1931

## Parents I should like to Boil

### (Continued)

day the mother had played on the girl's feelings until she persuaded her to abandon the idea of college; she set her among people who thought learning stuffy, and professional women a dowdy crew, and, the young being open to persuasion, Gwenda was conquered. She remains the casualty in her mother's battle against innovation.

But if one pointed out to Gwenda's mother that she had sacrificed her child to her own vanity, she would not understand. She cannot see that there has ever been a sacrifice. There seems to be nothing for it but boiling oil.

In Gwenda's case, it was the mother who needed boiling. In the Western case, I always blamed the father. The Westerns were a prosperous middle-class family. Mr. Western had an excellent family business of which he was very proud, and which he had fully intended to hand on to his son after him. But it so happened that the son was a genial, friendly creature with only one desire in life; he must be a farmer and ride to hounds. The elder girl, Hilary, was glad enough to leave school and come home to arrange the flowers and help her mother ice the cakes for tennis parties; but Dora was a tiresome young woman, bright as a button, sharp as a needle, plucky, pert, practical and clever as paint. Nature had clearly meant her to succeed her father in his business; but her father held no such intention. What? Dora go into the office like a boy? Dora change "Western & Son" into "Western & Daughter"? Whoever heard of such a thing?

Some of us had heard of such a thing. We murmured a few notable examples of successful business women; we suggested that Dora had just the head for bargaining and enterprise, that she was full of ideas, and had so much energy that it could not possibly all be expended upon arranging the flowers. Besides, Hilary already arranged the flowers, and Cook hated interference in the kitchen, and it was absolutely necessary, for the peace of the home, to find an occupation for Dora. But Mr. Western would not listen. It was not that he was not bursting with pride for his daughter's ability. He made quite a fool of himself quoting her pert remarks at the club. But he was not going to have it said that old Western could not afford to keep his daughters; he was not going to be teased by men in the City. Even if some young women had gone into business, he didn't hold with it, and that was that.

So Dora has gone home, and spends her energy in teasing Hilary and being rude to the curate and playing excellent golf and hunting when she can find a mount; and the world of business has lost a born director, and Mr. Western has no child to succeed him when he retires. But if we suggested to him that he has sacrificed not only Dora, but his whole family, to his sense of pride, he would be furious. He has never read Veblen's *Theory of a Leisure Class,* so does not know that gentleman's observations about conspicuous consumption, of which one form is a father's boast that he can afford to keep his daughters in expensive idleness. And even if he read it, he would not apply the criticism to himself. So there is nothing but boiling oil for Mr. Western.

Gwenda's mother and Mr. Western have no doubts at all of their own wisdom and unselfishness; but I sometimes think that Mrs. Marks must realise that she might have had more consideration for her daughters.

Mrs. Marks is one of those brave poor things who enjoy perpetual bad health at the expense of all their household. She has been bedridden on and off for several years now, and though she could well afford a nurse, she prefers to keep her three daughters as her attendants. They take turns to look after her at night, and together they watch over her slightest need by day. It is true that Rita's long engagement is wearing down her nerves, and that Rosamund has had to stifle her hunger for travel. But how could the girls leave home, with their mother in such a state? And while the girls are at home, why should their mother keep a nurse, eating her head off?

Ill-health is one famous family tyrant. The Marks story could be repeated for any period; but the case of Mrs. Burton belongs exclusively to this century. Mrs. Burton is not her name, and golf is not the only game she plays; but she is a pretty, wiry, tough, modern sportswoman, whose picture appears season after season in the *Tatler*, the picture of a smart, slender woman in perfect tweeds, resting after a game at Le Touquet or St. Andrews or some similar famous golfing centre. When she declares that she has a daughter of seventeen, people do not believe her, and she enjoys enormously their protestations of incredulity. For she has not only a daughter, but a daughter who adores her. Enid cannot play golf; she is not particularly clever; but she is a really charming young woman, with delightful, self-effacing manners, a gift for making people comfortable, and a pretty face. Moreover, she thinks her mother the most wonderful person in the world.

So when her mother suddenly drove up to Enid's school, and announced that she wanted the child to leave at the end of that term, Enid made no protest. But the headmistress protested, because Enid was to have taken her school certificate in the following term, and then she would at least have had some equipment for an independent life if ever she decided to cut loose from her mother's golf-clubs and find her way in the world on her own. But Enid made herself indispensable to her mother upon journeys. She would take the tickets and look after the luggage and turn hotel bedrooms into charming little temporary homes with flowers and cushions, and would massage her mother's wrists after a heavy game. So Mrs. Burton was inexorable, and Enid was swept away from school, bright, friendly, adoring, confident that her mother will always be the most wonderful of women, and content for the moment to live only as her shadow. But supposing she ever changes her mind, and tires of living in hotels among people whose golf talk she hardly understands, massaging the wrist of a mother who grows yearly less conquering and splendid? Well, Mrs. Burton gets her unpaid maid-companion, and, "What's the use of a daughter?" she sometimes asks, in the deep voice that Enid thinks so irresistible. "At least," she will add, in a laughing attempt at self-justification, "I'm very good for Enid's moral character."

Now that, it seems to me, is just what no one, mother or not, has any right to be. The Lord may send us troubles. That is his business. And they may be good for us. That is ours. But no one in the world has the right to lay troubles upon other people for the sake of their moral character. Sacrifice is something which may be offered, but never demanded. All parents who organise their home life on the assumption that sacrifice is good for the moral character of their children, should be boiled.

All parents who refuse to consider their children as individuals should be boiled.

# HORNBY TRAINS ARE BETTER THAN EVER NOW!

Even last year's Hornby Trains have been eclipsed by the wonderful new models! The locomotives are fitted with stronger mechanisms that give still longer runs, with still greater hauling power. The Rolling Stock is greatly improved, and many new models have been added to the range. The Accessories are more numerous and more realistic.

Hornby Trains, Rolling Stock and Accessories are supreme! Always the leaders, always the best, they are better than ever now! The Locomotives are the longest running locomotives in the world. In a recent test a Hornby No. 1 Locomotive, running light, covered the amazing distance of 182 ft. on one winding! Hauling three No. 1 Pullman Coaches, the same locomotive ran 150 ft. on one winding. This wonderful performance could only be accomplished by a Hornby!

For every boy who is keen on model trains this **must** be a Hornby Christmas! Get your boy a copy of the Hornby Book of Trains described here and let him make his choice now. If he prefers to have an ordinary price list, he may obtain a copy of catalogue No. 6 from any dealer, free of charge, or direct from Meccano Ltd., price 1d. Ask him to write to Department C.

## THE 1931-32 HORNBY BOOK OF TRAINS

Better even than last year! Read how our railway track has developed from crude rails laid on stone sleepers; how the modern passenger coach has grown from an open truck! Other articles tell about the special features of the four British groups. Page after page of fascinating information, and every page illustrated! All the splendid Hornby Locomotives, Rolling Stock and Accessories are depicted in full colour. There are details and prices of every item in the Hornby System.

Your boy must have this book! It can be obtained for 3d. from any dealer, or post free from Meccano Ltd. for 4½d. in stamps.

| PRICES OF HORNBY TRAINS | | | |
|---|---|---|---|
| M0 | Goods Set | | 5/- |
| M0 | Passenger Set | | 5/9 |
| M1 | Passenger Set | | 9/3 |
| M1 | Goods Set | | 10/- |
| M2 | Passenger Set | | 10/9 |
| M3 | Tank Goods Set | | 15/- |
| No. 0 | Goods Set | | 18/6 |
| No. 0 | Passenger Set | | 17/6 |
| No. 1 | Goods Set | | 25/- |
| No. 1 | Tank Goods Set | | 25/- |
| No. 1 | Passenger Set | | 28/6 |
| No. 1 | Special Goods Set | | 32/6 |
| No. 1 | Special Passenger Set | | 35/- |
| | Other Models up to 85/- | | |

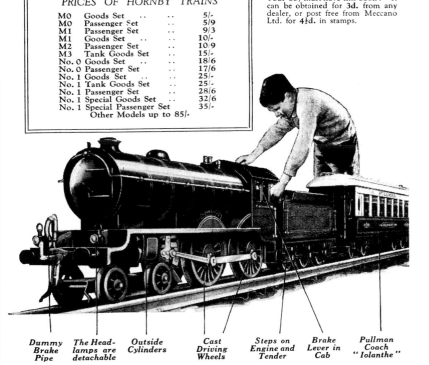

Dummy Brake Pipe — The Head-lamps are detachable — Outside Cylinders — Cast Driving Wheels — Steps on Engine and Tender — Brake Lever in Cab — Pullman Coach "*Iolanthe*"

# HORNBY TRAINS

## BRITISH AND GUARANTEED

*Manufactured by*

MECCANO LIMITED (DEPT. C) OLD SWAN LIVERPOOL

1931

1931

By Janette Stott

# Things you'll

### In July Anne Plays "Rollmops"

"You will roll in the long grass and the buttercups this month," we told Mac and Poodle, "and perhaps help at hay-making." But Mac said he would rather play "Rollmops." This is a game little Swiss children play when the sun has warmed the earth after hay cutting. ("Rollmops" is really a German word for pickled herrings—the sort rolled up tight and tied with a piece of string by cook. And you'll soon see why the game is called "Rollmops.") After a "he" has been chosen he is blindfolded and each player in turn comes up and touches his hand lightly and is told by "he" that he is allowed, say, only four hops or two jumps or six steps to escape when "he" blows a whistle. When everyone has been told how far they can go "he" blows his whistle and while he turns round three times the players take their steps or hops away from him. Then "he" sets out to catch them. They can either use all their stock of steps or hops at once or eke them out. Now comes the exciting or "rollmops" part. When they have exhausted their stock they can *roll* away from him indefinitely, but "he" must not hear them or he can catch them easily. It is exciting and a bit hot, especially as Mac and Poodle always give the show away by barking over prostrate bodies. But you try it on the next picnic, because it's very exciting.

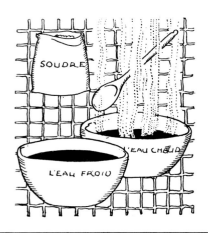

SOUDRE

L'EAU CHAUD

L'EAU FROID

### A Little Nonsense

When Anne was very young, she made friends with a rather clever girl named Pam. And the other day Pam wrote these verses and sent them to Anne, who loved them.

*The sea was shiny yellow,*
*The sky was black as ink,*
*The dear old cows were mad with joy,*
*Because the grass was pink.*

*The horses float about on wings*
*As happy as can be.*
*A startled pancake ups an' sings:*
*"Oh dear, what do I see?"*

*A flying tadpole bumps into*
*A leaping elephant,*
*So murmurs sweetly: "Pardon me,*
*I took you for an ant."*

*A black and golden grasshopper*
*Leaps into the sky,*
*And on a purple codfish*
*Goes sailing gaily by.*

*But as a tiger, creeping near——*
*I wake up with a scream,*
*And find that, luckily enough,*
*'Tis nothing but a dream.*
PAMELA TRUELOVE.

### Jeanne's Scullery

Jeanne is getting worried because you have now a kitchen, a larder (l'armoire à provisions), but no scullery (la relaverie), and she wants you to learn how to wash up (or, as she says, "Comment on fait laver la vaisselle"). Elle prend une grande poêle à frire, une cuiller de bois, un bol et un plat. Elle se dirige vers la relaverie, y emplit une bassine d'eau bien chaude, une autre d'eau froide. Elle met quelques cristaux de soude dans l'eau froide au sortir de la chaude pour la rincer, après quoi elle l'essuie avec un torchon. Elle lave aussi la poêle à frire et elle a fini.

She says by next month you must have drawn the scullery in your book, cut out the objects and stuck them in, writing the French names against them. "Et attention," she says, "qu'on sache tous les noms qui ont déjà été employés dans la cuisine et l'armoire à provisions!"

| | | |
|---|---|---|
| A | ⌀ | Apple |
| B | 🔔 ○ | Bell, Ball |
| C | ☿ | Cat |
| D | · | Dot |
| E | ⸮ | Emu |
| F | ∽ | Frog |
| G | ⅄ | Giraffe |
| H | ⊲ ⌂ ▷ | Hat |
| I | ☉ | Eye |
| J | ⊔ or ⊔ | Jam (pot) |
| K | ∟∕ | Keel |
| L | —∣ | Line |
| M | ⌒ | Mouse |
| N | ∕ ∖ | Needle, Nose |
| O | ∞ | Oyster |
| P | \∣∕ | Pin |
| Q | ♛ | Queen |
| R | ○◯ | Ring |
| S | ◎ | Snail |
| T | ⁒ ⊙ | Trumpet, Tadpole |
| U | ☂ | Umbrella |
| V | ⅗ | Viper |
| W | ⊞ | Wheelbarrow |
| X | ⚕ | Xmas Tree |
| Y | ? | Why? |
| Z | ⫴ or ᠁ | Zebra's Stripes |
| ? | Y | |

# like to Know

*Illustrations by Elizabeth Montgomery*

### Hands on Horseback

Have you heard people say that "hands" are a gift? That people are born with good or bad hands and it is therefore no use bothering. If so, don't believe it. Of course, some people have, by nature, better hands than others, just as some of us are better at music or games or anything else. As for not bothering, that is a fatal attitude.

To have good hands means telling the horse what you want through using the bit, so that he understands. To do this the first thing is to avoid just pulling. If you don't pull, the horse can't, because, as my riding-master always told me, "It takes two to pull." If your horse is going the pace you want, leave his mouth alone. When you want to steady him or pull him up, pull gently and "lingly," and the moment he responds, leave off pulling.

### Can you invent Signs?

The picture alphabet on the opposite page will give you exciting ideas for secret messages, and you will enjoy yourself inventing all kinds of new symbols which will be your own private sign-language, known to nobody in the world but you. And then, when you have worked out a whole new alphabet, for the competition this month I want you to translate and carry out the instructions written in secret writing at the bottom of page 62.

Two prizes of 5*s*. will be awarded, one for the best and most original attempt from competitors over 12 years, and the other for competitors under 12 years. Entries should be sent in alphabet form with the coupon on page 102 by July 27th. Mind you write your name and address clearly—in ordinary writing this time, not the secret kind!

### Bonville

This month you must begin to make Bonville's high street (la rue nationale) because Bonville is so terribly proud of it. A piece of brown paper covering the rest of your window sill or shelf can be roughly chalked to look like cobble stones—and there is your Rue Nationale. Plant twigs in plasticine at regular intervals down one side of the road for trees and try to raise with plasticine a low pavement (le trottoir) behind these. (You will remember the word trottoir because it is where people trot; the horses paw on the pavé or roadway.) A lane turns off by the farm and at the corner of the road. Opposite it at the corner stands the first shop (la boutique) of the village (le village) belonging to Monsieur Ronron the pork butcher. You see written above it Charcuterie, and that means pork butcher's shop. You must copy it from the drawing in the picture as you did the farmhouse. Rouf loves this shop with its bright counter (le comptoir) and its scales (les balances) of shining brass and its jolly butcher (le boucher) in a white apron (le tablier), its sausages (les saucisses), its liver (le foie), its pâtés de foie gras, its bacon (le lard)—very expensive and labelled finest English, because French people don't eat much bacon and what there is comes from England. All these made Rouf's mouth water. Now, if you have time, reproduce this shop three more times and name it differently, making one shop for the baker's (le boulangerie), another for the ironmonger's (le quincaillerie), a third for the draper's (les nouveautés). For Monsieur Panpan, the baker, you can make tiny pellets of bread into long loaves (le pain), and rolls (les petits pains).

In front of the shop I expect you wonder what all the small children are doing. They are little French schoolchildren. Do you see their satchels (les sacs d'écolier) on their backs and their little blouses (les blouses) and their clogs (les sabots)? French school-children work much harder than you do at school. They are up at 7 o'clock in winter and at 6 o'clock in summer drinking coffee and milk out of a bowl with a spoon and eating a slab of tartine. They sit in school from 8 o'clock to 12 o'clock and from 2 o'clock to 4 o'clock, and then you see them leap-frogging over each other going home, but still miraculously keeping their clogs on their feet!

**Swiss children playing " Rollmops "**

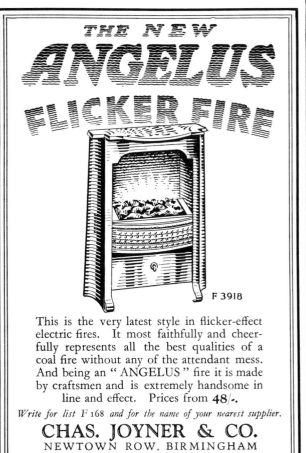

# After School

### By
### HELEN WELSHIMER

A house should have a cake tin,
For when it's half=past three,
And children hurry home from school
As hungry as can be,
There's nothing quite so splendid
For filling children up,
As spicy, crumbly gingerbread,
And sweet milk in a cup.

A house should have a mother
With smiles that never fail,
No matter what a boy brings home,
A puppy or a snail.
For children only loiter
When the bell rings to dismiss,
If no one's home to greet them
With a bun or a kiss!

*Illustration by*
*Clara*
*Elsene Peck*

Clara Elsene Peck

1931

# *Enter, Living Light!*

### The Vital Rays of Health in daylight cannot pass through ordinary window glass

Do your children spend the best hours of daylight behind ordinary glass windows, shut away from the greatest life and health-giving force known to mankind? Sunlight, blue sky and white clouds contain vital invisible rays which promote glorious good health and straight and sturdy growth, but these rays cannot pass through ordinary window glass. The light that comes into the schoolroom, the nursery and the home is drained of health as skimmed milk is drained of cream.

But now comes "Vita" Glass—the new inexpensive window glass—which lets through the health-laden rays that ordinary window glass shuts out entirely. "Vita" Glass floods your home with living light to tan the skin, enrich the blood and increase the vitality.

Put "Vita" Glass in your windows and let health stream into your home. Keep your children fit and resistant to disease so that they can ward off colds, influenza and more serious ailments during the winter months.

"Vita" Glass will pay for itself by saving the expense of patent medicines and special foods. It is already in use in many Hospitals, Schools, Offices, Factories and Private Homes. Supplies may be obtained from your local Glass Merchants, Plumbers, Glaziers or Builders. Send the coupon now for full particulars.

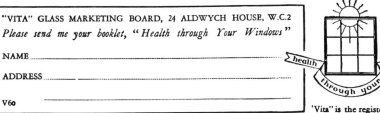

1931

*Sound advice from a schoolmaster's wife to mothers who are worried about the possible harmful effect of boarding school on the morals of their small sons*

# Morals and the
# Preparatory School

**W**HEN a mother decides to send her son away to a preparatory school at the tender age of eight or nine, or acquiesces in his being so sent, she not infrequently falls a prey to various worries as to what the future may hold in store for him. She may worry about his health, or his diet, or his treatment by masters or boys, about how he will acquit himself in this little world which seems so large to him. She may be terribly afraid of many things, but worse than all, sometimes, is the fear that he may lose his bright innocence; and if the mother worries at all about this it is a very bad worry indeed, for she usually feels singularly helpless about it. If she gets an opportunity when she visits the school, she puts to the headmaster's wife or the matron the question which, in varying forms, has been trembling on her lips all day, and receives exactly the answer she expected—that the tone of the school is excellent—and she goes away only half satisfied and continues to worry. Most mothers have heard at least one grisly story, concerning the boy of a friend's friend, and the story only serves to increase her fears without giving her any clue as to what precautions she may take in the case of her own son.

If the mother wishes to meet the difficulties of the case in a more effective manner than this, there are one or two facts which should first be realised. It must be remembered to begin with, that school and home are two quite different places. A boarding-school, any boarding-school, where boys are congregated together in numbers, forms a suitable soil under certain circumstances, for the seeds of undesirable things, seeds which have no chance whatever in normal family life at home.

This is one of the disadvantages of the public-school system, to which so many thousands of boys are bound inevitably from their cradles. There are people who think that because of this disadvantage and the risk which it entails, it is better never to send a boy away from home. Most people think that the advantages of the system, from the character-training point of view, outweigh the disadvantages, and that the risk is worth running.

The great point is that the mother who wishes to face the question boldly should realise that human nature in general, and small-boy nature in particular being what it is, the herding of small boys together in a school, away from their homes, creates a potentially dangerous situation for which the schoolmaster is not primarily responsible. More than that, when the schoolmaster has done all he can in every direction, when he has used all the care and vigilance that is possible or desirable the small boy can still outwit him—for a time—if he is bent on iniquity. Every sound schoolmaster acknowledges this fact, for it is a plain fact. One can conceive of a school where it would be impossible for two boys to whisper for a moment together, or to pass notes to each other, without detection, but it would not be within the accepted ideas of an English preparatory school, and it would hardly fit our English standards of education.

These remarks are not made with the intention of shifting responsibility from the schoolmaster, but to help the parent to understand a little better what he, and she, and the boy, are " up against." She must try not to think of the school as a wicked place waiting to corrupt her boy, but as a collection of boys, of whom hers is one, each

bringing his own contribution (with the headmaster as presiding genius), to the moral atmosphere of the place And this brings us to the practical side of the question.

We can perhaps view it better at this point from another angle, that of the much-debated subject of sex-instruction, upon which such widely different opinions are so firmly held by different people. The views of the present writer are based upon some years observation of preparatory school boys, and are given, where they seem to have some *Continued overleaf*

**Parents can prepare their little boys to play a useful part in the school world if they will only use sense in their early treatment**

1931

# Morals and the Preparatory School
*(Continued)*

bearing upon the matter in hand, not with the idea of laying down the law on the subject in general, but in an effort to throw some light upon it as it affects a particular class of boy going to a particular type of school.

Every young child lives, normally, in a state of complete innocence as to the differences and functions of sex. At this stage no questions trouble him, references to the subject often appear to pass completely over his head. He may ask where his baby brother came from, but the fact that the answer " God sent him to us " completely satisfies him shows the depth and sublimity of his innocence. It has always seemed to me that to break in upon this state of mind with information, however beautifully and mystically conveyed, about his own origin, is a highly questionable proceeding. On the other hand, it is difficult to understand how a mother can send a baby thus engulfed in innocence, away to even the most select and carefully guarded of preparatory schools. To do so is to ask for trouble almost as definitely as one can.

The difficulty is that the artificiality of modern life frequently prolongs this normal state of mind beyond its normal time. A boy of eight should have had ample opportunity of noting all he needs to know in a matter-of-fact manner, from his own observation. Nowadays he often has no such opportunities, and often he gets no help from grown-ups, who persist in suppressing all reference to such facts from their conversation in his hearing, and who will even, such is their determination to prevent his coming by his knowledge naturally, take care not to have any female dog, cat, or rabbit in the family, because of the " awkwardness " when the children ask questions.

It has long been a puzzle to the writer that parents whose children have thus grown up in unnatural ignorance should choose the most difficult and delicate point, namely their own origin, as a starting-place for definite information. It is my firm belief that there is in every child's life a time when that knowledge, awaiting the right moment, will come to him. It is not, I believe, anyone's business to choose that moment for him, but it is very definitely our business to give him the data to work upon, so that he may reach the point where the knowledge may dawn upon him rightly and naturally. The mother of a small boy of seven who seems still asleep on these questions may, of course, lead him into her room and close the door, take him on her knee and convey to him in tender and mystical language the secret of his birth.

Yet in my opinion she would do better, at whatever inconvenience to herself, to give him a mother rabbit in expectation of a family, and, as time went on, explain to him the whole matter (as regards the rabbit) in calm and matter-of-fact language, as she would talk about gardening or any other subject of common interest. He might suppose for a time that rabbits alone in the animal world exhibited this interesting phenomenon, but not for long. The growing intelligence within him would have something to work upon, and in due time he would arrive at his conclusion, by the right road.

Someone may ask what, according to this theory, is to be done with the boy who asks, point-blank, for information. I should answer that if a boy asks, he must be told; yet I should feel that things would have been better to go otherwise, that intelligence should not have been allowed thus to outstrip information, and that the answer might be a shock to him from which he would be slow to recover.

Parents sometimes spend much time in wondering whether or no they should " warn " a boy who is going away to school for the first time, about what he may hear and meet with. Sometimes the desire to put him on his guard is countered by a fear of " putting ideas into his head," and so the warning is not given. My own view is that a word of the right sort, in the matter-of-fact and not the sentimental tone, is a good thing, even if the warning is never needed. We sometimes forget that the small boy has often nothing to tell him at first that a certain kind of talk is wrong. It is mistaken to suppose that because he is *your* boy he must know by instinct. He will only do that if he has been very fortunate in his early training and associations, and if you have taken particular pains to impress his parents' habits of thought upon him.

Personally, though the suggestion is put forward very tentatively, I should always warn a small boy against allowing anyone else to touch him, in the bath-room, dormitory, or changing-room. Not fearfully or mysteriously, but in a straightforward way, telling him that his person is his own private property, and that he must never either finger other people's private concerns himself, or allow others to do the same to him.

The writer has met with mothers who feel that when a small boy goes to school where he must learn to do without the softness of home, it is kinder to harden him a little beforehand so that he may not feel the break so much. With this end in view and with the kindest of motives, they

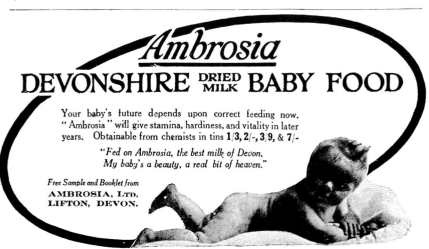

try to accustom him to doing without any family "petting" to which he has been used. Unfortunately, the affectionate small boy who has been used to a certain amount of petting, does not automatically cease to want it when it is withheld. Kipling tells us in his story of "Baa, Baa, Black Sheep" that a big boy of ten can put up with an astonishing amount of petting. The danger is not so much that he will suffer without it, but that if the wrong person should offer it to him, he will be more likely to accept it gratefully because he has ceased to look to his mother for it. Other mothers with the same danger in mind, choose the Spartan method of discouraging any kind of "fussing" even from the earliest nursery days. No doubt this is successful with some types of boy, though one doubts whether it would be equally so with all.

Enough has been said, it is hoped, to show the mother who is worried about the effect of school upon her boy's morals, that she need not, and should not regard herself as helpless in the matter. It is well to remember sometimes, not merely in the interests of the schoolmaster, but of the school, what his difficulties in the matter may be. Boys are sent to him at all stages of moral development, from a dangerous innocence to a still more dangerous knowledge. Yet he stands responsible for all that happens under his roof. The same batch of new boys that brings him four or five babies who have known scarcely any society but that of their own sisters and their nurse or governess, may bring him also that comparatively rare but not unknown person, the new boy who has already been contaminated by some boy at a

day school, or even by an elder brother at a public school. Happy is he if there is also in the batch a boy who has been properly prepared for school life, and who may be counted upon as a safe spot in the shoal of small fry.

In putting these thoughts in order the writer has often had in mind a boy whom she had the privilege of knowing years ago in his private school-days. He came to school a little before his tenth birthday, wise and knowledgeable, having learnt the broader facts of life from his father's troop of dogs at home. One remembers yet his almost fatherly affection for these same dogs, and his deep interest and concern about their family affairs. He had learned in advance and without knowing it, that fact which we long so much to bring home to all small boys, the fact of the utter, dreary, stale imbecility of the nasty story. His was not merely that passive, though steadfast purity, which many boys do mercifully possess all through their lives, but a sort of arc-light that consumed with scorn everything doubtful within its radius. The school does not exist that could have corrupted him; ten of him scattered through a school of sixty boys would have made things permanently safe for the remaining fifty; and even one of him was a very good thing to have. And I believe that this was largely owing, not to any magic gift that he was born with, but to the good sense and wise treatment of his parents, who had made out of a jolly little baby boy with a mind like a clean slate, such a very useful citizen of the school world. And what his parents did, most parents might do if they would give thought and care to the matter.

1931

1931

*A useful suit for a little girl is a plaid skirt with a white blouse and a jacket of one of the colours of the plaid*

Everyday clothes are best made on simple lines—

NICOLE ET DENISE

NICOLE ET DENISE

*Neatly made coat of heavy shantung, or of flannel, double breasted with turn-over collar and big cuffs*

*For a little girl this frock in dotted Swiss with smocked yoke and short sleeves would be attractive*

*Party frock of pale blue faille, with ruches of velvet ribbon at the hem, and a little fichu of white net finished with lace and a posy*

*On the right is a party frock of pale pink satin, the skirt in overlapping bands, and two bows poised in the front for the sole trimming*

FAIRYLAND

NICOLE ET DENISE

FAIRYLAND

# MINIATURE FASHIONS FOR LITTLE

WRITING about children's clothes is like writing about the weather. It is something that is more or less standardised in given locations, with only temporary fluctuations according to the degree of latitude. To talk too much about the mode and what is "in style" in connection with children's apparel, is pretentious and not suitable to modern ideas of bringing up the normal child. The average little girl adores clothes, but she adores pretty, becoming clothes, that resemble those of her friends, and not for one moment does the latest fashion have any part to play. The average little boy is bored with the whole subject, and asks only not to be dressed eccentrically. Aside from not being conspicuous, he does not care what he wears; in fact, he would rather err on the side of worn, commonplace, ancient raiment, than on the side of appearing too fashionable. Thank heaven he is like that; it is one of his charms.

Nevertheless, a girl's frock may follow more or less the lines of her mother's gowns. The waistline is normal during normal seasons, sleeves are full or tight according to the popularity of such things in adult fashions. Navy blue or bright scarlet leads according to its success in a more mature mode. But to exaggerate any of these tendencies is unchildlike and in bad

# —from hardwearing materials, such as tweed, serge & flannel

*The sketch on the left shows a sailor suit with long trousers of serge; a cotton twill blouse with trimming of navy is worn with them*

**1931**

NICOLE ET DENISE

NICOLE ET DENISE

*The above little boy's suit consists of a linen blouse trimmed with zigzag edge, and trousers of velveteen*

*Little boy's beach or bathing suit in wool jersey with the opening laced and an embroidered crab below*

*A well-made boy's coat, seen in the Bois, of beige flannel, with two buttons in the front and pockets, and a slight flair at either side*

*On the right a little boy's suit for formal occasions with sleeveless short jacket and shorts of tussore, and a blouse of handkerchief linen*

SEEN IN THE BOIS

SEEN IN THE BOIS

FAIRYLAND

# GIRLS AND LITTLE BOYS

taste, and the woman with common-sense steers clear of such pitfalls.

Personally, I have always thought that material played the leading rôle in youthful fashions. Novelties that are untried are out of the running. The many loosely woven jersey tweeds and fuzzy thin woollens or embroidered fabrics are not suitable because they pull. Anything but the closest and tightest surface will not stand wear. Even jersey has its drawbacks in this connection. It is pretty to look at, but with all the cleaning and washing that it must undergo, it cannot be expected to keep its shape as well as tighter materials. Tweeds, cheviots, serges, flannels, with some wool crêpes and challis, are much the best choice for little girls' school frocks and coats. These are known to withstand hard wear, and there is nothing to pull or get out of shape if they are carefully washed or cleaned. Wherever washing is scientifically done in soft water, almost all these materials may be washed instead of dry-cleaned, which is a help in itself. That, however, is a risky rule to lay down for the ordinary laundress, in spite of the fact that I know of many women whose small sons wear blue serge shorts in winter, and these shorts are always washed at home just as their blue linen ones are.

1931

# Cradle Wish

### By
#### Margaret Bell Houston

What do I wish for you,
Little New=born?
Hair that is yellow
As silk of the corn.

Eyes that are blue,
Lips that are red,
So you'll be wooed;
So you'll be wed.

Seas you may sail,
Roads you may roam,
So you'll be happy
To come back home.

*Illustrated*

*by*

*Anne*

*Rochester*

Gold a=plenty
To come at your touch,
So you'll not think about
Gold too much.

Roses to walk on,
If you choose;
Music to dance by,
Silver shoes.

Life is a moment,
A bite and a sup.
Full be your plate,
Brimming your cup.

Bright be the lights,
And when they are low,
May you be sorry,
Sorry to go.

By A. E. Wilson

*(author of
" Penny Plain, Twopence Coloured ")*

CARDBOARD

POLLOCK'S CHARACTERS IN THE SLEEPING BEAUTY.    Plate 3

*Published by B. Pollock, 73, Hoxton Street*

A LITTLE while ago I wrote a book about the Juvenile Drama—the little toy stage which was the popular pastime of Victorian children who spent their winter evenings in colouring and cutting out the sheets of characters and scenes of such favourite plays as *The Miller and his Men, Red Rover, Black-Eyed Susan, Jack Sheppard, Sixteen-String Jack* and *Mary the Maid of the Inn,* and then engaging (or attempting to engage) in a performance before an audience composed of their school-friends or, on special occasions, such indulgent elders as could be roped in for the occasion.

I assumed that the taste for this pastime among children was dead. Alas! the assumption is true; I have proved it to my own dissatisfaction. My enthusiastic description of this old delight and my demonstrations have met with a smile of superiority and often hardly concealed contempt from the sophisticated boyhood of to-day. They have no use for such an old-fashioned device; it is as though you offered a velocipede to a racing motorist.

Well, what can you expect in these days of toy cinemas and the other mechanical and scientific wonders of the nursery? What child is likely

# CLOWNS AND FAIRIES

*A rediscovery of the juvenile drama*

**SKELT'S LAST SCENE IN MARY THE MAID OF THE INN.**

to experience a thrill by the performance of the antique dramas of the swashbuckling type, with their bandits and fiercely-whiskered villains and their desperate combats and inevitable conflagrations so much favoured in our great-grandfathers' days? These dramas of the flesh and blood theatre are as dead as Kean, T. P. Cooke, O. Smith, Yates and Farley, and other famous actors who flourished in them, and although they gave so much excitement and pleasure to the adult audiences of a century ago, they would probably be deemed very silly by the child of to-day.

Besides, no modern boy could endure with patience the representation of such plays with the aid of tiny cardboard characters pushed on to the scene by the obtrusive tin slides which were an essential part of the machinery of the model stage. Accustomed to the vivid and continuous action of the screen, they would be exasperated by the immobility of the miniature actors, transfixed by the artist who drew them in an attitude not always appropriate to the sentiments supposed to be expressed by the actors or to the action in which they were engaged.

1932

# Best food for them — cheapest for you

Ripe Bananas are nourishment itself to growing kiddies. They're easily digested. Get the habit of buying a few Fyffes regularly. Save you cooking puddings. Fine for picnics and jaunts. Satisfying for play-time hunger; and oh so cheap! Now don't make the mistake of asking for bananas! Look for the blue label. That's Fyffes.

ELDERS & FYFFES LTD.

**BLUE LABEL**
## FYFFES BRAND
# BANANAS

snap! crackle! pop!

# CHILDREN LOVE THE FLAVOUR

And it's the easiest dish in the world to prepare. Just fill a bowl with Kellogg's Rice Krispies, pour on cold milk or cream and add a bit of fruit. There it is! Help yourself to this delicious treat. No cooking required.

Every one likes Rice Krispies because it's such a different cereal. Toasted rice bubbles that actually snap, crackle and pop in cold milk or cream. Delicious for breakfast. Splendid for the children's supper—so healthful and easy to digest. They invite sound, restful sleep.

Just ask your grocer for the red-and-green packet. Rice Krispies are always oven-fresh — protected by the famous Kellogg's inside WAXTITE Bag. *Quality guaranteed.*

*Use* COX'S INSTANT POWDERED GELATINE *and make this delightful dish.*

### LEMON JELLY
### (Six to Seven Persons)

1½ oz. COX'S INSTANT POWDERED GELATINE.
1½ pints of water.
¼ pint lemon juice.
½ lb. sugar.
Rind of 2 or 3 lemons thinly cut.
1 inch cinnamon.
2 cloves.     1 bay leaf.
Whites 2 eggs slightly beaten, and shells crushed.

Put the water and Gelatine in a saucepan and add all the other ingredients. Whisk briskly until almost boiling. Remove whisk and allow the jelly to boil up. Draw aside and leave to settle for three or four minutes. Strain through a scalded jelly cloth or bag till clear. When cool, pour into a wet mould.

Send for Sample (*complete with Recipes*) and enclose 3d. in stamps to :-
J. & G. COX Ltd., Dept. C, Gorgie Mills, Edinburgh

## Kellogg's
# RICE KRISPIES

Made by KELLOGG in LONDON, CANADA
KELLOGG COMPANY of GREAT BRITAIN, Ltd.
Bush House, London, W. C. 2

800

# For LEWIS CARROLL
## By Margaret E. Sangster

YOU gave the world the gift of gentle laughter,
Of magic touched with a prismatic gleam;
You taught us that life holds frail romance after
First youth is past and hearts scarce dare to dream.
Your people saunter by, a long procession
As mad as April and as sweet as May . . .
They are so real (and this is a confession!)
That I can see *them*, though my hair is grey!

THERE'S Alice and the Rabbit, walking primly,
The sobbing turtle, and the child that sneezed;
The croquet-playing Queens who shouted grimly,
The drowsy Dormouse, and the Hare that teased . . .
Your dear illusions never, quite, can pass,
Though you have wandered through the Looking Glass!

1932

# THE YOUNGER

*HARRODS*

*DEBENHAM & FREEBODY*

*HARRODS*

The "Winter Sunday" frock for the schoolgirl is chiffon velveteen, either cherry red, green, or blue. It has the fashionable slight flare and buttons down the front panel. There is a detachable, washable lingerie collar

A tailored coat in plain navy tweed is cut with wide, double revers giving the top-heavy 1932 silhouette which Miss Twelve-year-old must have as well as her mother. The underarm pointed insets are interesting details

Jerseys for little people are now made on exactly the same lines as grown-ups' and fit snugly at the waist with a deep band of ribbing. The almond green one above has broken, vertical stripes of pearl and a close round neck. Kilts reach to the waist. For the tiniest lady of all, comes a hand-made white organdie frock, ornamented with tucks and goffered frills; little brother wears hand-embroidered crawlers in natural tussore with a dropped back

# New Designs from the London Shops for Gym

# SETS CHOOSE THEIR AUTUMN OUTFITS

*The smart workmanlike coat worn by the six-year-old boy on the right is in winter-weight Harris tweed in tones of woody brown and has trousers and stitched hat to match. The fine flannel shirt is in the same shade and severly tailored*

*Daniel Neal's new design for a gymnasium tunic places the fullness at the sides, instead of the front, as deep, inverted pleats. It is in strong navy serge, with a round neck, and the school colours can be embroidered in the centre front*

DANIEL NEAL

DEBENHAM & FREEBODY

*The little person on the left wears a frock of red and blue checked washing woollen material, with white crêpe de Chine collar and cuffs and a yoke piped with red and ornamented with red buttons. Her playmate has a coat and hat of sand and coral fancy tweed, warmly lined and interlined. The buttoned-over scarf collar is very chic, and the belt fastens trimly around the natural waist. Hat to match*

# nasium Tunics, Frocks Coats and Jumper Suits

# Is it Right to pass on one's

1932

*Should youth work out its own salvation?*

*Or is it wiser that parental judgment should*

*have control over children's decisions?*

C.V.M

CAN one pass on one's own experience to children? Does one? Would one, if one could? Has one any serious hopes of so doing? Has one, even, any serious wish so to do? Is it better to let them find out things for themselves? And anyway, won't they insist on finding out things for themselves, in spite of our interference? The days of Cautionary Tales are surely over. The young no longer listen—if, indeed, they ever did listen—for wasn't that an amiable delusion of their parents? Most modern parents say with a sigh of resignation that their children no longer even pretend to listen. And they let it go at that.

Still, I wonder.

It saves trouble, of course, to let your little boy cut his finger with a knife, instead of pointing out to him that he will cut it. It saves trouble in the end, because although you have to produce immediate lint and a bandage to tie up the injured finger, which is bleeding most unpleasantly over the orange at breakfast, you will probably not be obliged to produce it again on a similar occasion, because the similar occasion will not be renewed. Other accidents will occur, but not exactly the same accident. So, gradually, by letting your children work their way through all the possible accidents of daily life, you will attain to a certain immunity. They will have learnt. It is a Spartan method. It demands some self-restraint and some self-control. Some things one must of course prevent by the exercise of authority. One must prevent one's little boys from walking along the ridge of the roof. One must call out firmly and say, "Come down at once. If you slip, as you certainly will, you will be killed." (And then, during the descent, one covers one's eyes in terror; and when they have reached earth in safety, one shakes them violently, boxes their ears, and sends them supperless to bed.)

Yes, there are certain accidents that one must prevent, however high and Spartan one's principles. Even a Spartan parent would hesitate to let his child be killed, just in order to prove to that child that he *would* be killed. One must draw the line somewhere. One draws it at walking along the ridge of the roof; not at cutting a finger at breakfast.

So, in early life, the problem remains comparatively simple. It is only in later years that the real problem arises.

Supposing, for instance, that your son falls in love with a most unsuitable young person. Your own wisdom and experience, laboriously acquired, tell you that the connection is prophetically rich in disaster. It is no longer a question of your little boy cutting his finger or even of breaking his neck, but of your son breaking his heart. Well, is he to be allowed to break his heart, just in order to prove to him that he *will* break it? Ought you to warn him? Young love is notoriously impatient of warnings. Yet he may thank you, in the end. He may, having failed to make his mistake, come to you and say, "How right you were!" This moment will be very sweet to you. If, on the other hand, he makes his mistake and then comes to you in sorrow asking how on earth he is to get out of this mess, you will no doubt be able to stop yourself from saying, "I told you so," and will be able to apply your mind without undue smugness to the problem under consideration.

Whether your children listen to you or not depends of course largely on your own previous wisdom. If you have nagged at them continuously over little things ever since they were able to crawl, they are not likely to pay much attention. They will realise that you always say "Don't" as a matter

# Experience to one's Children?

## By V. SACKVILLE-WEST

*Howard and Joan Coster*

*Illustrations by C. V. Mackenzie*

of principle, whether it really matters or not. It is better to save up one's warnings for the really solemn occasions.

It seems to be an accepted fact that we are less consistently severe with our children than were the parents of an earlier generation. I think our grandparents and great-grandparents (who are rapidly dying off) would agree. Even the inquiring minds of our public bodies appear to be aware of a change in the attitude of parent towards child. There is a significant section in the questionnaire recently issued by Sir William Beveridge through the B.B.C. in association with the London School of Economics. This questionnaire, which is headed "Changes in Family Life," includes amongst other things the following paragraph: "What are the chief changes, as between your

parents' generation, your own generation, and the generation after yours, in . . . the relation of parents and children, including such matters as choice of careers, choice of partners, and claims to respect or obedience?" I hesitated a long time as to how I should fill in the answer to this question. I wanted to be perfectly honest; and the anonymity of the questionnaire allowed me full scope for perfect honesty. Eventually I wrote down: "Reasonable co-operation; discussion; and, invariably, ultimate agreement." And I think I answered it truly.

I thought, in other words, that I might say without undue boastfulness that my children would turn instinctively to me and/or to their father in any crises of their young and present lives. I thought they would trust our judgment in preference to anybody

else's judgment, or, more importantly, to their own judgment. The "claims to respect or obedience" of the B.B.C. questionnaire have a slightly old-fashioned ring. Respect—yes, if you mean that your parents are reasonable people with a longer and therefore deeper experience of life than your own. Accord it, then, by all means. Obedience—no, if you mean that you must blindly follow your parents' dictates simply because your parents are older than yourself. Refuse it then, by all means; refuse obedience, if you have little or no trust in the wisdom of your parents. Obedience is a horrid word, a word destructive of independence and self-respect; it is frequently cut out to-day even from the marriage service, and should be cut out of the unwritten service comprising the duty of children towards their *Continued overleaf*

1932

*A Nonsense Rhyme*

> Robert the Bruce
> Drank hot spider juice,
> When Patrick, his Jester,
> Came for a sequester.

> Catherine of Aragon
> Munched cold toast and tarragon,
> When especially blue,
> Henry Eighth might, too.

> William the Quiet
> Fussed over his diet,
> And shunned orange gorse
> With Sweet William sauce.

> Mary of Modena
> Liked duck (nothing plainer,)
> Ducklings and cream
> Made her sparkle and dream.

> Cardinal Wolsey
> Broke all the rules they
> Made, and Welsh Rarebit
> Became his harebit.

## Is it Right to pass on one's Experience to one's Children ?

### (*Continued*)

parents. (This unwritten duty, in any case, is an outrage : children owe no debt of gratitude to their parents for bringing them into a difficult and probably painful world. The debt is all on the side of the parents, for the interest that their children revive in them.)

But to return to the answer I gave in the B.B.C. questionnaire. " Reasonable co-operation ; discussion ; and invariably, ultimate agreement." I realised, after I had sent it off, that the answer was vainglorious in the extreme. It meant that I had succeeded in getting my children to accept my experience, and/or their father's in lieu of their own. It meant, that we could persuade them into almost any point of view. It meant that they accepted our judgment rather than their own young judgment. Surely a dangerous influence to exert over the young ? One must be careful, very careful, in exerting it. It was a triumph, certainly, to have gained their confidence to that extent, but how could we be certain that the advice we should give them would be the best advice ? And was it not possibly more healthy to let them make their own mistakes instead of profiting by the mistakes of other people ? Would not the muscles grow flabby if they always leaned on the prop of somebody else's strength ?

Influence over others is a power to be wielded gingerly ; it is good to have it in reserve, but not good to make wanton display of authority or persuasion. That was the conclusion I came to. And the necessary, desirable influence, I thought to myself rather priggishly, was to be acquired by suggestion rather than by precept. Sermons were useless. Confidence was everything. Nor was it the slightest use pretending to one's children that one was omniscient: that bluff might work very well in the early years, but sooner or later it would be called. One would be exposed as inadequate and a fraud. No, much better to practise an engaging frankness, and to say, on occasion, "I don't know. That is a thing which nobody can know—not the wisest man in the world. If you want to know what I think, this is what I think, but remember that I may quite likely be wrong. This is one of the things you will have, someday, to think out for yourself."

In spite of, or perhaps because of, such qualifications and reservations, I found that my children would listen to what I had to say. They might listen critically; the point was, that they would listen. They would weigh my arguments, and discuss them, agreeing or disagreeing. At any rate they knew that I wasn't trying to impose an arbitrary point of view; they never suspected me of trying to treat them as unreasonable beings. What they didn't know, was that I deliberately wanted to make influence and not coercion my creed.

So I have hopes (but I may be living in a fool's paradise) that if my children come to me later on in some crisis of their

---

*Have you bought the new Sixpenny Quarterly, "Cooking by Electricity"?*

---

lives they will come without the anticipation of any brow-beating. They will know that I have not bothered and badgered them from the cradle with blind severity or dogmatic advice about this, that, and the other—unnecessary things. They will know, I hope, that so far as it was possible, I let them work out their own salvation; and put on a grave face only occasionally, when it became really urgent that I should intervene. But alas, life and our good intentions being what they are, it is far more likely that my sons will compare notes and say to each other in exasperation, "I do wish that she would *sometimes* give us a jolly good cursing."

For, if it is difficult to grow middle-aged, it is equally difficult to be young. The world is a large place to flounder about in; it is rather like being thrown into the ocean when one has only just learnt how to swim, and indeed the simile is exact, for even the art of swimming would not bring one to the safe coasts of the ocean. It must therefore be pleasant to know that there is a boat within hail, and that a helping hand will be stretched out if one is in immediate danger of sinking. There are moments when one is tired and frightened and baffled and buffeted, and when one likes to be taken on board and given a little respite while somebody else assumes the responsibility. But, if one is to become a real swimmer, that helping hand must not always be in the neighbourhood at the first signs of distress. The helping hand must certainly be firm when grasped, but it must not be immediately available, nor must it stretch itself out to every hysterical signal. The helping hand . . . but it is tiresome to labour a metaphor, and so I desist.

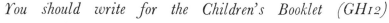

# The Children's Charter

*An explanation of the important Children
and Young Persons Act of 1933*

1933

## By
## HELENA NORMANTON

THE Children and Young Persons Act of 1933 is a codification of the bulk of the law affecting juveniles in this country. More than twenty years ago the Rt. Hon. Sir Herbert Samuel, M.P., who was then Home Secretary, conceived the idea of enacting legislation which should be a serious advance upon the then existing state of the law concerning children. Success to a certain degree crowned his efforts, and the Children Act of 1908 was passed. We look back to-day upon that Act merely as a milestone, but in 1908 it was a very big thing to secure as many beneficial changes as that Act contained. It must be recalled that it was not so very many years before that that the infamous Jane Dyer was hanged for her hideous wholesale baby-farming. Queen Victoria is said to have declared that Dyer's death warrant was the only one she ever signed that did not cause her pain. It is true that the day of Oliver Twist and Dotheboys Hall had long been passed, but things were a long way off from what was really desirable even in 1908.

It is not surprising, therefore, that a large part of the 1908 Act should have concerned itself with the prevention of the ill-treatment of children. Perhaps the most obvious feature of that Act to the ordinary person was the presence of children outside public-houses whilst their parents were partaking of refreshment inside, for the 1908 Act made it illegal to take children inside licensed premises. Of that part I was personally never enamoured, for I do not like to think of a public-house as a place where it is a wrong thing for a man, a woman, or a child to be found, and I should have preferred the reform of the public-house into a place more resembling the Continental café. However, opinions differ, and I do not condemn the fine 1908 Act because it contained one provision not particularly approved of by myself.

A score of years passed, and Sir Herbert Samuel again became Home Secretary, with the Hon. Oliver Stanley

as Under-Secretary of State for Home Affairs. One cannot but admire the Hebrew race for their genuine love of children, and it is not surprising that Sir Herbert again turned his mind to the need for further legislation to benefit children and adolescents. More than one Royal Commission had sat upon questions relating to the young—such as the one on Criminal Assaults on Women and Children—and the whole idea of dealing with the young delinquent had undergone remarkable changes as a result of the experiments by the Birmingham magistrates, Sir William Clarke Hall's writings, teachings and practice concerning Children's Courts, and of such other persons as Mr. Lovat-Fraser, M.P., here and Judge Lindsay in the U.S.A.

Prevention, privacy, probation, reform and scientific study of the young wrong-doer were all facets of the new system which silently developed within the

## The Sections of the Act

**I.** The Prevention of Cruelty and Exposure to Moral and Physical Danger.

**II.** Employment.

**III.** Protection of Children and Young Persons in relation to Criminal and Summary Proceedings.

**IV.** Remand Homes, Approved Schools, and Persons to whose care Children and Young Persons may be committed.

**V.** Homes Supported by Voluntary Contributions.

**VI.** Supplemental.

score of years between 1908 and 1928.

A large number of readers of GOOD HOUSEKEEPING have asked that I should give a sort of summary of the new Act, so, for this occasion only, like a *prima donna* who "comes back" after she has warbled her farewell, I am once again writing a legal article in this magazine. So here for it!

The Act is divided into six sections, which are listed in the panel on this page.

From these section headings may be deduced the fact that the 1933 Act is a blend of the 1908 Act and a number of new reforms. As a matter of fact these new reforms were embodied in a Children and Young Persons Act of 1932, and the present Act is a sort of codification of the two, omitting those portions it was felt wise to repeal. The whole 1933 Act occupies a hundred pages in our Statute Book, so that it would really take a series of articles to summarise and comment upon it all. However, most people will want to know mainly about the first three sections which concern Cruelty and Physical and Moral Danger, Employment, and methods of trying young delinquents.

Section I (Cruelty, etc.) provides suitable penalties for each of the following offences against the young: neglect causing injury to health; suffocation by over-lying in bed; causing or encouraging seduction or prostitution of girls under sixteen; allowing persons under sixteen to be in brothels; causing persons under sixteen to be used for begging; giving intoxicating liquor to children under five; causing or allowing children to be in bars of licensed premises; taking articles in pawn from persons under fourteen; purchase of old metals from persons under sixteen; vagrancy so as to prevent children from receiving education; exposing children under seven to risk of burning; and failing to provide for the safety of children at entertainments.

For the purposes of the above provisions, any person who is the parent or legal guardian of a child or young person *Continued*

# THE CHILDREN'S CHARTER

### *(Continued)*

or who is legally liable to maintain him is presumed to have his custody. A father is not deemed to have ceased to have custody because he does not in fact reside with the mother. This seems just if the father has merely deserted the mother, but if they have separated by consent, it seems liable to cause hardship. A mother who has deserted a father leaving the child with the father does not seem to be similarly liable—that is as I construe the Act.

The section on Employment first places many restrictions on the employment of children. It has, so I read, already caused it to be an impossibility to include a baby as a character in any film shot in this country. No Jackie Coogans here! Opinions will differ as to the entire good of such a limitation.

The following are the prohibitions:

*Children under twelve must not be employed :—*

(*a*) Before close of school hours on school days.
(*b*) Before 6 a.m. or after 8 p.m.
(*c*) For more than two hours on any school day.
(*d*) For more than two hours on any Sunday.
(*e*) For lifting or moving things heavy enough to injure them.

Local authorities may, by by-law, modify certain of the above provisions. The bad feature of the powers entrusted to them is that they may differentiate between the sexes. One knows of yore that by-laws ostensibly protecting girls work out to their economic disadvantage. Women town-councillors, etc., should be extremely vigilant upon these matters.

Local authorities have similar powers to deal with the employment of young persons under eighteen years of age. Several M.P.s including women such as Lady Astor raised the point during the passage of the Act through Parliament that the young persons between fourteen and sixteen were not sufficiently protected under the Act. Here again, actual vigilance upon the part of those caring for adolescent life will be of enormous value in assessing the dangers that still remain.

No young person under sixteen may engage or be engaged in street trading. Apparently the multimillionaire who began life as a newsboy is to become a being of the past, like the juvenile chimney-sweeps of Kingsley's day.

Sections 22 to 25 of the Act deal with restrictions on children taking part in entertainments. The details here are voluminous. Perhaps the kernel of them all is that when it is desired that a child of twelve or over may be licensed by a local authority upon certain conditions to take part in a series of entertainments, and when such local authority refuses to grant the licence, the applicant may appeal to the Board of Education. No persons under sixteen may take part in public performances in which life or limbs are endangered and no person under twelve may be trained to take part in such except under the terms of a licence granted for the purpose. Licences to be trained for dangerous performances may be granted only by petty sessional Courts, after notice has been given to the local Chief of Police, who may oppose it if he thinks fit.

One of the most valuable sections of the Act deals with young persons going abroad to perform for profit. Readers of the League of Nations reports and of other informative literature will remember

only too well the terrible pitfalls which a large number of such engagements have proved to be to young and ill-advised girls, and what a powerful subsidiary some of them have been to the White Slave Traffic.

A licence must be obtained for all young persons under eighteen from a Police Magistrate, and the licensee must be at least fourteen. Important conditions must be observed before it is granted—the parent or guardian must have consented; the engagement must be a definite one; the licensee must be fit for it; there must be proper provision for health, kind treatment, personal supervision, and return from abroad; the licensee must be given a copy of the contract of employment showing its terms and conditions in a language he/she understands. Here again the Chief Police Officer must have notice of the application and has power to oppose its grant upon proper grounds. Moreover, the licence lasts only for three months unless renewed after the magistrate is satisfied about the observance of the terms.

The third section of the Act covers for the most part ground that has been previously well traversed in this magazine and elsewhere. It might be summed up in the words: Children's Courts and Probation. The golden words of the Act are: *Every court in dealing with a child or young person shall have regard to the welfare of the child or young person and shall in a proper case take steps for removing him from undesirable surroundings and for securing that proper provision is made for his education and training.*

Juvenile Courts sit in privacy and their proceedings are not reported. In the provinces the magistrate must be assisted by a woman Justice of the Peace; in the Metropolitan Area he may be, but it is not yet compulsory. It is rather a pity from one point of view that these Courts sit and work without any publicity, because the public has in consequence little chance of realising their good work.

Apart from modes of trial, certain other reforms have been enacted. No child now can be guilty of any offence, nor can any young person be convicted of felony. A child can no longer be imprisoned, or sent to penal servitude, nor be imprisoned because a fine incurred cannot be paid— that is, unless the Court certifies that he is so depraved or unruly that detention in a Remand Home is impracticable. No longer can sentence of death be pronounced upon any young person under eighteen—instead, a young person guilty of murder must be detained in such place and on such conditions as the Home Secretary may direct.

There was a sharp conflict of opinion between the House of Commons and the House of Lords about birching boy offenders. The Commons desired to abolish it entirely, the Lords to retain it in suitable cases. All the other Lords' amendments were agreed to by the Commons, except this one. However, the House of Lords made it clear that they would not pass the Bill without it, so the Commons reluctantly had to give way. As the Home Office is striving strenuously to obtain benches composed of men and women of a much younger average age it may be assumed that they will have rather less regard to King Solomon's adages than the elderly folk hitherto presiding. After all, Solomon was by no means a successful parent from the point of view of rearing well-behaved children!

For three and sixpence any interested person may purchase a copy of this tremendously important Act. It may also be remarked that it is expressed in clear and comprehensive English.

*1933*

1934

*Walter Bird*

## Advice to the Young on the correct

# BRINGING

### By

## SEWELL STOKES

be reckoned as the younger generation, I have no hesitation whatever in saying that it is largely the fault of the children. We are most to blame for the continual strife. And this is because so few of us take the trouble even to try to understand our parents. As for bothering to educate them to our way of thinking, such an idea has probably never occurred to most of us. Well, it is high time it did.

Nowadays we hear a great deal on the subject of how to bring up children, but nothing at all about the education of parents—which is a great pity, for between the ages of sixteen and twenty-one nearly everybody is confronted by this extremely ticklish problem. Please do not think, because the idea of educating parents sounds rather topsy-turvy, that I am not in earnest over it. I am in deadly earnest.

You see, it is not so very long ago since I undertook the education of my own parents, and with excellent results. I am convinced that if only all young people would endeavour to do the same, instead of shelving their responsibility, they would soon find their homes far pleasanter places to live in, and their parents far pleasanter people to live with. Therefore, for those who have sense enough to make the experiment for their own, as well as for their parents' sake, I have drawn up a few rules and suggestions—the results of practical experience—which they might do well to follow.

One of the very first jobs that we, of the younger generation, should set ourselves to accomplish, is the job of really getting to know our parents. Few of us ever attempt to do this, consequently we know far more about the characters of our recently-acquired friends, than about those people with whom we have lived all our lives, and in whose care we have been brought up.

"A contemporary stranger," says Mr. Shaw, "is a novelty and an enigma, also a possibility; but a mother is like a broomstick or like the sun in the heavens, it does not matter which, so far as one's knowledge of her is concerned. Whether the child is beaten by it or warmed and enlightened by it, it accepts it as a fact in nature." How true that is! How true it is, too, that we never imagine

I AM thirty. Which means that I am not quite old enough to be regarded as a hoary Methuselah by my juniors, nor quite young enough to be thought a flippant baby by my elders. Consequently I find myself in the unique position of being able to entertain the confidences of both children and parents. In fact, whether I like it or not, I am constantly dragged into the heated arguments with which every family in the country is only too familiar.

My advice is sought by desperate young revolutionaries in the home, declaring themselves to be misunderstood by parents whose outlook on life would be better suited to the Stone Age than to the present day. My sympathy is enlisted by those same parents, who, a little wistfully, ask, "What *are* children coming to these days?" It is a sad, harmful state of affairs, and to prevent the atmosphere of destruction which it creates, some remedy ought certainly to be found. But by whom?

Is it for the children, or for

*" The discontented child, whose choice of a career fails to meet with parental approval."*

their parents, to bring about this much-needed change in family life? In other words, whose fault is it, mostly, that in nine homes out of ten—homes in every sphere of life—the peace is so frequently disturbed by the cries of one generation upbraiding the other? As a member of what I suppose may still

## *way of handling the Older Generation*

# Up Parents

### *An article which is not as flippant as it sounds*

*" Do not forget, when taking your parents out, to see that they are dressed suitably."*

our mothers as having had youth, passions, and weaknesses, or as still growing, yearning, suffering and learning! But these are the very things that we must always bear in mind.

Having begun to know our parents, the next step is to encourage their confidence. As a rule we make no attempt to share the problems which beset them, or even realise that they have any. Full of our own concerns—which seem of burning importance—we forget how much our sympathy might mean to them. Yet nothing has a more humanising influence than an exchange of confidences. Be human enough to sympathise with your parents sometimes, and they will more readily sympathise with you.

We all know, of course, that parents are apt to view life through spectacles that have gone out of fashion. Their thoughts run in an opposite direction to our own. But is that any reason why we should not strive to bring their mentalities up to date? This, for the sake of peace in the home, is most important. Nearly always we are unjustly impatient with our parents' views on art, literature, and the drama, and every other subject under the sun. A discussion on nearly every general topic invariably leads to an unprofitable exchange of heated words, followed by painful silence. Whereas, with very little trouble, these futile misunder-

standings could be dispensed with altogether. We have only to acquaint our elders (who, it will be discovered, are willing enough to learn) with some idea of what writers, artists, dramatists, and other leaders of thought are trying to express. That shouldn't be difficult. After all, how can we expect middle-aged people to discard their own (often obsolete) views, if we don't take the trouble to inform them (with the minimum of abuse, please) of the newer views which have come to take their place? Teach them, tactfully, all that you have learned. You'll find them surprisingly good pupils.

*" Take your parents about the place, introduce them to a new atmosphere."*

*Illustrations by Marcus Campbell*

1934

# Fashion Bulletins

With yellow linette shorts goes a white cellular cotton blouse. The small girl has a very smart Tobralco frock with white spot muslin frills. It is charming in apricot. The seated baby wears white muslin that is ruffled and pintucked and has a blue ribbon at the waist

HARVEY NICHOLS

Shorts and jumper in closely knitted wool. The jumper has cable stitch panels over the shoulders. White coarse canvas belt

Under her coat on the opposite page, the little girl has a dress of pale yellow heavy crêpe de Chine, with minute white organdie frills. Little brother wears white wool-linen trousers with a cream crêpe blouse (shown left)

JAEGER

FORTNUM & MASON

Barefoot sandal for holidays and gardens—brown leather, leather sole
DANIEL NEAL

Hand-plaited sandal in scarlet and white with light, flexible leather sole
DANIEL NEAL

This tan calf bar-shoe for the school-girl is available in many fittings
LILLEY & SKINNER

# for the Nursery

The small girl on the immediate right wears a washing-silk frock and knickers from Jaeger, sprigged with pastel blues and bound with scalloped blue. The pale pink pin-spot muslin from Treasure Cot has a square ruffled yoke and a bodice dipping to a deep V. The other damsel has a green checked cotton crêpe with two useful pockets bound with white. Also Treasure Cot

JAEGER          TREASURE COT

Dressing-gown in pink Jaeger flannel lined with silk and bound with white. White animals appliquéd on the pocket and hem

JAEGER

FORTNUM & MASON

White wool-linen coat for three-year-old boy with half belt and deep inverted pleat at the back. A new light-weight material, slightly speckled. The little girl's coat is in a canvas tweed. This one is buttercup-yellow, but it is good in any pastel colour. White lawn collars and cuffs stitched with yellow and a bonnet trimmed with buttercups

Scarlet, white or blue sandal in washable calf with leather sole

DANIEL NEAL

White kid toeless summer sandal with crêpe-rubber sole and heel

LILLEY & SKINNER

Tan leather strapped sandal of new design, with crêpe-rubber sole and heel

LILLEY & SKINNER

1934

**REMARKABLE TESTIMONY**

*Mrs P thinks it may interest the Chilprufe Co, to know that the Infant's Vests bought in 1912 have been used & lent for NINE babies since that date & are still in good, use-ful & useable condition*

*Nov 26th 1933*

This remarkable testimonial (the original of which can be seen at our offices) again emphasises the wonderful durability of CHILPRUFE. Surely there is no other underwear which will give 21 years' hard service. The economy of provid-ing CHILPRUFE is obvious.

Apart from its durability CHILPRUFE really does afford the greatest protection from the risk of chill to children of all ages.

# CHILPRUFE For CHILDREN

There is also a range of **LADIES' CHILPRUFE** equally protective, in fashionable styles and at moderate prices. Ask for particulars of the CHILPRUFE RENOVATIONS SERVICE

Enquire from the *Chilprufe Agent of your District for the* **ILLUSTRATED CATALOGUE**

**THE CHILPRUFE MANUFACTURING CO., LEICESTER.**
(JOHN A. BOLTON, Proprietor

1934

# THE WISH

## By Sara Henderson Hay

*Illustrated by James Montgomery Flagg*

FOUR candles marked the number of his years—
My neighbour's little boy—
And he was dazzled by a cake with tiers,
And many a brave toy.
But when the day turned golden in the skies,
And he as well went drowsily to bed,
He sighed, and mournfully winked his dewy eyes.
" I wanted a gun," he said.

ACROSS his tumbled curls our glances met—
His mother's and my own—
And starkly, hideously, in her eyes was writ
The brutal Word all motherhood has known,
That twisted sword, the ominous phrase addressed
To gentle Mary's breast !

AND quiet between us, rosy with dreaming, slept
The Child Humanity, the thoughtless one,
Dear, foolish, reasonless, the world's small son,
Wanting a gun !

" GOD keep him from his wish," his mother said,
And caught her quivering lip, and suddenly wept.

1935

Ann, Elizabeth and

# "Jour de

Telling delightfully of the
that befell the author's chil
them and Anne Rea to do

"A thoughtful, hopeful
and slightly impish look
on Elizabeth's face"

## by Sylvia Thompson

"I had asked whether
they would like the
screen between their
beds removed. They said
no, it was far more
fun to look round it"

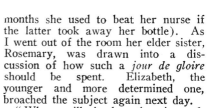

WHEN my two little girls were
seven and five years old, they
learned the Marseillaise. They
learned and sang it with great
enthusiasm, for they have a French-
Swiss governess, have spent a good
deal of time in France, and talk
French most of their day. Indeed, the
house fairly rang with those stirring,
patriotic notes. Every evening when
I went to say good night to them, a
moment at which they usually sing to
me or I to them (the songs most in
demand in my repertory are *Two
Little Sausages, The British Grenadiers*
and *A Bicycle made for Two*) they at
this time preferred that we should all
join in chorus in the Marseillaise.

One evening the younger one, still
breathless from the singing of "*Aux
armes, citoyens!*" said, "Mummie,
what is exactly *le jour de gloire*?"
I said, "Oh, well, I suppose a day that
seems peculiarly glorious. For
instance, for you a *jour de gloire*
would be a day on which everything
seemed exciting and you did exactly
what you liked, and you kept on feeling how splendid everything was."
Her answer, with a slightly wondering
and saddened expression, was "The
*jour de gloire* never seems to arrive
to me." So I said, with that
optimistic and non-committal lightness
characteristic of grown-ups, "Well,
one day you shall have a *jour de
gloire.*"

"And do exactly what we like?"
"Yes."
"All day?"
"I expect so."

I observed a thoughtful, hopeful and
slightly impish expression on her face.
She is a young woman of immense
determination (at the age of six

months she used to beat her nurse if
the latter took away her bottle). As
I went out of the room her elder sister,
Rosemary, was drawn into a discussion of how such a *jour de gloire*
should be spent. Elizabeth, the
younger and more determined one,
broached the subject again next day.
"When will it be, the *jour de
gloire*?"
"Not yet."
"Well, when?"
"Oh," said I, realising that there

was indeed going to be a *jour de
gloire,* "sometime this summer." It
seemed to me that there would be
fewer possibilities of disastrous
experiment in good weather.

Let me say here that my daughters
are not brought up on any extreme
or particular theory of liberty or of
restriction. They are expected to have
proper manners, and to be reasonably
obedient. In short, to behave, once
they have passed the first stages of
babyhood, so that they are neither

142

# "Rosemary have a Gloire"

## gay and sorrowful things dren on the day she allowed exactly as they pleased

1935

*Illustrations by*
*Isobel Lucas*

"At seven they were to give one another a bath. Screaming and giggling, each pair in turn played nurse to the other one"

ing, being read to, a few lessons (which they enjoy) eurhythmics, drawing and painting, according to a schedule arranged by their "grown-ups"—they could choose themselves which of these things they would do and when they would do them; or, alternatively, they could decide to do none of the usual things and find ways of filling their no longer organised leisure.

I made certain stipulations whose necessity they themselves acknowledged. I said that they were not to light matches; that they were not to go out of their depths bathing; and that they could not go out for walks alone on the high roads. I said that the day would begin at 7 a.m. and end, like Cinderella's Ball, at midnight. A little friend was expected to stay with us about three weeks hence, Anne Rea, the daughter of Lorna Rea, whose novels will be well-known to you. Anne is twelve. We decided that the long-promised *jour de gloire* should take place during Anne's visit. Anne is a very gentle and nicely behaved little girl, so that I knew that she would not add any turbulent element to the activities of the day.

The day dawned—alas, rather rainy! Undeterred by this Anne Rea and Rosemary and Elizabeth got up on the stroke of seven, washed each other's faces like three little cats —neglected. I suspect, to do their teeth—and dressed themselves primly. They usually at the seaside wear sweaters and shorts on bad days and bathing dresses on good ones. However, they got out what a generation or two ago would have been known as their Sunday dresses, put on overcoats and gum boots and went out to play before breakfast in the garden. I saw them going down the staircase and watched them out of the

"Rosemary . . . looking like a small Lady Macbeth and protesting that she was so *very* tired"

very noisy when there are people about who would dislike the noise, nor excessively talkative when older people want to talk, nor shy and awkward when they are expected to be sociable and friendly.

The idea for them of a day of freedom did not therefore represent, as it might have for a child fifty years ago, a complete reversal of a rigid routine! It simply suggested to them that instead of doing things that they mostly like very much—games, bath-

*Continued overleaf*

## "JOUR DE GLOIRE"
### (*Continued*)

window as they stood in the rain with that mixture of vivacity and vagueness, that look of expectancy and idleness and self-importance which characterise a crowd waiting to see a procession or a coronation.

Breakfast, like the other meals in the day, had been ordered by them in advance; with simplicity and good taste they had chosen scrambled eggs and coffee-in-their-milk. At 8.30, with unwashed hands, they breakfasted; a lengthy affair, for at 9.30 I found them still at table sipping their milk with a dash of coffee, to make this unusual taste last as long as possible. I asked them what they were going to do during the morning. They answered vaguely, but with very elated expressions, that they were going to talk, and later they were going on the beach by themselves.

I noticed them until about eleven o'clock sitting about in arm-chairs making occasional remarks to each other. There seemed to be nothing very much in the way of sustained conversation, and finally they seemed relieved at their own decision to go out. They departed, arm in arm and sucking toffee, with an air of gay defiance. They returned about one for the luncheon they had specially ordered—sausages and mashed potatoes (and "*no greens*"!); after which they ate steamed treacle pudding mixed with vanilla ice, and then little bits of cheese; and then Edinburgh Rock and toffee and some stale bits of biscuit which one of them produced from a miniature tin.

Then came the glorious occupation of having no rest, or rather (for I had asked them beforehand whether they were going to do without their after-luncheon sleep altogether) of going up to their rooms to lie on their beds and during the hour usually appointed for rest to talk and fidget and roll about and make each other laugh. They usually have a screen between their beds. I had asked whether they would like this removed. They said no, it was more fun to look round it—a process I suppose which involved a delicious feeling of sin. The three of them took up books and towards the latter part of their "rest" Anne, who can read, tried to read to herself; Rosemary, who can read, but won't, pretended she was reading aloud, inventing out of the book in front of her; and Elizabeth, who toils daily in an unaided effort to teach herself to read, lay spelling out words so loudly and persistently that the others groaned. They came downstairs about three o'clock looking, I thought, a little out of sorts; it may have been the mixture of treacle pudding and ice cream.

What they did in the dining-room between then and five o'clock tea I couldn't really make out. The "crowd waiting for the Coronation" was definitely less vital and gay than it had been in the morning. The Procession hadn't yet come; the first glamour of anticipation had worn off. . . . There was still a kind of excitement in waiting for this glorious and overwhelming Thing that must

certainly sooner or later come to pass (There had been no doubt in their minds before the Great Day that there would be in some way a sort of revelation or apotheosis of happiness). But, by the middle of the afternoon, I think this particular crowd felt that it could do with a little incidental amusement, or even occupation. However, you don't come to a coronation to mend your stockings! So from three to five passed in a state of even slightly irritable anticipation. Anne read to herself and felt that she oughtn't to; Rosemary walked about a good deal, and Elizabeth moved in a fidgety way from the house to the garden and back again. But at five, there was tea—and alone. There was chocolate cake, and they ate it walking about; they poured out their milk and didn't finish it; they sat on the floor and spilt crumbs; and altogether behaved in what they conceived to be the most unconventional tea-party manner possible.

After tea, to their unspoken, but probably unspeakable, relief, the little girl next door, who is a young woman of charm and initiative, invited them to play with her, so that the use of the hours between five-thirty and seven was solved for them. Anyway, seven o'clock was a landmark, because then one of the definite projects for the day could be realised. They were to give one another a bath. Their spirits revived, they retired screaming and giggling into the bathroom, where each pair in turn played nurse to the other one, and where their wit and their interest in each other seemed to revive. (I have noticed that the most apathetic women become similarly friendly and loquacious in a Turkish bath). They then emerged, damp, if not clean, to array themselves in their best dresses—Anne in yellow, Rosemary in pink, Elizabeth in green—and to descend with extremely ladylike airs to a candle-lit dinner table and to a meal of green pea-soup and bananas and custard.

It had been in my contract with them that neither I nor the governess would interfere with them in any way, but I did murmur during the afternoon that if anybody wanted to be read to I was, of course, there to do it. During dinner they asked me if I would read to them afterwards, Elizabeth adding, "And I shall stay up till twelve." But at least four times I saw her nod forward in the candlelight, her eyelids dropping with an air of almost sodden sleepiness; then she jumped herself upright again and glanced quickly round the table to see if this shamefully childish lapse had been observed.

After dinner, they gathered round a fire in the drawing-room and there was great talk of the many hours still ahead of them, for indeed it was only half-past eight. One of them even asked that a clock should be put on the mantelpiece so that they, should see the glamorous minutes ticked away one by one. With unglamorous providence I went upstairs and fetched their night-things, dressing gowns and slippers and put them to warm at the side of the fire. (It was one of those wet August evenings whose only charm lies in the pretence at December.) I then settled down to read aloud from *The Jungle Book*. After I had read two or three pages, Elizabeth said, "I think I should hear better if I was lying down on the sofa." A few pages after this, Rosemary said, "It would really be better if I had some cushions and was lying on the floor," and by nine o'clock even Anne remarked that it was rather nice to curl up in an arm-chair.

Shortly after nine I said in a detached and amiable manner that I thought it would be fun now if they were to put on their pyjamas, so they did this and folded up their clothes and put them in a corner. Then I said it would amuse me to brush their hair in the drawing-room, an oddness which appealed to them as part of a festive evening. So I fetched their three hairbrushes, green and red and blue, and they sat very upright, asking at intervals what the time was and calculating how many hours it would be until midnight. Then they began to feel their spines curling down on to the sofas again, and asked me, I thought with a somewhat forced enthusiasm, to go on reading. Anne said that she would sit with Elizabeth on the sofa, but Elizabeth gave her little irritable pushes with her feet, and Anne moved back to her nest of cushions in the arm-chair.

I went on reading.

Then, suddenly, punctually at 9.45, Elizabeth burst into tears.

Not such sad or sleepy tears, but hot, furious floods of tears accompanied by screams of chagrin. I hardly asked what was the matter. It was much more difficult for her to explain than it was for me to realise what this awful emotional collapse portended. I seized her in my arms (she is still small enough for this) and carried her upstairs, still weeping and screaming, and laid her in bed. As I did so, the screams quieted into long, angry sobs, and I began to distinguish mutterings of "I hate the *jour de gloire*. . . It wasn't a bit nice. . . It wasn't nice at all." I said firmly and as reassuringly as I could,

"Some of it was nice; think of your bath and the sausages," for it really seemed too bitter that at the age of five years and one month she should be suffering from that most agonising sensation of wasted pleasure and lost chances of delight. I added, "And you can have a lovely last thing to console you. You can have the curtains back and go to sleep watching the sky."

The unfamiliar stars and the familiar pillow then soothed her chagrin; the sobs stopped; the tears stopped; and within two minutes even the snufflings and sniffings gave way to the regular and peaceful breathing of sleep.

Then I went downstairs. In the hall I found Rosemary with round and tragic eyes, a white and brooding face, and her dark hair scattered about her shoulders, like a small Lady Macbeth, moaning and protesting that she was really so *very* tired that she didn't think she would ever stop being tired, and that not even going to bed and sleeping could possibly make any difference to her extreme unparalleled and unprecedented exhaustion. She too, she pointed out, must be carried to bed, so staggering under her considerable length and weight, behaving indeed like an amateur fireman with more courage than strength, I carried her to bed too. She sank back with a dramatic moan of relief. "I don't like *jours de gloire*," she said.

I perceived that disillusion was in fashion.

"I never want a *jour de gloire* again," and she added, romantic that she is, "Now we shall always want to do what we're told."

The Life of Pleasure was being succeeded by Remorse. Unromantically, I pointed out that she had enjoyed some of the day and that later we might have another *jour de gloire* and that perhaps we could arrange the next one better.

Anne meanwhile had come uncarried to bed. Perhaps her riper years, perhaps her Scottish blood, had made it possible for her to survive the curiously intangible but perfectly real disappointment of the day. She got into bed looking like a very sensible Botticelli angel; and went to sleep, unimpressed by Rosemary's already half-dreaming protests that *no* sleeping would make her any *less* tired.

The way that the *jour de gloire* worked out is to some extent an answer to the educationists who say that children should manage their own lives. For as many experienced educationists of the opposite school have pointed out, the mind and intelligence of even the cleverest child develop unevenly. The organisation of a day and the organisation of time is a definite strain on a child's mind; in attempting to arrange its own life it assumes a responsibilty for which it isn't yet ready. It wastes energy in trying to decide what to do—that same energy it can use so happily in the many things that the older person gives it to do. On the other hand, I don't at all believe that one should over-organise a child's time. I think that as it gets older, organisation of its own day and choice of its own pursuits are among the things it should learn.

By this first experiment, I have learnt that children of five and seven are not fitted to arrange their own lives even for a few hours; and I suspect that they themselves came to the same conclusion. But I shall try the same kind of experiment about every six months, and if I don't find that as time goes on they show a capacity to keep themselves occupied and happy and reasonable for a day at a time, I shall feel that I am in some way to blame in the training of their characters.

1935

The music of " God Save the King " rose from trumpet and horn.   Drums
beat . . . and Geordie saw the King.   He threw all the fervour of his
pent-up emotions into a long, penetrating look . . . and the King saw him !

## How Geordie MacQueen of Garlochry
## shared celebrations
## with His Majesty King George V

LITTLE George MacQueen stood on
the top step of the three that led to
his father's bicycle repair shop
wearing, pinned on his breast, the large
Jubilee medal sent to him all the way
from London by his Aunt Aggie.  He
was so small, his little chest so narrow,
and the medal so large that it hit you
in the eye the moment you looked at

him.  And everybody did look at him.
No one could help looking at him
because his figure, tiny as it was in the
deep, dingy doorway, seemed symbolic
of noble elation in great achievement.

His mind was, in truth, almost overwhelmed by two emotions, pride and a
great pity for those who were not as he
was.  His eyes glowed with pride, his

neck was stiff with it, but his lips wore
a pitying smile for the passers-by, none
of whom wore Jubilee medals, and particularly for Alec McKay, his greatest
friend, who to-day was removed from
him by a gulf impossible to bridge.
Alec stood across the way in front of
his mother's tobacco shop, barefoot and
dirty, as he always was, staring in bewildered envy at the friend now so far
above him.

The medal had come in a wee sma'
box addressed to Geordie himself.  It
was the first time he had ever got a
package by post and shivers of excitement ran along his spine as his mother
carefully untied the string and unwrapped the box.  Inside, in a nest of
cotton-wool, lay the medal and a card on
which was written, *With love from Aunt
Aggie.*  Aggie was Mrs. MacQueen's
sister, who had been a waitress in a
London restaurant for six years, and
who came home to Scotland once every
year for a week's holiday.  She was very

### The Silver Jubilee's Most Delightful Tale

# TWA KINGS

## by Mazo de la Roche

*Illustrations by Isobel Lucas*

fond and proud of her nephew George. She thought he was superior to all other small boys. Often, waiting at table, she felt contemptuous towards the people she served, remembering the superiority of her own family. They were, without exception, clean, neat and industrious. Angus MacQueen too, had all these virtues and, like his wife and sister-in-law, he was small, pale and even fragile-looking, but he had their spirit and determination and he had worked so hard that last year he had found himself able to afford a second-hand motor-bicycle which he had bought at a great bargain. Now, on the Sabbath, instead of taking George by the hand and his wife on his arm for a walk on the hills beyond the village, he mounted his motor-cycle and, with wife and child in the side-car, disappeared in a whirl of dust to parts, before now, unexplored. It was glorious.

When the medal had been brought to view and Mrs. MacQueen had explained that it was made to celebrate the King's Jubilee, Geordie asked at once:

"Can ah hae it pinned on me to-day, Mither?"

"Weel," answered Mrs. MacQueen thoughtfully, "I dinna think that would be quite right. I think it ought tae be kept for the day itsel'." As always, she was anxious to do the right thing.

"But, Mither," declared Geordie vehemently, "Ah want ye tae pit it on me right awa'! Ah want Alec McKay tae see it."

"I think ye'd better wait, Geordie." But she had no strength to oppose him.

"It's ower long to wait. Ah canna."

He had his way. Not only was he allowed to wear the medal, but he was allowed to wear his Sunday suit as a fit background for it. He also had his face and hands washed and his hair licked with a wet brush. Ah, but he looked grand when at last he stood outside the shop door, with the medal on his breast and his heart swelling almost more than he could bear! No wonder everyone stopped to look at him and Alec McKay's bare toes turned up in envy!

There was trouble the next morning when again he demanded to wear his Sunday suit, his Sunday boots and his red Sunday tie.

"But ye'll ruin yer Sunday claes!" expostulated Mrs. MacQueen.

"Na, na, Mither, ah'll no ruin them. Ah'll no be playin' in the mud wi' Alec. Ah'll juist be standin' by the door for a' the folk tae see."

Stand by the door he did, all day long, with short intervals for rest. He was only six years old and the medal had changed the course of his life. He had his father's support. Angus MacQueen thought that the child should be humoured, indeed both parents thought that the child should be humoured. They were as proud of him as he was of the medal.

He took to asking questions about the King. How big was he? How old was he? When he learned that the King was nearly seventy, he exclaimed:

"Havers! Ah hope he'll last!"

Though he did not explain why or for how long, his mother took it for granted that he meant during his own lifetime. She did say, however:

"It seems queer that a Scots laddie should set sae much store by an English king."

Little Geordie's face was a study in disappointment.

"Ye're no' tellin' me, Mither, that the King is an Englishman!" *Continued overleaf*

*(Continued)*

"Ay, he is that."

Geordie's face went crimson but he controlled himself. He drew in his chin so that he might the better see his medal. He gained strength from it to bear his disappointment. The next day he came into the kitchen radiant.

"Mither!" he cried, "Ah've juist heerd tell frae Duncan MacTavish that the auld Queen was a Scotswumman! He tuk me intil his ain room and shewed me the medal he had for her Jubilee. It was fine, but no sae big as mine. He telled me how she lived in Balmoral and he has a picture of her and her bairns in a plaid shawl and kilts!"

Duncan MacTavish was a retired schoolmaster who boarded above the provision shop on the corner. He took a great interest in the little boy and had prophesied more than once that he would be a remarkable man. Consequently Mrs. MacQueen thought him a very astute man, though she knew that anyone with an eye in his head could see that her son was born for greatness.

She said, mixing her scones, "Weel, I'm glad tae hear that Queen Victoria was a Scotswumman. I hadna heerd tell of it before."

"Ah'm thinkin'," went on George, "that our King taks after his Scots grannie."

"I daursay."

"It 'ud be an awfu' thing if he was a' English, wouldn't it?"

"Ay, it would." She looked tenderly at her little boy, standing straight and proud, with his medal on his chest.

Just as she was taking the scones from the oven he came again to the kitchen.

"Ah maun tak' a wee rest," he said, and seated himself on his little stool by the fire. She looked at him with concern, noticing how pale his face was, how set his mouth.

"Ye'll wear yersel' oot wi' this flummery-dummery!" she declared. "I wish ye'd play aboot wi' the ither bairns."

"Ah canna," he answered. "Nane o' them hae medals. Ah canna play till the Jubilee is past."

"Will ye eat a scone, then?"

"Ay. Ah'll eat a scone."

She broke one open steaming hot and spread it with treacle. Fortunately, she thought, his appetite was better than she had ever known it. When he had eaten he went back to the door to show himself.

As he stood motionless he had time for long thoughts. They were concerned almost entirely with the King's Jubilee and his own share in the rejoicings. With each succeeding day his share loomed larger and larger till, at last, it almost equalled that of the Sovereign. They both bore the name of George. They both celebrated their birthdays on the third of June. They were both giving themselves over with Royal magnificence to the celebration of the Jubilee. There was the King in his Palace waiting for the great moment. Here was he, in front of his father's shop, his medal on his breast, the cynosure of all eyes in Garlochry. Sometimes the lads made fun of him, jeering as they passed, even throwing a small stone or two at him. But the effect of

this was only to increase his prideful elation. And, at last, the other boys became proud of him too and pointed him out to any passing stranger.

"Yon's Geordie MacQueen! He's celebratin' the King's Jubilee."

Each day as Duncan MacTavish passed on the way to get his morning paper he saluted the little boy with, "Guid morning, your Majesty. And I hope this fine weather holds out for your Jubilee."

One day he remarked, "It's a remarkable thing, Geordie, that your surname is MacQueen. You must come by your Royal proclivities honestly."

The little boy did not understand him, but he felt for the first time that both his names were associated with the Royal Family. His chest seemed scarcely big enough to contain the swelling of his heart.

Every night he laid his medal on his bed and knelt by it to say his prayers, which now always ended with the words:

"Lord, please gie us a fine day for it. Amen."

Mrs. MacQueen, for her part, would be glad when it was all over and her son was restored to normal again. She was thrown into excited perturbation by a letter from her sister urging that they should all go to London for the celebration. Never in their lives again might they have the chance to see such sights. Little George would remember it to the end of his days.

She was almost afraid to make the suggestion to her husband, so sure was she of disappointment. He was all for careful living and saving up for George's education. But, almost without a moment's hesitation, he threw himself heart and soul into the scheme. Considering the way, he said, Geordie

had been impressed by the Jubilee medal, it was their bounden duty to give him the opportunity to be still more impressed by the celebrations in the capital. He had his motor-cycle. They would make the journey to London in good time so that they might secure places in the front row on the kerb and hold them down throughout the night, as Aggie said. It was his duty to Geordie and he was not a man to shirk his duty.

Geordie was so overwhelmed by the news that he was to see the great procession and the King himself, that he walked round the kitchen in a circle, with a dazed look in his eyes, not knowing what he was doing. But, when he did take it in, his elation reached the point of a high serenity It was then

1935

Ah, but Geordie looked grand when at last he stood outside the shop door, with the medal on his breast and his heart swelling almost more than he could bear. No wonder everyone stopped to look at him and Alec McKay's bare toes turned up in envy!

that he began to feel pity for those who were not as he and the King. One night at supper he said suddenly:

"Fayther, ma Sunday suit's no' guid enough to wear tae the Jubilee. Ah maun hae a kilt. Ah'd like fine tae show the London folk what like a Scot in his kilt looks."

His mother laid down her knife dumbfounded. But Angus MacQueen, after a long look into his son's eyes, said calmly:

"Aye, laddie, ye maun hae a kilt."

"Ah, the pair o' ye!" cried his wife. "Ye'll hae us impoverished!" But her eager mind flew to the details of a grand Highland costume with velvet coat and sporran and a bonnet with ribbons to it.

From that day Geordie's appetite failed him. He could scarcely sleep for excitement. Luckily there was only a short time till their departure, barely enough for the acquiring of a Highland costume, a little on the large side but still becoming. Oh, how grand the Jubilee medal looked when it was pinned on the velvet jacket! Geordie's ribs ached from swelling out his chest. On the last day he did not stand at the door of the shop for long intervals but, like Royalty, showed himself for only a few moments at a time to the gathering of children, with a few grown-ups, who collected for the spectacle. It was Duncan MacTavish who encouraged them to cheer Geordie at each reappearance.

The little boy was pale and tired before ever they set out for London, which they did as soon as the shop closed at noon on Saturday. But still his eyes were bright with courage, though the thought of going so far from home, which he had never left before, loomed fearfully in his mind.

Mrs. MacQueen packed a substantial meal to eat on the way; the Highland suit was carefully wrapped in clean paper, but Geordie carried the Jubilee medal in its little box clasped in his hand. Through the bewildering maze of roads he clasped it. He held it tighter when they passed through crowded towns, thinking of the folk who might so fiercely snatch the prize from him, if but once they glimpsed it. All the way his mother held him on her lap, softening a little for him the jarring and *Continued overleaf*

## TWA KINGS
### *(Continued)*

jolting of the machine.

Under the clear starry sky they sped, their three faces growing whiter and more wan. They had a few hours of restless sleep in a crowded inn on the highway and at sunrise they were on their way again. With every mile the traffic became more pressing, more raging, more like a flooding river urging towards the sea.

They stopped to drink ginger beer and lemon squash. Ice-cream was bought for Geordie. Ellen MacQueen's headache got worse and worse and, at long last, they raged into London.

Aggie had arranged for a place where the motor-cycle could be left without charge. The friend with whom she shared a room had gone home for the week-end, so Aggie was able to take her relations completely under her wing while they were in London. Neither her sister nor her brother-in-law had been there before, and, now that they were there, it seemed doubtful if they would have the strength to enjoy it, so completely done out were they.

But Aggie made a pot of tea, of a strength that can be only achieved by a Scotswoman, and after three cups apiece of it (Geordie having six lumps of sugar in each of his) they were able to look forward to the Jubilee with eager anticipation.

Mrs. MacQueen and Geordie stretched their weary bodies on the lumpy bed and a quilt was laid on the floor for Angus. Almost instantly he fell into a heavy sleep, but Ellen and Geordie felt the vibration of the motor-cycle in all their nerves. Their legs twitched, they threw their arms about and moved their heads uneasily on the thin pillows. The air in the room was very close, and beyond the grimy panes of the open window a steady roar of traffic came. Through the window Geordie could see a cluster of dark roofs and chimney pots which, after a while, were richly gilded in the sunset.

It seemed to Angus MacQueen that he had scarcely slept when he was woken by the return of Aggie, who had come to tell them that it was time to be off if they were to secure places worthy of their great endeavour. There was just time for another cup of tea and a bite to eat, and, much more important, the dressing of Geordie in his Highland costume.

He could scarcely believe that the great moment had come. He stood trembling with excitement while mother and aunt stripped his clothes from him and exclaimed at his general griminess.

"Ye'd never believe, Aggie, that he was scrubbed from heid tae heel before we left home! But na wonder he's dairty, puir bairn! Mony a time I thought we'd be smothered wi' the dust."

"Dinna fret, Ellen! I'll gie him a wipe wi' my flannel an' he'll shine like the new medal, won't ye, Geordie?"

The two women stood back from him when he was fully dressed and they felt weak with admiration and possessive love. Angus MacQueen, washing in the water left over from Geordie, felt that no sacrifice was too great for such a son. Geordie looked grand. His kilt hung to perfection. The buttons on the velvet jacket gleamed like lesser stars beside the constellation of the medal. But it was the bonnet, placed jauntily on his fair head, that most truly set him off. His mother's eyes filled with tears as she looked at him. His father took him almost solemnly by the hand as they preceded the two women down the stairs, covered by drab linoleum.

Everyone in the crowded 'bus stared at Geordie, or so it seemed to the relatives who guarded him. The 'bus man said "Hoots, mon," to him as he collected the fares and more than one person called, "Hello, Scottie!" when they saw him. Everyone seemed to be excited and in good humour, yet they were all rivals for the best place to view the procession.

Geordie had been disappointed at what he had first seen of London. It had seemed overpoweringly crowded and the houses dingy and dour. But, after they had left 'bus and tube and had walked through several streets he stood at last before a scene that was beyond all he had imagined. He saw a green park with brilliant flower beds set among the trees. He saw water where white swans calmly sailed, as though the flood lighting was truly sunshine. All this was surrounded by great gleaming buildings each one of which might well be the palace of the King. These were festooned with flags and bunting and all the street was like a fairyland of Venetian masts and banners and little pointed pennants and lights of blue and gold and crimson. He wished there were not quite so many people or that he were taller so that he might drink in all this bewildering beauty. He wished his friends in his own village could see him, but, in truth, all his thoughts were confused by the kaleidoscopic movement before his eyes.

The MacQueens would have been nowhere without Aggie. As it was she was almost distraught for a time with the seeking out of a good place for them. Hundreds of people were there before them, stolidly planted on the spots they meant to hold. There seemed no room anywhere but at the back. Then suddenly a big grey-haired woman saw their anxious faces, saw Geordie's Highland kilt and gave a friendly smile to Aggie.

"Come along," she said, "get in here in front of me. You're little and I'm big. There's room for the lot of you." The friend who was with her was not quite so genial, but she made way and Aggie and the MacQueens were established in the front row in a position from where they could see the Royal Standard above Buckingham Palace and where nothing could come between them and the sight of the King. The new moon was up in the sky. Aggie gave Geordie a red lollypop on a wooden stick to suck. They prepared to face the long hours of the night.

Again Geordie was an object of interest in his kilt and tartan caught on his shoulder by a gleaming clasp, the bright buckles on his patent leather shoes. Angus MacQueen would have to work many a day to pay for all this finery. He and his wife and Aggie could scarcely take their eyes off the boy. His decorations were more to them than the decorations of all London.

Geordie felt his heart so strong within him that all sense of fatigue was gone. He stood bravely at the kerb, conscious of admiring glances, now and again moving his body so that his kilt might swing. But his small vanity was insignificant compared to his stark northern pride in his fellowship with the King. A golden cord seemed to join him to the Royal form in the Palace.

"Twa Kings," he murmured to himself. "Twa guid Kings."

Men went about selling hot coffee and chocolate and little flags. Aggie offered to buy a flag for him but he graciously refused it.

"Na, thank ye, Aunt," he said. "Ah'll no' wave a flag."

There was much chaffing among the crowd and, now and again, a burst of song. This was led by the strong, clear soprano of the stout grey-haired woman. Geordie stared up into her face as she sang. He liked the looks of her. She took his little

hand in hers and beat time with it to the song.

Some had brought stools or cushions and sat on these to rest, but for the most part newspapers were spread on the pavement. Aggie had brought some and she and Ellen and Angus sat down on these as the night drew on and Ellen took Geordie on her lap.

He fell into a restless sleep filled with confused dreams of little villages flying past, great human faces looming above, while, in a reddish sky, his medal shone like a sun. His bonnet fell over his eyes, his mouth hung open, his small hands hung limp.

He was woken by a blast from a bugle. He started up terrified, not knowing where he was.

"It's naething to be frighted of," comforted his mother. "It's juist the bugle fro' yon barracks." She sat him up and straightened his bonnet.

"Ah'm no' frighted, Mither," he said, and scrambled from her knee to his feet.

The bright sky arched above. The air quivered beneath its brilliance. Geordie saw that his medal was in place. He took off his bonnet and bowed his head. He murmured:

"Thank ye, Lord! Ye've gied us a fine day for it."

Ellen MacQueen rose with difficulty from her cramped position. Indeed, she scarcely could have risen, had not the stout woman taken her under the arms and given her a heave. If it had not been for Geordie she could almost have wished herself back in Garlochry. But a bun and a drink of hot tea from Aggie's thermos put new life in her. She moistened her handkerchief at her lips and wiped Geordie's face and tweaked and patted the intricacies of his Highland costume into seemliness. Angus lifted him on to his shoulder that the newcomers surging up behind might have a look at him. He said sneeringly out of the side of his mouth to his wife:

"Ye'd think these Londoners had never seen a Scots laddie afore."

"I don't suppose they have, puir things," she said complacently.

It was grand for Geordie sitting on his father's shoulder. Even though Angus was a small man it seemed a long way up. He could see the greenness of the park, the new leaves fluttering in the breeze, the Palace with the Royal Standard floating above it. A band marched by playing a Scottish air.

"It's a guid thing," muttered Geordie to himself, "that the auld Queen was a Scotswumman."

There was always something new to look at, new relays of policemen, officers trotting by on splendid horses, the purple and gold draped stands filling with ticketholders. But the sun came out hotly, beating down on the patient people, the breeze fell and the pavement gleamed hot and bright. Ellen and Aggie removed their coats and appeared in thin blouses. But Geordie's fine Highland costume made him feel the heat greatly though he would not acknowledge it or remove his bonnet to cool his head. Yet to himself once he murmured:

"Lord, ye need na hae made it quite sae fine."

Nothing ruffled the good humour of the stout woman. Again and again she led the singing, shouting the words of the old war-time songs. Over and over she sang —*Pack up your troubles in your old kit-bag* and *Tipperary*, while the sweat gleamed on her ruddy face and the sun beat without mercy on her grey head.

Now the crowd wanted to cheer. They were in the mood for cheering and when cars passed bearing guests to the service in St. Paul's they were cheered as though

*Continued overleaf*

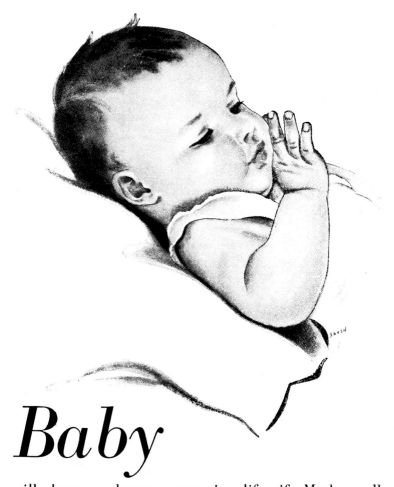

# Baby

will have a better start in life if Mother allows Treasure Cot to help her, and Mother will find that she saves money this way. We particularly advise expectant mothers to read the introduction to the new Maternity catalogue. Please send for any of these free booklets.

## TWA KINGS
*(Continued)*

they were doing something remarkable.
Field-Marshals, Statesmen and Rajahs
with their ladies looked severely ahead or
exchanged humorous glances with the
crowd, according to their nature.

Then all that the people had waited for
began to happen—music, glittering uniforms, haughtily-stepping, shining horses.
Again and again Geordie asked, " Is it the
King ? "

His father would answer through the
cheers, " Na, laddie, it's one o' they
Princes."

The stout woman knew who they all
were. She pointed out each notability by
name. She knew all about the little Princesses.

Suddenly she grasped Angus by the arm
and said, her voice quite hoarse from much
singing and shouting :

" Here they come ! Their Majesties !
Put him right in front, Mister, so the King
can see 'im an' 'e can see the King ! "

The people stirred like a field of corn
bending before a wind. The music of *God
Save the King* rose from brazen trumpet
and horn. Drums beat. Deafening shouts
of " God bless Their Majesties ! " drowned
all other sounds.

He did see the King. He threw all the
fervour of the pent-up emotions of the past
weeks into a long, penetrating look into
the smiling blue eyes of the grey-bearded
man in uniform. And the King saw him !
There was no doubt about it. Everybody
said so. The stout woman looked about
truculently as though she dared anyone
in the crowd to deny it.

" 'E looked straight at 'im," she declared, " straight at little Scottie, 'ere, an'
smiled. I wouldn't 'ave missed it for
anythink ! "

" Twa Kings," murmured Geordie to
himself. " Twa guid Kings."

They stayed where they were, in the heat
and sun, till the processions returned. This
time Geordie had only a glimpse of the
King, but he was quite satisfied. He had
had his great moment.

It was hours before they were back once
more in Aggie's room. What a lucky
thing for them that the store, in the
restaurant of which Aggie was a waitress,
was closed for the day. And Aggie, being
a waitress, was not nearly so tired as the
others. Again she made Ellen and
Geordie lie down on the bed while she and
Angus lay, in different corners, on the
floor. But they were all too excited for
sleep. They could not stop talking. One
of them was always recalling some in-
cident, thrilling or amusing, and must re-
peat it to the others. Aggie insisted that
they must not return to Scotland without
taking Geordie to the Palace that night,
for it was whispered that Their Majesties
might show themselves on the balcony.

The third journey by Underground and
'bus made no impression on Geordie. He
had seen too much, felt too much already.
Like a puppet he moved where he was led.
His glazed eyes looked straight ahead of
him seeing only the figure of the King in
his gilt state coach drawn by six white
horses. When he found himself once again
in front of the Palace it seemed to him that
he had never left there. But now a vast
throng had gathered in one great block, all
gazing intently at the aloof façade of the
Palace. He saw no other children. He
was suffocating down among the legs of
men and skirts of women. His father
lifted him on to his shoulder, but there was
no stout grey-haired woman to protect
them. They were swayed like seaweed in
the tide of the crowd. The crowd sang,
shouted, stood stolid, and sang again. The
floodlights blazed. An illumined aeroplane

sailed far above. A bugle sounded from
the barracks.

Then someone cried out, " There They
are ! " Geordie, safe on his perch, saw
two figures on the balcony of the Palace.
" God bless the King and Queen ! Long
Live Their Majesties ! " Geordie saw the
King vigorously waving his arm. He took
off his bonnet and waved it with all his
might. " Ah'm here too ! " he shouted.
" See me ! "

The crowd roared itself hoarse. It
surged forward towards the great gates.
Geordie saw Aggie sink down out of sight
among the moving feet. His mother
screamed and his father put him into her
arms, then rescued Aggie and struggled
with her limp body towards the Victoria
Memorial where other fainting women
were receiving succour.

Geordie looked at the poor things with
mingled pity and contempt. He knew that
they were not dead, for he saw them re-
viving, sitting up with bewildered faces,
being swallowed again in the crowd.

Soon Aggie recovered her senses and the
four made their way towards the Underground station. All the rest was a blank
to Geordie till he found himself sprawling
on his mother's lap in the side-car of the
motor-cycle and on the way back to Garlochry.

On and on through the clear bright night
they sped, till they reached the open
country, and the sun rose above peaceful
woods. Geordie slept and woke and ate
and slept again and still his father bent
above the handle-bars of the motor-cycle,
and the day passed and the bright young
moon showed herself in the twilight
sky.

They were within a few miles of home
when a motor-lorry, coming round a bend,
took more than its greedy share of the
road. The lorry struck the motor-cycle
and the three riders were hurled into the
ditch in a sort of sandwich, Geordie being
between his parents.

Although Angus was at the bottom he
was the first to rise to his feet and gather
up his wife and son. The motor-cycle was
demolished. Geordie was unhurt, but Ellen
had rather a bad cut on her hand to which
she paid no heed whatever, but clutched
Geordie frantically to her feeling him all
over to see that he was sound.

Good fortune followed them. A motor-
car directly behind them was driven by a
doctor who saw their accident. He bound up
Ellen's hand and took the three MacQueens
into his own car. He also took the name
and number of the lorry driver and gave
them to the traffic officer who now approached. He said :

" I saw the whole thing. The driver of
the lorry was entirely to blame. I'll give
evidence to that. This poor woman shall
get damages and her husband a new motor-
cycle ! "

Deposited in their own home the Mac-
Queens could scarcely believe in their good
fortune. They had been to the Jubilee.
They doubted if any there had had a better
view of the great happenings than they.
They were to have a new motor-cycle, to
say nothing of damages for Ellen. Geordie
had been admired almost as though he were
Royalty.

Now he stood examining the havoc of his
Highland costume. A tear rolled down his
cheek. He held the medal in his hand,
looking at it dolefully.

" Dinna greet, laddie," comforted his
mother. " I'll send the kilt an' a' tae the
cleaners an' it'll coom back as braw as
ever."

" I ken that," he answered glumly.
" But, Mither," he turned a look of re-
proach on her, " ye need nae ha' bled on
the Jubilee medal ! "

1935

**1935**

**4344.** *For one's first grown-up nightdress, this pattern is suitable for making up in any of Courtauld's lovely real and artificial silk satins or crêpes. Seams above the waist in front and below it at the back mould the figure smoothly, and the shoulders may be tied or joined with a seam. For size 34, 3¼ yds. 36-in. material are required. In bust sizes 32–42 in. Price 9d.*

**4473.** *Pyjamas cut like a man's and in striped Clydella like a man's, will please the six-year-old. This suit is easy to make, and takes only 2⅞ yds. material for size 8 (available from 4 to 16 years). Clydella at 2s. 6d. a yard can be bought in innumerable gay pyjama stripings. Pattern price 1s.*

**4839.** *A sturdy but light-weight wrap-round dressing-gown for girls in their teens is made in Tootal's Lova—plain trimmed with plaid to tone at 2s. 11d. and 4s. 11d. respectively. Available in bust sizes 30 to 46 in., and taking 4¼ yds. plain and 1 yd. plaid material for size 34. Price 9d.*

**4858.** *This is the classic nightdress pattern for girls and can be made as shown, with long sleeves, collar and buttoned closing for winter, or with shoulder-sleeves and open neck for summer. Nursery Clydella, which has just been reduced in price, costs only 1s. 11½d. a yard in delightful pastel-coloured flower prints, and 3½ yds. will be required for size 10. Available from 2 to 14 years. Price 9d.*

4773          4353

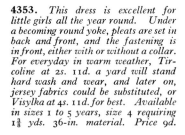

**4773.** *Long or short sleeves are provided with this demure little dress, and the pattern includes panties. It is very easy to make, and Printed Viyella at 3s. 11d., which washes well, is just the right weight for early autumn. The sizes are for 2, 4 and 5 years, 2⅛ yds. being required for size 4, with ⅜ yd. contrasting material. Price 9d.*

**4353.** *This dress is excellent for little girls all the year round. Under a becoming round yoke, pleats are set in back and front, and the fastening is in front, either with or without a collar. For everyday in warm weather, Tircoline at 2s. 11d. a yard will stand hard wash and wear, and later on, jersey fabrics could be substituted, or Visylka at 4s. 11d. for best. Available in sizes 1 to 5 years, size 4 requiring 1⅜ yds. 36-in. material. Price 9d.*

4839

4344

4473

4858

Patterns for all these designs can be obtained through Good Housekeeping Pattern Service, 153 Queen Victoria Street, London, E.C.4, at the prices given and post free. All are hand cut and have full instructions and cutting guide

1935

# PATTERNS

## for

## the Younger

## Generation

4897   3940   4922   4838

**4897.** *This attractive " best " dress can be made for the coming months in uncrushable velvet such as Artvel, at 7s. 11d. a yard, with kilted trimming round the wide collar, or in a flowery Liberty silk. Puff sleeves and a plain round collar are also included in the pattern. In sizes 6 to 15 years, requiring 3⅝ yds. 36-in. material for size 12, and 2 yds. collar pleating. Price 9d.*

**3940.** *Gauging and smocking are very fashionable just now, and there is no more attractive trimming for children's clothes. This pattern depends upon squares of gathers at shoulder and waist for its fit and graceful lines. It can have smocked elbow sleeves or long ones gathered into a cuff, and a collar or plain square neck. Heavy shantung silk is perhaps the best choice of material, and for size 12 allow 2¾ yds. Available in sizes 4 to 14 years. Price 1s.*

**4922.** *This excellent everyday dress is made with a single-pleat panel at the back and a double one in front. The double collar is fastened with a large or small bow, or a tie may be worn. One of the scores of interesting Viyellas should be chosen, as these are washable and in excellent designs, all price 4s. 11d. Available in sizes 6 to 14 years, requiring 3¼ yds. material for size 12 and ¾ yd. plain for double collar. Price 9d.*

**4838.** *Another good dress for the schoolgirl is this one with a pleated panel leading to a shoulder yoke in the front, and a back with inverted pleat in both bodice and skirt, to give plenty of room for movement. The neck can be closed up to the throat if desired. Suitable for any light woollen fabric, taking 2 yds. in 54-in. width for size 12. In sizes 6 to 14 years. Price 9d.*

4248   4252

**4248, 4252.** *These two little suits provide a popular " brother and sister " outfit. The blouses are identical, with a tab-like extension on the yoke that accommodates a pocket. The fastening is on the shoulder. For the boy the pattern includes tailored trousers, and for the girl, a pleated skirt set on a bodice-top. Jersey fabrics would make up excellently. Each blouse requires ⅝ yd. in 54-inch, with ½ yd. for trousers, ⅜ yd. for skirt and ⅜ yd. bodice-lining in 36-in. material. Available in sizes to fit 2 to 6 years. Price 9d. each.*

1936

# *Does your* Child *know these signs of the Happy Healthy* OVALTINEYS?

*Boys and Girls!*
*Join the League of*
*Ovaltineys to-day!*

Send a postcard to-day to THE CHIEF OVALTINEY, The 'Ovaltine' Factory (Dept. 67), King's Langley, Herts, asking for the Official Rule Book and full details of the League.

P214A

MANY thousands of boys and girls are enthusiastic members of the League of Ovaltineys. They get endless fun and amusement from the secret high-signs signals and code. And more important still, they are told how to be always fit and vigorous.

The League of Ovaltineys was founded by the proprietors of 'Ovaltine' in the interests of children everywhere. Parents welcome the League because they appreciate its objects and the great benefit which 'Ovaltine' confers on the health of their children.

Delicious 'Ovaltine' is the perfect food beverage for children. It provides every nutritive element required to build up a strong, sturdy body, sound nerves and abundant vitality. For this reason make 'Ovaltine' your child's regular daily beverage. And be sure, too, that he or she joins the League of Happy Ovaltineys.

# 'OVALTINE'
## *Builds up Brain, Nerve and Body.*
*Prices in Gt. Britain and N. Ireland, 1/1, 1/10 and 3/3.*

# Lots to Do and Lots to See

by Dorothy Shearer

## NECESSARY

I WONDER where did the big wind go
When he went rushing by—
A-ruffing up my dog and me
And shaking the tree tops high !

I'VE got to find out where he went—
A-singin' his bustly song—
And follow after him because
He took my hat along !

## BY AND BY

MY DADDY takes his hook and line,
Grasshoppers for his bait,
And goes a-fishin' in the stream
Beyond the meadow gate.

I CAUGHT two 'hoppers of my own
Out in the field one day.
They're in my pocket here right now,
All safely tucked away.

AND some day when my dad asks me
To go a-fishin', too,
I'll have my bait all ready.   See ?
Guess I'll catch 'nother 'n' or two.

1936

*Drawings by*
*Dorothea Warren*

## A LITTLE BOY'S DAY

AT MORNING, when the world grows light,
The sun comes peeping up so bright !
He looks at me and seems to say :
" Get up—for here's a bran'-new day !
There's lots to do and lots to see.
Come, let's be at it, you and me ! "

THEN darkness comes.   And in the sky
A silver moon goes sailing by.
He looks at me and seems to say :
" You've been so busy all the day !
It's time for you to go to bed
And rest your tousled little head.'

## DISSENT

NOW, big folks say a boy ought not
To run and play about
With pockets looking very queer
Because they lump and stick right out.

O' COURSE mine's crammed brimful of stuff—
Things any boy might need :
Some loops of string, my tiny truck,
My top—an' then some 'sturtium seed.

A PAIR of wheels, an apple core,
And several rusty nails.
My marbles, too—and somewhere there's
A matchbox full of worms and snails.

BUT, oh, I want to save 'em all,
No matter what you say !
Boys have to have nice things like these—
We use 'em every single day.

1936

" My elder girl
seemed to be
born civilised "

# Children Like Discipline

### declares
### SYLVIA THOMPSON

"My second daughter was gaily, vitally and unflaggingly

WHEN my children were very small I read books on child psychology, and articles on the management of children, and one of the most emphatic ideas among their authors was that one must not " order a child about" too much, nor give it complexes and inhibitions by imposing a very strict morality upon it. If one did so, I understood, the child, feeling cramped when it needed freedom, would assuredly grow up to have a fearful reaction: the good little girl (made good by an imprudent nurse or mother) would assuredly turn out a murderess, or a lady of doubtful virtue; and the nice-mannered little boy—so unwisely trained as to come quite quietly into a room full of grown-up people—would certainly repay the discipline which brought him to such a pass by a fling of criminality, or by sowing wild oats all over Europe.

As I say, I read the books. So did my friends. Some of them had children, already of school age, brought up in the name of freedom-in-the-nursery. Not only did their parents spare the rod—they even went so far as to hand it, figuratively, to the children to beat their nurses with, if such a wayward fancy should seize their young and unbridled imaginations.

I went to tea with some charming friends whose six - to - ten - year - old children came into a London drawing-room with dirty legs and hands, shouting loudly, and discussing sex problems with a vigour and detail that would have shamed many a successful playwright. I went home, confirmed in my determination that I would at least moderate my children's early freedom. I would not, I thought, let them decide everything for themselves while they were hardly out of the pram.

Still—I had a conscience in the matter, and determined not to fall into the wrong and tiresome reaction of disciplining too much. I would try to co-operate with them, and not force them more than I could help.

My elder daughter reached the ages of three and four with a character which made discipline not very necessary. She seemed to be born civilised. She had, in babyhood, a nice, affectionate, but firm-willed nurse, who probably crushed out all sorts of liberal wickedness while the child was still in its pen: anyway, by the time she became my problem she wasn't, in that particular way, a problem at all. Her moral feelings seemed very much of the grown-up sort, and naughtiness of the old-fashioned, recognisable nursery sort wasn't her line.

The second daughter was a very different problem. She had a tremen-

"naughty . . . she interpreted liberty by throwing her food on the floor"

*The author, who is herself the mother of two children, opposes modern ideas on child management*

*Illustrations by Isobel Lucas*

dously strong, and not at all temperately exercised will; from the early days when, at six months, she beat her Nannie for taking away her half-finished bottle! Every night for a year and a half she screamed with rage at the prospect of going to sleep, and broke into delightful chuckles if she got some placating grown-up person to come in and see if, perhaps, after all, the poor little thing had a pain!

By the age of one year she was one of those children to whom my psychological works would have had me allow liberty—she was not, in theory, to be repressed. But I was, in those early stages, forced to compromise, in fact even—I confess it now—obliged not to spare the rod. She was gaily, delightedly, vitally and quite unflaggingly naughty. Unless such "immoral" measures as commands and punishments were applied, she interpreted liberty by throwing her food on the floor, playing all night in bed, screaming when she came out of her bath, lighting matches and putting the flame up her nose, gargling with her milk, and a hundred ingenious deviations from sober conduct which had never occurred to her sister. In special bursts of high spirits she would try to go head first downstairs, and at the age of two invented songs of rollicking impropriety which she sang when visitors came to tea. (I suppose psycho-analysts would have urged that those songs were a wholesome release, but they did, at times, make social life with a more prudish generation rather difficult!)

In fact—by any but modern standards—she was a naughty child, but a gay one.

After a good deal of careful reflection on her *Continued overleaf*

"The second girl . . . a different problem"

1936

8159

8162    8182    8184    8183

8162.   Party frock with hand faggoting, in four sizes from 2 to 8.   Allow 1⅜ yds. 36-in. fabric for size 4.   Price 1s.   8182. Dress with plain bodice and gathered skirt, in five sizes from 4 to 12.   Allow 2½ yds. 36-in. fabric for size 10, with ½ yd. contrast.   Price 1s. 8184. Princess dress buttoning down the front, in five sizes from 4 to 12. Allow 2⅝ yds. 36-in. fabric for size 10, ⅜ yd. contrast. Transfer for buttons included. Price 1s.

8183.   Sailor frock with box-pleats back and front, in four sizes from 4 to 10.   Allow 2 yds. 36-in. fabric for size 6, with ½ yd. contrast.   Price 1s.   8159. Simple dress that the child can fasten itself, in four sizes from 4 to 10.   Allow 1⅝ yds. 36-in. fabric for size 6, with ⅜ yd. contrast.   Price 1s.   8188. Three blouses in one pattern, bust sizes 30 to 42.   Allow 2⅛ yds. 39-in. fabric, size 34, for full-length blouse. Price 1s.

8188

*Styled by*
**Good Housekeeping**
FASHION SALON

SELECTED    PICTORIAL
PATTERNS

## CHILDREN LIKE DISCIPLINE

*(Continued)*

character—which, during a nurse's sudden illness, tried my patience to the aforementioned point of spanking her with a slipper—I decided to try, after all, the method of letting her do what she liked. She was then two and a half. So when, as I came to dress her, she beamed, and said, as usual, "I don't want to be dressed," I said: "All right, darling, you stay in bed and I'll bring your breakfast there," she burst into tears of rage at once, and continued to scream with chagrin for an hour. Then she implored me to dress her, but cried with baffled rage all the time I was doing so. Later, when she said she wouldn't eat, I said of course she needn't, and she screamed again. All through the day she continued to revolt against her unexpected liberty, and by six o'clock—when she duly proclaimed that she would not go to bed, and when I said that she should, of course, stay up as long as she liked—she gave a roar of anger, and threw herself on the sofa, crying "I want to be punished, *I want to be punished!*"

This attitude of mind, fantastic as it sounded, expressed with kicks and sobs by a stout and refractory two-year-old, is, I am convinced, an expression of something quite fundamental in the mind of almost all children—from the time they are conscious and desiring beings at all, they "want to be punished!" In other words they want to be naughty, and they expect to be punished! If you take away the possibility of being naughty, you deprive their life of that most human, most natural, most age-honoured charm—of deliberate sin and the sweets of sin. And if there are no "roses and raptures of vice" for them, there must equally be no "lilies and languor" of virtue.

In fact, if you try to imply that all conduct is equally unpunishable, you may make their immorality seem dull (which, as a theory, is all right as far as it goes), but you will also make virtue, goodness or good behaviour non-existent. (This is what is wrong, just now, with a good deal of adult morality.)

You cannot set the child a good standard unless you admit (and by admitting punish) what is bad. And where there is no standard there is no real civilisation. However much your open-minded child-psychologist may urge against discipline, etc., in doing so he attacks something fundamental in human tradition and in human instinct. There is, and has always been for human beings, Good and Bad.

Children know this instinctively. The smallest baby begins to apprehend it.

The bigger child grasps, as a matter of course, that there is not only Good and Bad, but that the two are opposed. He goes on, by sheer instinct, to perceive a certain value in trying to be good. And when he is bad he goes, equally instinctively, through all the stages of sin—hesitation, excitement, pleasure, followed—according to his strength of character—by fear or repentance, by surfeit and despair, or by remorse and confession. But, just as he knows that there is a kind of grandeur about being good, he equally knows that being naughty ends in some kind of badness of feeling, quite apart from punishment. Punishment—one sees this over and over again—he regards as a kind of expiation. It cleans up his sin. He can start afresh.

Only the other day I overheard my elder daughter discussing with a schoolfriend whether it was better to be punished, or not.

1936

## '*Just what the doctor ordered*'

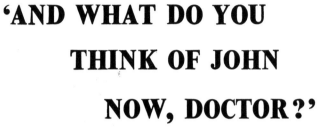

# 'AND WHAT DO YOU THINK OF JOHN NOW, DOCTOR?'

'Well, what does John think of himself?'

'Dad's given me a new football, and I kicked three goals with it yesterday.'

'He's put on such a lot of strength since you saw him last, doctor. Do you think it's that Crookes' Halibut Liver Oil you ordered?'

'Never a doubt of it! Do you know what that stuff actually contains?'

'You did tell me about its vitamins, but ——'

'Look here, this is something you ought to learn by heart. Vitamin A is the vitamin that helps to protect our bodies against infection, and Vitamin D is the bone-forming one. Now cod liver oil possesses a good supply of both, but—

**There is 80 times more Vitamin A in Crookes' Halibut Liver Oil than in the finest ★ cod liver oil, and 30-40 times more Vitamin D.'**

'So you can't do better than go on with Crookes'. A drop instead of a spoonful—what could be easier to take?'

## VITAMIN CONTENT GUARANTEED

★ *This means over 300 times more Vitamin A than in average cod liver oil.*

Healthy children (and adults too, for that matter), no less than those who have been weakened by illness, need Crookes' Halibut Liver Oil. They need an adequate supply of Vitamin A to help to protect them against infection, and of Vitamin D to build up sound bodies and sound teeth. They get that supply, *with guaranteed certainty*, in Crookes' Halibut Liver Oil, made at the famous Crookes Laboratories. Be sure it *is* Crookes' you are getting—not a cheap substitute made from low-grade oil that Crookes have rejected. The green label on the carton is your safeguard, for it guarantees a high and *standardised* vitamin content. *What other oil does, or can do, this?*

*A single drop of Crookes' Halibut Liver Oil is equal to a teaspoonful of finest cod liver oil.*

# CROOKES'
## PURE HALIBUT LIVER
# OIL

'COLLOSOL' BRAND (Regd.)

### Obtainable *only* from Chemists

In liquid form, with dropper, per phial containing sixteen days' full adult dosage **2/-**. In capsule form, per bottle of **25** capsules, each containing a full dose **2/6**. Of all chemists.

There are three other preparations of Crookes' Halibut Liver Oil: HALIMALT, HALYCITROL and HALYCALCYNE. *The Crookes Laboratories, Park Royal, London, N.W.*10

# Creatures *from a* Zoo *that never was*

*Described by*

THE

MARCHIONESS

OF

CARISBROOKE

## THE CHIZZY WIT

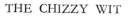

The Chizzy Wit is sleek and stout,
And no one knows what he's about,
Because he crawls around at night,
He can't stand day or candle light.
I'm told by someone who once saw
The Chizzy Wit, that every claw
He has upon his twenty toes
Is white, and that he has a nose
Exactly like a sucking pig,
And also that he wears a wig.
Perhaps if you sit up at night
There is a tiny chance you might
Perceive this funny little beast—
    Who knows ?

## THE KIKRIKEE

Try to avoid the Kikrikee,
He's old and lives up in a tree,
He won't wear collars, no, nor boots
And feeds on dandelions and roots.
He's awfully mean and very sly
And teases insects till they cry,
Small birds he tips out of their nest
(In fact, he is an awful pest).
The birds and insects, one and all,
Refuse to speak to him at all ;
He therefore leads a lonely life
(He cannot even find a wife).
If he across your path should stray
Will you just quickly look away ?
Now please remember my advice
Because I know he isn't nice.

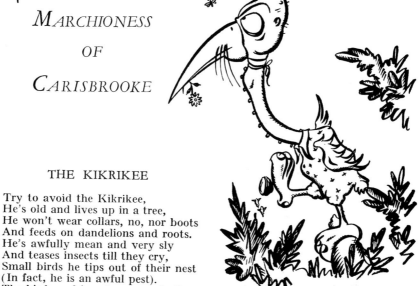

*Sketches*

*by*

*Ian Fenwick*

## THE OUZEL MOUSE

I've never seen the Ouzel Mouse
Who lives alone in Ouzel House
Right under ground and out of view
Of stoats and owls and foxes too.
The Ouzel Mouse is very shy
And won't, no matter how you try,
Be tempted from his earthy lair
(In fact, he seldom takes the air).
What food he eats—well, no one knows;
Some say it's ants and beetles' toes
All stirred into a lovely stew
(I wonder if it's really true).
Others believe it's mole-tail soup,
For that, I'm told, cures flu and croup,
And as he gets the croup at night
Perhaps that last surmise is right ;
Still, never mind if we don't know
The life he leads far down below;
The reason is to me quite clear—
We are not meant to interfere.

## THE PUSSY-CHUBB

The Pussy-Chubb is very snug,
He's half a cat and half a pug,
He's got a lovely heart, you'll find
(I've never known him be unkind).
If you should lose a tennis ball
Among the bushes he will crawl,
And even if it pours with rain
He'll look until it's found again.
If you fall down he'll always rush
To help and give your clothes a brush,
And if you have a streaming cold
He'll say, " Please, may I make so bold
As to lend you my hankcherfee "
(He has words of his own, you see).
Now that you know he is so sweet
Do try the Pussy-Chubb to meet,
And the first moment that you're free
Do ask him out to lunch or tea.

# Going back to Kindergarten

1937

1. This attractive jumper suit is for the girl of perhaps five or six years. It is in a soft shade of silver-grey edged with scarlet, and hand-embroidered with daisies in scarlet wool round the neck. *Lilley & Skinner*

2. A charming little coat in old rose tweed with a beautifully gored skirt emphasised by arrow-heads. It is neat and very tailored, and comes from *Daniel Neal*

3. A small girl's frock and knicker set in Check Clydella. The abbreviated skirt is joined to the short bodice by diamond-shaped smocking ; the short puff sleeves are quite delightful. *From Lilley & Skinner*

4. A buster suit for winter wear with neat check top in all-wool taffeta, and button-on knickers in wool repp material. The colours available are green or brown check tops with knickers to tone. *Lilley & Skinner*

5. Here is a charming little coat for a small boy, in soft, pure wool tweed with a stitched velvet collar and flap pockets. At the back it has an inverted pleat and a stitched half-belt. It is lined throughout with Chilprufe. Ages two to five years. *Lilley & Skinner*

golby

*1937*

6.  Another little coat for the small boy or girl in a sturdy woollen material, made with matching cap.    The collar and the pockets are piped with contrasting velveteen.   In several pastel and dark shades.  Daniel Neal

7.  He may be the dunce of the class at figures, but this little fellow standing on the stool is beautifully turned out, in a misty-blue stockinette suit.    It has plain-coloured trousers and a striped blue-and-white jersey, bearing an anchor monogram on the pocket and a blue Lightning Fastener.  Daniel Neal

8.  This very demure-looking little girl is wearing a jade-green velveteen dress with a natural-coloured Shantung collar, which has scalloped edges and embroidered French knots.   The bodice is darted at the waistline and the skirt is flared.  Lilley & Skinner

9.  A cosy frock for the growing-up toddler in Nursery Viyella.  This model is long-sleeved, and charmingly trimmed with smocking below the yoke.    From Daniel Neal

10.  Chic in the nursery world is always a matter of neatness, a quality which this Nursery Viyella frock possesses in a marked degree.   There is some nice detail work round the yoke and triangular smocked pockets.   Daniel Neal

11.  Scottish and proud of it !   She is only five years old, but already swirling a kilt with quite an air !  The whole outfit is in pure botany wool in a gay shade of red and tartan lines of white and green.  From Lilley & Skinner

1938

# Time for SCHOOL CLOTHES again!

### says the CLOTHES CONSULTANT

RUST is the colour! That's the first bit of news I have for mothers-of-daughters, and good news, too, for both dark and fair wearers look well in this practical, cheerful shade.

Next, a style note: tweeds are gaining on plain, smooth materials. Not so long ago the plain navy suit went into every schoolgirl's trunk, spring and autumn alike. This season, more and more who are not bound by school regula-tions are choosing nice, sturdy Harris tweeds, in clear, soft blues or the characteristic Harris brown, while some of the schools are even switching over on their "uniforms."

As to cut, that has changed a little, too. Remember the time when the jacket of a suit was cut almost square, whether you were eight or eighteen? Not so with the styles I've been seeing. They're simple, schoolgirlish and essen-tially tailored in appearance, but backs are panelled to give a good line and buttons chosen for their decorative value as well as for mere fastenings.

As with more mature fashions, colour-contrast gives a sparkle to autumn - into - winter frocks of favourite novelty jersey or fine wool and angora fabrics. Scarcely one that does not have contrast pipings, appliqué and belt; gay-toned embroidery or just a discreet touch of colour intro-duced into buttons and tassel-topped zip. Besides the rust tones (generally allied to green), a warm mid-blue, old gold and grass green head the list of frock colours. Generally, a darker tone such as navy or brown makes effective contrast.

Shirt-frock styles lead, but although they look demure, the square and shape-less look associated with "juvenile" clothes has completely disappeared. Bodices are darted to fit, and even if skirt hems flute out into sunray pleats, the hips are neat-fitting. Pleats, in a modified form, continue strong favourites, but if you've no affection for bills for repleating, choose the "pinch-pleated" kind for *your* girls. Stitching along each pleat makes them "stay put" for ever. The Wolsey model sketched is a good example, but then Wolsey do excel at this kind of practical but attractive frock. This season's range comes in three groups—the "Wee Folk" models for nursery youngsters, the "Minor Miss" group for the junior school-girl and the "'Teen Age" fashions for the elder girls, so, as you might guess, the styles are particularly appropriate to the age of the wearer.

For nursery-age daughters I've just seen something spanking new that appeals to

*Above, left: Harris Tweed suit with shaped back and leather buttons. Excellent finish. In Harris brown or soft blue. Sizes for 12–18 years. Price, all sizes, 49s. 6d. Daniel Neal. Centre: beautifully tailored "reefer" in wool freize, with jaunty little hat in same material. Rust or blue. Sizes 32–38 in. Similar style for older girls. Rising 1s. 6d. per size, from 38s. Daniel Neal. Right: "'Teen Age" shirt-frock in firm wool jersey with contrast appliqués and stitching on collar to echo the colour of the novelty buttons. In the following combinations: ol. gold/dark royal; mid blue/dark blue; navy/rose; rust/brown; green/rust. Sizes 41–44 in. From about 35s. Wolsey*

me as having distinct possibilities. It's a frock that fits without fastenings; simple enough for a five-year-old to get in and out of by herself. The secret lies in lastex. You remember the marvellous one-size-all-figures swim suit, the "Slix"? These frocks, made on the same principle, have been christened "Chix." The lastex is introduced in a sort of honeycombing effect at neck and waist, and very effective it looks, too. I liked a white-dusted angora woollen dress (also in the rust tone) with a cute polo neck and embroidery in blue and gold. I also saw some very lovable little pinafore frocks, carried out in fine, washable flannel with smocked waists and little check blouses.

I haven't mentioned coats, and these, I must admit, remain fairly conservative. The princess style with nice, full skirt and little round collar, perhaps of stitched velvet, takes a lot of beating for the young person of five to eight; while for the older lass the "reefer" with high revers, double- or single-breasted bodice closing, fitted back and slightly flared skirt, com-petes with the good old straight-cut, belted classic. If your daughter has a reasonably good figure, she'll look rather nice in the reefer, but should she incline to solidity around the hips, the straight style will probably be safer.

I've sketched a reefer that seems to me

## TIME FOR SCHOOL CLOTHES AGAIN!

perfect of its kind. Well-proportioned, well-detailed and of good, firm, woollen freize cloth that feels as comfortable in December as September. It comes from Daniel Neal in sizes 32–38. Very properly they consider that in larger sizes the style should be a little more grown up, so they take away the half-belt at back and add a little more stitching and detail. For the fifteen to seventeen-year-old it could hardly be bettered. All sizes; colours, a rich "kind" blue and the favourite rust. Price for 32-inch size 38s.; rising 1s. 6d. per size. This includes the little matching hat.

Much as I applaud the coats, dresses, knitwear and the rest, it's in the matter of undies that I feel the young people of to-day score.

Take the case of gym knickers. The newest streamlined pants, brief and tailored, seem in a different class from the old bulky, baggy stockinette 'bloomers." They have lastex at waist and knee, cutting out the old "my knickers want fresh elastic" bogey, a neat pocket and a specially shaped double gusset that makes for longer wear.

Wolsey and Viyella both do a model, each perfect in its way; the former of superb quality pure Botany wool, the latter of the famous Viyella mixture yarns. Look at them both; I think you'll agree they're excellent value.

Talking of Viyella; those of you who know and "swear by" Viyella materials will be glad to know that this season they're styling quite a lot of "wovenwear" or knitted underthings for children and grown-ups. One of the best "lines" is a toddler's knicker of silky-soft, wear-indefinitely, warm-as-wool fine tricot (knitted from standard Viyella yarns) with a minute lace edging and a lastex top. Sizes 1–3; colours, peach, sky, cream; price about 2s. 11d. For small brothers they suggest a "training pant," also with lastex top, and with wrap-over front open-

*Left above : Viyella " knitted" pyjamas—won't irritate the most sensitive skin. Very warm and snug. Peach, sky, nil, with white. Sizes to fit 6-14 years. Size 28 in. chest, about 12s. 11d. Gossard combinaire for the schoolgirl whose figure is not yet developed. Sizes 30–36. No. 1511; about 9s. 6d. Practical girdle for 'teen-age girl whose figure needs discipline. Broché with lastex net panels. 1 in. sizes, 24–31. Gossard No. 10621. 21s. Rayon satin and lace " bra." Sizes 32–38. No. B018 ; about 6s. 11d.*

ing that eliminates buttons. Same price, but cream only.

Amongst the schoolgirls' range, I was particularly struck by a tricot pyjama suit with round-necked "sweater" top. You can choose it in peach, sky, nil or white, all with contrast trim. Very good-looking and safe for endless wear. The 28-inch chest size retails at about 12s. 11d.

One of the most encouraging things about progressive schools to-day is their realisation that a girl's figure needs taking care of as soon as it begins to develop. Not only do spreading hips and pro-tuberant "tummies" want a certain amount of gentle discipline, but youthful breasts need very careful support. If your girl suddenly shows signs of "getting a figure," take her to your local shop and have them show you the new Gossard Junior foundations. For the young woman who may be dubbed "hefty" they do a girdle in lastex net and figured baptiste (figured in an endearing "doggie" design, incidentally) that has a slightly built-up front, and over-hip and back panels of the baptiste. These "hold in" beautifully firmly, but the whole thing is so slight, soft and airy that even the most tomboyish won't find it too confining. The No. is 10621, 1-inch sizes 24–31, the price 21s. A shorter and softer model, without the side and back material panels, No. 10162, costs 18s.

To wear with the first girdle there's an excellent "bra" of rayon satin with just a small part of the top section in lace. It's sensibly built up under the arms, will stand-up to any amount of boarding-school wash and wear and comes moderately deep. Sizes 32–38. No. B018, price about 6s. 11d.

For the slighter girl, or the one who is

only just beginning to develop her figure, you can't better a Kestos brassière. They're sensibly made in sizes from 28 ins. (models B1, B5, B14), give a beautifully balanced and natural support and last for ages. Prices from 3s. 11d., with a special new number considerably priced at 2s. 11d.

If one-piece foundations seem preferable, look at Gossard No. 12021. The same family as the girdles, with a reinforced, shaped back to control without discomfort and a light lace "bra" section. Price about 21s. For younger girls, who are in the "puppy fat" stage, and who have scarcely begun to grow curves, there's a thoughtfully de-signed broché combinaire. It has deep elastic insets over the hips, a short front to give lots of freedom, but a longish back to neaten the line. Well-placed suspenders at side-back don't get in the way when sitting down. Low back, built-up shoul-ders and just a little shaping over the bust; Gossard No. 1511, sizes 30-36, the price 9s. 6d.

Well, so much for the girls! Just a word, though, before I pass on to the "grown-ups." Tropical wear! If any of you are going out east, or west, and are rather perturbed as to what you should take for the youngsters, whether they're babies or older, get on to Treasure Cot of Oxford Street. They're perfect ency-clopædias on the subject, and issue some extraordinarily informative catalogues for those who live out of town.

Lately I've been having so many requests for "warm but pretty" undies, for trous-seaux and general wear, too, that I want to tell you something of the new autumn ranges. I've seen so many excellent de-signs that I can't mention them all now, but here are notes of a few that struck me as outstanding in their way:

(1) Crochet-top lace wool camibocker by Wolsey. Very dainty, lacy design, yet not too open; ribbed waist. Fine neat braid finish and straps. Lovely for wear under slim frocks, for there's no double thick-ness around the waist. The style "Cobby's," the price about 8s. 11d. (women's size). Also made in young matron's fitting.

*Left : sweater-topped botany wool buster suit, with practical lastex-topped pants. The gay duck trimming will surely please small wearers. Soft blue, green, fawn. Sizes 16 in. and 18 in. From about 12s. 6d. Matching cardigan and sweater for small sisters. (Wolsey, " Wee Folks" range.) Right : wool and angora jersey in trim style with pinch-pleated sunray skirt. Green, blue, coral rose, rust and navy, all with contrast-covered zip and pompon. Sizes 30–39. From about 21s. 9d. (in the " Minor Miss" styles from Wolsey).*

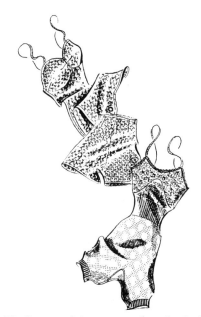

*Viyella yarn cellular weave trunks and " bra" vest. A grand new idea. Sizes S.W. and W., about 4s. 11d. each. " Cobby's." Exquisitely feminine, but so warm ! Lace stitch all-wool cami-bockers from Wolsey. Size W., about 8s. 11d.*

# *Ladies in waiting—*

All eager to see the show. And what a picture they themselves make in their gay Tobralco frocks. Quite a part of the decorations. And long after the rejoicings are over they'll continue to look decorative. For Tobralco is one of those permanently pleasant and cheerful things we may enjoy every day. In it the children always look their best — yet it's not too precious for everyday wear — even for knockabout frocks. Nothing stands up to hard wear and repeated washing like Tobralco. Nothing keeps its colour so well. or has such wealth of colours and patterns to choose from. See the many lovely designs in the children's range — gay pictorial, ABC, nursery rhyme and floral patterns. All guaranteed, for Tobralco is a Tootal fabric.

# TOBRALCO

## SO EASY TO WASH — SO HARD TO WEAR OUT

Now only 1/6 a yard.    36 inches wide.    Name on selvedge.

TOOTAL BROADHURST LEE COMPANY LIMITED (DEPT. 5)   56 OXFORD STREET, MANCHESTER 1

# DISAPPEARANCE
## by Ogden Nash

Have you seen Linell?
She was three years old;
Her eyes were grey,
And her hair was gold.
She had three dolls,
They were all named Maggy;
She wore pyjamas,
And the knees were baggy.
She wore a dress,
It was sprinkled with flowers;
She left her blocks—
I can see the towers;
She wore a hat,
With an Indian feather,
And galoshes, in case
Of nasty weather;
And when she was sick,
She went to bed;
And when she was better
She got up instead.
Oh, where she is hiding
I can't tell.
Has anybody possibly
Seen Linell?

Has anybody seen
My absent child?
She seldom fussed,
And she often smiled.
She threw a penny
To the organ=grinder;
Wherever she is,
I want to find her.
I looked in the corner,
I looked on the stair;
I couldn't catch a glimpse of her
Anywhere.
Is she in the cupboard?
Or a bureau drawer?
I tried and I spied,
But I never saw her.
She had a bike
With a jingly bell.
Has anybody possibly
Seen Linell?
Did she tell the postman
She was his?
Why, who's that coming?
Here she is!

169

# The FIRSTBORN

### by LAURENCE HOUSMAN

*Author of the "Victoria Regina" series of plays*

*IN the Ante-room of the Royal Private Apartments, the Head-Nurse is in attendance, with other Nurses at call. Within half-drawn portières, folding doors lead to the inner chamber, where only yesterday took place the happy event—not quite so happy as had been hoped—for which the whole Nation had been waiting expectantly. At the Ante-room door comes a discreet knock. The Head-Nurse sails importantly across, while the door is opened by one of her underlings. One of the Prince's Gentlemen presents himself; he is allowed to enter.*

GENTLEMAN: His Royal Highness has sent to inquire how is Her Majesty this morning?

HEAD-NURSE: Doing very nicely, Sir. Her Majesty has had a good night and is well rested. Her Majesty is still asleep.

GENTLEMAN: The doctor informed His Royal Highness that he would, perhaps, be able to see Her Majesty for a few minutes to-day, if you would be good enough to send word what time would be best.

HEAD-NURSE: When Her Majesty has wakened and had her breakfast, His Royal Highness shall be informed. But he is not to stay, tell him, more than five minutes. Her Majesty mustn't be excited.

GENTLEMAN (*stiffly*): I will tell His Royal Highness what you say.

HEAD-NURSE (*as one accustomed to have her orders obeyed*): Ah! Mind you do!

(*The Gentleman moves towards the door, then pauses.*)

GENTLEMAN: And Her Royal Highness, the Princess—how is *she*?

HEAD-NURSE (*proudly*): Well, Sir, for a one-day-old—and I've seen hun-

dreds of 'em—*I* say she can't be beaten

GENTLEMAN: Very satisfactory, I'm sure. Quite healthy?

HEAD-NURSE: Healthy! You should have heard her! Ah! She's got a will of her own already—like her mother *I* say; and I ought to know, for I came to Kensington Palace as under-nurse when Her Majesty was the one herself And a nice handful she was!

GENTLEMAN: Dear me! Very interesting. ... (*then ingratiatingly*). Nurse would it be asking too much—would you allow *me* just to see the little Princess for a moment—only for a moment!

HEAD-NURSE: *You*, Sir? No, Sir certainly not, Sir! Not till His Royal Highness himself has seen her is anyone else going to. Not if *I* know it.

GENTLEMAN: I humbly beg pardon of Your Majesty.

HEAD-NURSE: Granted!

# A delightful glimpse of a proud and happy moment in the great Queen's life 🎋 🎋 🎋

1939

GENTLEMAN   Have I Your Majesty's leave to retire?

HEAD-NURSE: Go along with you! (*The Gentleman proceeds to back out of the room: a performance which is lost on the Head-Nurse, who abruptly turns her back on him. From the inner room enters the Under-Nurse; stepping cautiously, she speaks in a whisper.*)

UNDER-NURSE: Her Majesty is waking up. At least, I think so.

HEAD-NURSE: Then go along and get Her Majesty's breakfast quick and sharp.

(*The Under-Nurse goes. The Head-Nurse enters the inner room and draws back the bed-curtains.*)

HEAD-NURSE: Is Your Majesty awake?

THE QUEEN: Yes, Nurse, I'm awake. At least I'm going to be. What time is it?

HEAD-NURSE: Six o'clock, Your Majesty.

THE QUEEN: Morning?

HEAD-NURSE: Yes, Your Majesty; it's morning now. Your Majesty has had six hours' good sleep; and 'll have another, after Your Majesty has had her breakfast.

THE QUEEN: I don't think I want any breakfast—not yet.

HEAD-NURSE: No, Your Majesty; but your breakfast wants *you*.

THE QUEEN: Not till I have seen the Prince, I mean.

HEAD-NURSE: Your Majesty can't see His Royal Highness the Prince till you've had your breakfast. No! It's doctor's orders.

THE QUEEN: Then let me have it at once.

HEAD-NURSE: It'll be here in a minute, Your Majesty· I've sent for it. (*Under-Nurse enters with tray.*) Ah! here it is. Bring it in, Nurse. Put it down. (*The tray is deposited. The Head-Nurse proceeds to officiate.*)

THE QUEEN: What's that?

HEAD-NURSE: That's what we call a feeding-cup, Your Majesty. It's the same one Her Royal Highness, the

*Continued overleaf*

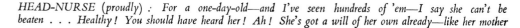
*HEAD-NURSE (proudly) : For a one-day-old—and I've seen hundreds of 'em—I say she can't be beaten . . . Healthy! You should have heard her! Ah! She's got a will of her own already—like her mother*

## *On November 21st, 1840, the bells rang out for the Princess Royal, who was to become German Empress*

(*Continued*)

Duchess, had when Your Majesty was born. Yes, the same one.

THE QUEEN: Oh? How interesting. It's the first time I've ever used one.

HEAD-NURSE: Ah! and it'll not be the last—let's hope. Now Your Majesty has only got to lie still. Don't move. I'll give it you.

THE QUEEN: While I'm taking it, will you send word to the Prince—to come and see me.

HEAD-NURSE: Word's been sent, Your Majesty. His Royal Highness will be here as soon as we are ready for him. Now then—this is going to do us good, please, Your Majesty. . . . Now a little more. . . . And a little more. . . . And now just to finish it. . . . Oh yes, you can; you can, if you *try*. . . . There! . . . And good and gracious, you've done it. . . . Does Your Majesty hear the bells ringing?

THE QUEEN: What are they ringing for?

HEAD-NURSE: What for? Why, for the Princess, to be sure.

THE QUEEN: The Princess? Ah, yes, of course. (*She sighs.*) Oh, I do so want to see the Prince!

(*The Head-Nurse goes out into the ante-room, where the Under-Nurse is waiting.*)

HEAD-NURSE: Go, and say that His Royal Highness can come now. (*Then returning to the bedside.*) There! Now I've sent word. His Royal Highness will be here in another minute.

THE QUEEN: Tidy me, Nurse. Tidy me! How do I look?

HEAD-NURSE: (*as she does the tidying*): Your Majesty's looking very nice indeed. Just a little pale; but that's to be expected.

THE QUEEN: Let me look at myself. . . . (*The Nurse holds up a hand-mirror.*) Oh, Nurse, I look dreadful.

HEAD-NURSE: You don't, Marm. You look sweet—and like a *mother*.

THE QUEEN: How's Baby?

HEAD-NURSE: Oh, she's all right. Your Majesty needn't worry about *her*. She's having her twenty-four hours' sleep, and having it well.

THE QUEEN: Twenty-four hours' sleep? Impossible.

HEAD-NURSE: No, Your Majesty; it's what babies always have to do when they first come . . . to get over the shock.

THE QUEEN: The shock of what?

HEAD-NURSE: Of being born, Your Majesty. It's hard treatment they get sometimes, poor little things!

THE QUEEN: Did *she* have very hard treatment?

HEAD-NURSE: No, Your Majesty treated her beautifully, like as if you'd been the mother of twelve.

THE QUEEN: Oh! Does that make it easier?

HEAD-NURSE: Sure, it should, Marm! Now Your Majesty must lie still, and not talk till His Royal Highness, the Prince, comes.

THE QUEEN: When he does come, Nurse, you must go.

HEAD-NURSE (*horrified*): Go, Your Majesty?

THE QUEEN: Yes; I wish to see him alone.

HEAD-NURSE: But I *mustn't* go, Your Majesty. It's doctor's orders.

THE QUEEN: This is the Queen's orders. You will do as I tell you.

HEAD-NURSE: I've never done such a thing before; but if Your Majesty really means it.

THE QUEEN: I really mean it, Nurse.

HEAD-NURSE (*hearing the outer door open*): Well, here His Royal Highness is, then.

(*She bustles forward to meet Prince Albert as he enters, shown in by the Under-Nurse.*)

PRINCE ALBERT: Mrs. Nurse, how long may I stay?

HEAD-NURSE: (*her stature restored to her*): Only five minutes, Your Royal Highness, *please*.

PRINCE ALBERT: Very well.

(*He looks at his watch and goes forward to the inner room. The Head-Nurse drives out the Under-Nurse with a*

*Only yesterday there took place the happy event—not quite so happy as had been hoped—for which the whole Nation had been waiting expectantly*

1939

*look; then takes up her stand within the screen which shuts off the outer door. Thus, out of sight and hearing, she obeys the orders.)*

ALBERT: *Weibchen!* . . . *Liebes, kleines Frauchen! Wie gehst du?* (*He bends over and kisses her.*)

VICTORIA: Oh, Albert darling, have I disappointed you?

ALBERT: Disappointed me? But how? Why, *Weibchen?*

VICTORIA: That it wasn't a boy?

ALBERT: You wished it to be a boy?

VICTORIA: Albert! Of course. How could one have wished anything else for an heir to the throne? The heir to a throne *must* be a boy—if possible.

ALBERT: Well, Vicky, I do not know that that has *always* to be. For if you had been your bruder instead of yourself— *this* would not have happened.

VICTORIA: "This?"

ALBERT: I mean that I should not have then married you.

VICTORIA: Then you are not disappointed?

"*Oh, Albert darling, have I disappointed you?*" "*Disappointed me? But how? Why, Weibchen?*" "*That it wasn't a boy. . . . The heir to the throne must be a boy—if possible*"

ALBERT: Oh, there is plenty of time, Vicky; you may yet be a mother of twelve.

VICTORIA: That is what Nurse said.

ALBERT: Oh! Did she? Well, let us hope that she was right.

VICTORIA: No, Albert, I don't want to have twelve—not quite. You see, it would be such an interruption to my being Queen.

ALBERT: Yes; I suppose. But while that was so, I could be looking after things for you, perhaps. No?

VICTORIA: No. . . . No, Albert, that would never do. My people wouldn't like it.

ALBERT (*sadly*): So?

VICTORIA: No. Two or three will be quite enough, I think. Perhaps I wouldn't mind four . . . in time. So you really don't mind? Oh, how good you are to me! I was so afraid I hadn't quite done my duty.

ALBERT: Well, Vicky, if it is anyone's fault, it is my fault, too.

VICTORIA: Oh no, Albert, no! The father has nothing to do with whether it is a boy or a girl.

ALBERT: Indeed? You seem to be very learned in the subject, Vicky. You surprise me. I thought it was something nobody knew anything about.

VICTORIA: Oh yes! I am quite sure of it. I have thought so much about it, you see—lately. So I *know.*

ALBERT: Well, if it is all your doing that it is a girl, let us hope that it will be good like its mother.

VICTORIA: But not clever like its father; a girl can't be. That is not possible.

ALBERT: Perhaps not—as a rule. But being clever is not everything. And if one cannot use one's cleverness, what use to have it?

VICTORIA: What do you mean, Albert, "not use"?

ALBERT: Oh, nothing, nothing! not that matters just now. Besides (*looking at his watch*) it is time I went. Nurse told me I was only to be here five minutes.

VICTORIA: Nurse told you!

ALBERT: Yes; and she was quite right. It was doctor's orders. And when doctors order, Kings and Queens must obey. . . . So now, for a little, good-bye. (*He kisses her.*). . . .

VICTORIA: Again! (*They kiss.*) . . . Again! . . .

ALBERT: No, no! not again. You must not so excite yourself. . . . Good-bye.

(*Going out he meets the Head-Nurse at the door.*)

Have I been more . than my five minutes, Nurse? No. . . . But it was a little hard to obey. . . . And now, if you will let me, I would like to look at Her Royal Highness, the Princess.

HEAD-NURSE: She is in here, Your Royal Highness—asleep.

ALBERT: Ah! then we must be careful that we shall not wake her. You think it will be quite safe?

HEAD-NURSE: Quite safe, if Your Royal Highness will allow me to go in first. This way.

ALBERT (*half returning*): Oh, Vicky! What a thing to be a father! *Das ist wunderlich!*

(*The Nurse goes in. He tiptoes after her.*)

VICTORIA: Oh! he's pleased! really pleased! Well, dearest, if you want twelve you shall have them. Anything —*anything* to please *you.* But oh, I do wish it had been a boy—a boy!

(*From the next room comes the loud screeching of a baby; the Princess Royal has woken, with a will of her own, which nothing is ever going to take from her.*)

 *Illustrations by Stanley Herbert*

# Butter short?

1939

# Give your children
## salads dressed with
# Heinz Salad Cream

*57*

Those vital butter fats that children need to keep them healthy are all in Heinz Salad Cream. And a great deal more good nourishment too! For Heinz is made now—just as it always has been—with plenty of cream, new laid eggs and pure olive oil. Take fresh vegetables and fruits and dress them with Heinz delicious dressing. That's properly balanced nourishment—with mineral salts, vitamins, proteins and energy fats all complete. And don't children love the mild, creamy flavour of Heinz Salad Cream!

For those who prefer a cream to spoon on top of a salad instead of to mix with it—there is Heinz Thick Whip—made of exactly the same pure rich ingredients as Heinz famous Salad Cream.

Made in our London Kitchens
Other varieties: Mayonnaise,
Tomato Ketchup,
Baked Beans', Spaghetti, etc.

*1940*

ONCE again it is the season of holly berries, carols, panto-mimes and Christmas cards. It does not matter whether we are carefree young-youngs or young-olds with memories, we are sure to enjoy ourselves and be caught up by the festive spirit. For several weeks our thoughts will linger lovingly round the idea of a party. And why not? Every party is a success if you play amusing games, and here they are, waiting for you! You will find games to suit every type of party: the party with aunts, grandmas and the youngest grand-daughter; the party consisting of the oh-so-clevers; the party —well, after all, what does it matter? All your guests will enjoy themselves, if you choose the right types of games

# Games for Parties

## by MARY VIVIAN

### Bed Time

ON a table at one end of the room put two boxes of matches, two candles in candlesticks and two old cushions to represent babies. The players divide into two equal teams at one end of the room. At the word "Go" the first players run to the table, light a candle, grab the baby and carry both back to their team, passing all the way round it and then proceeding back to the table. Here they put down the baby, blow out the candle and run back to their places. The next player then follows on and does exactly the same. The first team back in its original place is the winner. Needless to say, any player whose candle blows out before it should must return to the table, light it up and begin the putting to bed all over again.

### Stamp Hunters

BEFORE the party hide a number of used stamps of every value you can collect, including foreign ones. This collection will not be so difficult at Christmas-time, when parcels and cards are an everyday occurrence. No stamp should be absolutely covered by anything else, and if you have young visitors none should be placed too high to be reached easily.

All the guests are invited to make a collection of these stamps and allowed twenty minutes to find as many as possible. At the end of that time the numbers are counted up. Each halfpenny one counts one point, each penny one two, and so on. Foreign stamps count two if they are ordinary countries and three if they come from colonies, irrespective of value. The winner is the one with the highest number of points at the end of the game.

### What's in the Shopping Basket?

THIS attractive competition needs only a little preparation beforehand. Before the party put a dozen things to eat (each one beginning with the same letter) into a shopping basket, each object being put into a paper, or better still, a material bag, and tied securely so that nothing may escape. Number each packet.

Each guest is provided with paper and pencil, and the shopping basket is brought in. In turn each object is taken out and passed round among the guests, who are allowed to feel it and then write down what they guess it to be. At the end of the time the correct list is read out, and the winner with the highest total is given a small prize.

The letter S is an excellent one to choose. Here are a dozen suggestions for this: (1) Sultanas, (2) Sugar, (3) Salts, (4) Salt, (5) Soda, (6) Sage, (7) Sago, (8) Semolina, (9) Suet, (10) Sausages, (11) Tin of Sardines, (12) Sherbet.

The players should, of course, be told in the first place the initial letter with which all the words begin.

### I Resolve

EVERYONE is given paper and pencil and is asked to write the word RESOLUTION twice down the left-hand side of the paper, the letters arranged so that the R is on top, E below and so on. Everyone then begins to write down New Year resolutions, the first set being "I Resolve To Do So-and-so" and the second "I Resolve Not To Do So-and-so." In each case the first word of the resolution must begin with the given letter. Thus the first set might begin: "Read good books instead of rubbish," "Entertain more friends," "Save as much money as possible," and so on to the end of the word. Everyone should be invited to make the resolutions as amusing as possible, as they are read out at the end of twenty minutes.

### The Perfect Rose

THIS is a restful game which will be enjoyed by all. Into a bowl put a number of ordinary pins—sufficient for every guest to have one—and a packet of rose petals such as are sold for weddings.

The guests sit round in a circle, and while music is played the bowl is passed from hand to hand. As soon as the music stops whoever is holding the bowl takes out a pin, which represents a stalk. The aim of every player is to collect in this way one pin and five rose-petals, but nobody may take more than one petal at a time. As soon as a player has a complete flower by putting the five petals on to the pin, he cries out "I have a rose," and is proclaimed the winner.

The music should be played as for Musical Chairs, but for very short periods of time only.

### Cushion Circle

THIS is played on the lines of Musical Chairs, only cushions are used instead of chairs and placed in a circle, leaving spaces between them. There *Continued overleaf*

## ON THE KITCHEN FRONT

# How to eat wisely in wartime . .

**So much of our food comes from overseas, using valuable shipping space, that care and skill in its choice and preparation is now an urgent national necessity.**

TO eat wisely in wartime we should vary our meals as much as possible. There may be a shortage of some of the foods we usually buy but there will always be others to take their place. To keep fit and well we should choose something from each of the four groups below, every day.

## THE FOUR FOOD GROUPS

### (1) BODY BUILDING FOODS:

*Milk, cheese, eggs, meat, fish.*

### (2) ENERGY FOODS: *Bacon and ham, bread, butter or margarine, cheese, dried fruit, dripping or suet or lard, honey, oatmeal, potatoes, rice or sago, sugar.*

### (3) PROTECTIVE FOODS

(Group 1): *Milk, butter or margarine, cheese, eggs, liver, herrings or salmon (canned or fresh).*

### (4) PROTECTIVE FOODS

(Group 2): *Potatoes, carrots, fruit (fresh or canned but not dried), green vegetables or salads, tomatoes, wholemeal bread.*

## ISSUED BY THE MINISTRY OF FOOD

## Games for Parties
### (*Continued*)

should be one fewer cushions than there are guests.

While music plays the guests walk round, as soon as it stops each sits down on a cushion. This is never as easy as it sounds, for in the excitement of the moment one is apt to land on the floor. When this happens the player is out, just as much as if he had been without a cushion at all. One cushion is removed after each round, the winner being the one who succeeds in sitting accurately on the cushion in the final round.

### *Filling the Gap Backwards*

ALL the players except one join hands in a circle and the one who is out goes round the outside of the circle touching any player he chooses on the shoulder. He then continues his way round the circle as before, but now backwards. The player who has been touched proceeds round the circle in the opposite direction to the other player, also travelling backwards. The player who first gets into the gap left by the first player remains there, while the other less fortunate one proceeds on his way in a forward direction until he chooses to touch another player.

### *Ham and Eggs*

YOUR guests will thoroughly enjoy this novel competition. Before the party write out each of the following descriptions on a separate numbered card, putting them up in prominent positions round the room.

When you are ready to play the game, provide all the guests with paper and pencil and invite them to guess the answers to the descriptions. Explain that the odd number solutions begin with HAM and the even with EG or EGG.

1. Ham that is an English county (Hampshire).
2. Egg that is a going out (Egress).
3. Ham that drives in nails (Hammer).
4. Egg that is conceited (Egotistic).
5. Ham we connect with the Pied Piper (Hamelin).
6. Egg that is a bird (Egret).
7. Ham which hangs from two trees in the garden (Hammock).
8. Egg that is sweet-briar (Eglantine).
9. Ham that is a famous Court (Hampton).
10. Egg that is a man's name (Egbert).
11. Ham that is found on the Continent (Hamburg).
12. Egg that is an old exclamation (Egad).
13. Ham that is a small village (Hamlet).
14. Egg that is self-conceit (Egotism).
15. Ham that is taken on picnics (Hamper).
16. Egg that is foolishly distinguished (Egregious).
17. Ham that was a friend of Nelson's (Lady Hamilton).
18. Egg that urges people on (Egg).
19. Ham that is found at the back of the knee (Hamstring).
20. Egg that is self (Ego).

Keep the answers handy, and award the prize to the player who first brings you a correctly completed list.

---

### IMPORTANT

Owing to the paper restrictions during the War it will be necessary for readers to place a definite order in advance with their Newsagent or Bookstall for their regular monthly copy of GOOD HOUSEKEEPING

---

1940

I WONDER if you can remember a series of discussions on the Cinema arranged by the B.B.C. two years or so ago? Herbert Hodge, the philosophic taxi driver, was in the chair, and week by week he sat at the microphone interviewing film producers, actors and actresses, news-reel men and script writers—he even cross-examined the Film Censor. In the opening discussion he interviewed a number of us at Broadcasting House—a suburban house-wife, a man from the country, a member of the Film Society and a schoolboy. I was cast for the part of the man about town, who goes to see the new films when they are first shown in the West End; the sort of person who scorns the two-feature pro-gramme, plus organ solos, plus publicity film and local announcements.

I didn't quite recognise myself in the part. Still, I said my little piece, refusing to let Hodge label me as either highbrow or lowbrow, and stressing one thing: I said that I did want a film to do its primary job—that is, to have action. All this was readily endorsed by the schoolboy, who delighted me by saying, with much emphasis, that he was sick of "sloppy love stuff at the pictures."

I was reminded of all this the other day when I attended a Mickey Mouse Chil-dren's Matinée at the Odeon, Wealdstone.

The programme consisted of a Disney cartoon, *Beach Picnic;* the last instalment of a Western serial, *Oregon Trails,* appro-priately called *The End of the Trail;* and the first instalment of a new serial, *Flash Gordon's Trip to Mars;* and a full-length Western, *The Western Trail,* starring Bob Baker.

The opening announcement of the Disney cartoon, which showed the familiar drawing of Donald Duck, got a loud shout, but the cartoon itself didn't amuse the children

quite so much as others I have seen, such as *Goofy and Wilbur* and *The Band Concert.*

How those youngsters love excitement and action on the screen! When the hero galloped off after the villainous band, alone, they followed his every move with rapt attention. There wasn't a sound in the cinema except the noise of galloping hooves from the sound track. It was just the same when Flash Gordon went off into space in his rocket ship, but whenever the hero showed signs of falling in love, or even talking to the heroine, the silence was broken and the youngsters started talking. They did not talk loudly, but one could sense that their attention had slackened. A small boy near me expressed what every-body felt when he burst out, "It's only 'er again!"

Now the cinema is the ideal medium for children, it tells a story in pictures simply and directly, and with action. The char-acters come to life and live and move before them. That much will be agreed, but more and more people are wondering about the influence of the cinema on children. What is the extent of its influence? Is it a good

influence or a bad one? If it is bad, can it be improved?

It should be remembered, I think, that these problems have only been posed since the coming of "talkies" in 1929; since when a new generation of children have become regular filmgoers. Almost every day bishops deplore some film or other. Public morality councils report on films which they consider unsuitable for children. Welfare workers talk of juvenile delin-quency and of the effect of films on the young, and some magistrates hint that gangster films make crime attractive to the young.

I confess that I am very suspicious of people who talk of "the child," who proceed to elaborate some argument or other on the harmful effect of the cinema on "the child." That is as much a fiction as "the average man" or "the man in the street."

But it is not enough to say that this or that film is unsuitable for children. What are these people who complain doing to encourage a better supply of films for chil-dren? Everyone agrees that there are not enough suitable films.

I must say that I sympathise with the people who do organise special children's matinées, who often go to endless trouble to book films, barely covering their expenses, for children's matinées do not bring in the revenue of the ordinary public perform-ances. To organise them the manager or the circuit has to show an enthusiasm that is not measured by £ s. d. Some of the big producing companies will not release any of their films for children's matinées at all, others will not release them until they have exhausted their bookings in the ordinary cinemas, and by the time they are available for children's matinées they are probably three or four years old.

These are some of the practical difficul-ties in the way of those who are trying to

arrange special children's cinema shows. When the war broke out, one circuit, the Odeon, had 150 Mickey Mouse Clubs organised at their various cinemas, repre-senting a membership of 100,000, but that number is not anything like large enough to encourage the producing companies to make films specially for children.

And what films do children like? After deducting all the films which are "For adults only;" the number which children enjoy wholeheartedly is very small. A friend of mine, a school-master evacuated from London to St. Albans, has been making enquiries of his own scholars for me. He teaches a class of 33 boys, all of them between 12 and 14 years of age. First of all he asked them what they con-sidered to be the best film of the year. This bothered them a bit, so he asked them to write down the names of the films they liked best and remembered. Then, having got a list of titles, they began to classify them and compiled a list of twelve classes. A number of boys then called out the names of films which did not fit into any of the twelve classifications, so they finally extended that list to seventeen.

These are the seventeen classifications, in the order of their popularity, as drawn up by this class. Some of them, frankly, surprise me, but here they are:

| | |
|---|---|
| 1. War films | 8. Child characters |
| 2. Detective films | 9. Sport |
| 3. Mystery thrillers other than de-tective films | 10. Cartoons |
| | 11. Tragedies |
| 4. Sea films | 12. Geography and travel |
| 5. Gangsters | 13. Society films |
| 6. Cowboy and Westerns | 14. History |
| | 15. Nature |
| 7. Comedies | 16. Musical films |
| | 17. Love |

That list is full of surprises. I am sur-prised to find war films top of the list, for example, though that does not mean news reels, but action pictures such as *The Lives of a Bengal Lancer, Gunga Din* and so on.

I confess, too, that I was rather sur-prised to find cowboy films and Westerns so low down on the list, because they are the special diet of the children's matinées, but that again is because they are the only films available in sufficient quantities to run children's matinées weekly.

# CHILDREN AT THE CINEMA

1940

ADOLESCENCE is a difficult period for both children and parents. Much patience and understanding are needed by the latter to help children over this worrying transitional time, so that they may become normal, uninhibited adults. Lack of understanding and impatience with the adolescent may lay up a store of trouble for him in the future, therefore all parents must consider the best way to manage their children during puberty.

I think it is important to prepare the child for the changes that are going to take place. It is extraordinary how, even in the present day, many parents are too shy to discuss the subject in anything like a normal manner with their children. It is easier for mothers to prepare their daughters and fathers their sons, so that their children are not shocked by idle gossip at school or elsewhere.

The age at which puberty begins varies, and it is a little difficult to choose the right time to broach the subject, but so long as it is early enough, it doesn't really matter. A child will not absorb any information before it is ready for it.

As a rule girls start developing at the age of about eleven or twelve, and boys a year or two later. One can usually notice changes both physical and emotional taking place about this time. In girls the body begins to alter, they get plump, and breast tissue begins to form. They also get fits of moodiness, lose their tomboyishness and become more interested in their personal appearance and domestic affairs. With boys the physical changes are less marked, though the voice of course breaks, and they are apt to develop acne. They become rather restless and irritable, and are apt to despise the companionship of girls with whom they had previously played quite happily. Later on they become dreamy and romantic in their outlook. Children of the lower classes reach puberty earlier and pass through it more quickly, partly because they begin to earn their living earlier and therefore develop the independence of the wage-earner sooner; also they do not lead such sheltered lives, but live in close contact with adults, and so appreciate the meaning of the difference of the sexes, and take it far more as a matter of course than do children of the middle and upper classes.

If the parents themselves are leading a happy and normal physical life there should be no difficulty in ex-

### Wise parents can do a lot to help their children pass through this trying phase with ease and spirit

plaining to their children the physiological changes of puberty. The way should be prepared during the whole upbringing of children by answering the questions they almost certainly will ask about birth and pregnancy. The arrival of baby sisters or brothers, puppies or kittens, is bound to arouse their interest, and parents should explain these matters simply and truthfully. This prepares the mind and prevents a child being shocked when he or she is old enough to understand these matters. In explaining the onset of menstruation to their daughters, mothers should make certain that they themselves understand the reason for it, so that they can do this simply. It is important to avoid letting a child think she is in any way an invalid at this time. She should be encouraged to lead as normal a life as possible during it, and to take it as a matter of course. As a rule games and sport, with the exception of swimming, should not be interfered with, but if the mother notices that the child suffers a good deal, either from pain or from excessive loss, she should advise taking life quietly for the first day, and explain that during the establishment of the cycle things are often not quite normal, but that they will become so. The important thing is not to suggest to a child that she will have more than a little discomfort and inconvenience. Often, if a girl is growing very fast and working hard at school, she tends to become anæmic during puberty, and this makes the periods more severe. In this case medical advice is needed.

Puberty is a definite physical and emotional strain, and unfortunately coincides usually with a child's entry into the outside world of school and hard work and play. It is important to watch children's physical health during this time—such things as eyestrain, spinal curvature, flat feet and sheer out-growing of their physical strength must be looked for and treated as they arise. Adequate sleep and diet must be ensured. Nervous children in particular should not be pushed in their work or even in their play, though reasonable fresh air and exercise are always good.

An adolescent has not only his own rapidly changing body and emotions to cope with, but is also beginning to go out into the world and face new experiences. He meets unkindness, competition, injustice and perhaps bullying. The world is no longer the nice safe place it was before. It is now more than ever important that he should be able to rely on the affection and understanding of his parents. When life proves unhappy or difficult he must have some refuge to turn to, to regain his self-confidence and courage, and this is where good parents prove their worth.

It is difficult to hit the happy medium between giving too much sympathy, causing a child to feel he has been unjustly treated, and giving too little. You must always make him realise that you take his troubles seriously, and also that, however irritating his behaviour, he can rely on his parents' love.

Adolescents are very sensitive about their changing appearance. Be careful not to tease them about this, and help them not to mind being laughed at by others. Do your best to get them to mix with other children of their own age, so that they do not feel unique. With shy children this is not always easy, but can be done if you try hard enough. Also get treatment, if it is necessary, for the disfiguring acne that often accompanies puberty and causes both girls and boys much misery.

A trying side of puberty is the hero-worshipping type of friendships that arise. These are normal, and the best way to treat them is to exercise patience and let them run their course. They do not usually last long unless met with opposition. Laughing at the relationship is harmful, as it tends to make the child hide his natural reactions and become introverted.

Another important point for parents to realise is that with the onset of puberty comes the development of independence. It is difficult not to be possessive over one's children, especially if they are of the dependent type, but it is very important to realise that from puberty onwards they must learn to stand on their own feet. They must develop into individuals with their own ideas and thoughts. The longer

1940

# LUCKY DIP

## to amuse both holiday-makers and stay-at-homes

### SPOT THE TWINS

Well, children, if you were walking along the beach and met these six nigger minstrels, what would you think? That they were as alike as six peas in a pod? If so, you would be wrong. Only two of them are *exactly* alike.

## Current Events Crossword

### Clues Across

1. Coming from abroad, they provide us with more than food for thought.
3. Rather a costly impression nowadays.
7. Iron ones are carried by the men on active service.
9. Political garden ?
10. You might hire one, thanks to the team.
11. Quite novel in one way.
13. He takes the lead in certain foreign affairs.
14. Depressed capital due to the war.
16. Such a hat might enable you to keep your head during a raid.
19. Flying cards ?
21. We are fighting to be.
22. What we like to hear from Our Gracie.
23. Something for the troops to do with their arms.
24. See 17 down.

### Clues down

1. It may sound a timely warning.
2. When drawn up it may be looked down upon.
4. It provides some sleeping accommodation for the army
5. Where a soldier might choose to take French-leave ?
6. A matter of burning interest to the A.F.S.
7. A country flier ?
8. Those of the enemy may scuttle away.
11. A catchy aid to camouflage.
12. Conquered, and now back.
15. Their crews certainly don't have a smooth passage.
17. A "nasty" decoration with 24 across.
18. Obviously a man's gun.
20. You wouldn't sun-bathe during a cold one.
21. What you might feel while in danger.

## ASSOCIATIONS

With which of the under-mentioned places were the following people connected ?

1. John Dunlop.
2. Charles I.
3. Charles Lamb.
4. Richard II.
5. John Ruskin.
6. Andrew Carnegie.
7. George V.
8. Horatio Nelson.
9. Sir John Falstaff.
10. Mrs. Fitzherbert.
11. The Duke of Monmouth.
12. John Crome.

Lyme Regis.    Bognor Regis.    Brighton.
Belfast.    Margate.    Dunfermline.    Burnham
Thorpe.    Conway Castle.    Caister Castle.
Carisbrooke Castle.    Norwich.    Coniston.

# HOW DO YOU RATE
## as a parent

1. Do you open your children's letters?
2. Do you make it easy for your children to entertain their friends?
3. Do you give your children an " allowance " which they have to budget themselves, rather than paying all expenses, and giving just " pocket money " ?
4. Do you allow some choice in the matter of clothes?
5. Do you show your children the good manners you expect from them, *e.g.* by always thanking them for small services?
6. Do you allow your children to share in both the work and the privileges of home-making, by asking them to perform some definite job, and by giving a say in such matters as the planning of the family holiday?
7. Do you cultivate personal interests and friendships, so that you do not act as a " tie " on your older children.
8. Do you insist on staying up or keeping awake for your older children when they have an evening out?
9. Do you recognise your children's right to have friendships and opinions of their own, and refrain from petty criticisms?

# HOW DO YOU RATE
## as a son or daughter

1. Do you rely on your mother to " get you up " ?
2. Do you keep your eyes open for odd jobs about the house that you could well do?
3. Do you expect menus to be planned around your food preferences?
4. Do you take it as a matter of course that your mother should do " extras " for you, such as ironing a dance frock at the last moment?
5. Do you, in making plans for the evening or weekend, take care not to overlook your parents?
6. Are you unscrupulous about borrowing your parents' personal possessions?
7. Do you treat your home as a free boarding house?
8. Do you automatically regard your parents' opinions as old-fashioned and therefore worthless?
9. Do you always say " Just a minute " when asked to do anything?

1940

# FOURSOMES

Here is a fascinating game for old and young alike. It's good fun for the children, and grown-ups will find that there is plenty of opportunity for skilful play.

Make a large-scale copy of the " board " on a sheet of paper, and place black counters and white counters (draughtsmen will do) in the positions shown. (If you like, you can play the game on a section of a draught-board.)

Two people compete, playing alternately, and " white " moves first. You are allowed to move in any direction, horizontally, vertically, or diagonally, but only one square at a time, and not into a space already occupied. The object is to get your four counters in a straight line in adjacent squares, horizontally, vertically, or diagonally. The player to do so first is the winner.

# NAVAL RANKS

### The rank of a Naval Officer is shown by the gold stripes he wears on his sleeves.

(1) Admiral of the Fleet. (2) Admiral. (3) Vice-Admiral. (4) Rear-Admiral or Commodore 1st Class. (5) Commodore 2nd Class. (6) Captain. (7) Commander. (8) Lieutenant-Commander. (9) Lieutenant. (10) Sub-Lieutenant. (11) Warrant Officer. (12) Middy or Naval Cadet. (13) Lieutenant R.N.R. (14) Lieutenant R.N.V.R.

The special duties of Petty Officers and men are indicated by sleeve badges, incorporating, for instance, a diver's helmet for a Diver, an anchor for a Leading Seaman, and a 'plane for an Air-Gunner. From left to right, the badges illustrated are worn by a Gunlayer 2nd Class; Leading Torpedo-man; Visual Signalman; Trained Operator; Telegraphist; Leading Stoker and Stoker 1st Class.

## STAMP QUIZ

1. What colour was the penny Victorian stamp issued in 1840?
2. What British possession issues a $\frac{1}{4}d$. stamp?
3. What is the rarest stamp in the world?
4. In what values were the George V Silver Jubilee stamps issued?
5. How is mourning usually shown on stamps?
6. What country last year issued stamps to commemorate an international Girl Guide camp?

1940

# WHO ARE THEY?

Here are photos of six celebrated authors, poets and playwrights, showing them as they appeared some twenty years ago, or earlier

1     2     3     4     5     6

# Games to Warm You After a Swim

| Red Prisoners |
|---|
| White Team's Base |
| JORDAN |
| Red Team's Base |
| White Prisoners |

## Jordan

You need a court marked out roughly as in the diagram. You also need a big rubber ball, and any number of players. Divide into two teams, which we will call Red and White. Each team is in one base, and the game starts by a bounce between a Red and a White player (who return immediately to their own bases). The one who gets the ball throws it at the players opposite, trying to hit them anywhere below the knee. Anyone who is hit must go to the appropriate Prisoners' section, and must not cross the line dividing it from the other team's base. However, if the ball comes within the reach of the prisoners, they may throw it at the enemy team, trying to take them unawares from the rear. If they prefer, they may pass the ball over the heads of the opposing team back to their own. Similarly, players in the bases may pass the ball over the other team to prisoners from their own side, in the hope that they may be able to hit an "enemy." No player may step into "Jordan" upon pain of becoming a prisoner. If the ball goes into "Jordan" and cannot be recovered by either team, it should be bounced again between representatives of the two teams. To avoid the ball you may step aside, jump, catch it in your hands, and so on, but you should not squat down and cover your legs with your arms. The game goes on till all the members of one team have been made prisoners.

## Five Passes

You need a football or big rubber ball, and any number of players. No court need be marked out. Divide the players into two teams, which should mingle and scatter. The referee (who can quite well play also) bounces the ball between two players, one from each side, who both try to catch it. When you obtain the ball you throw it to a member of your own team, while the other team tries to intercept it. Each time a team achieves five consecutive passes, it scores a point. If the ball touches the ground, or if the other team gets it, any passes you may have made are cancelled, and you start counting afresh—only five complete passes score. Count aloud as the ball is passed, to avoid disputes. Rough play is banned, but you can jump to catch the ball or knock it from another player's hand.

# For London Visitors

London's larger collections, such as the Elgin Marbles at the British Museum and the Eumorfopoulous Collection at the Tate Gallery, are world-famous, but there are several smaller ones which are no less fascinating and well deserve a visit. Here are notes on a few:

## The Wax Effigies of Westminster

In the Upper Chamber of Abbot Islip's Chapel at Westminster Abbey you may see wax images of William Pitt, Lord Nelson, Queen Elizabeth, Queen Anne, William and Mary, Charles II and Frances, Duchess of Richmond (heroine of a story in the present issue of GOOD HOUSEKEEPING). All are clad as they were in life—though under his really gorgeous court suit Charles II was found to be wearing no less than five shirts! These effigies, by the way, are a survival of the Roman custom of having ancestral images carried at a funeral.

(Open every weekday: admission 3*d*.)

## Flower Pictures at Kew

In the small, square red-brick gallery near the Lion Gate at Kew are displayed the Flower Pictures of Marianne North, a mosaic of glowing colour. Marianne North was born in 1830, and during frequent journeys abroad with her father she began to develop the talent for flower-painting which later grew to a passion. After her father's death she devoted the rest of her life to depicting the flowers of Europe, Asia, Africa and the Americas, travelling continuously despite the difficult conditions of those days. She herself presented her pictures to the nation, together with the gallery in which they are so appropriately housed at Kew.

(The North Gallery is open every day: admission free.)

## Victoriana in Kensington Gardens

One of the most charming statues of Queen Victoria is that sculptured by her daughter, Princess Louise, fittingly placed outside Wren's dignified Kensington Palace, where the Queen spent her childhood. Under the careful personal direction of Queen Mary (whose early home was also Kensington Palace),

*Continued*

1940

## Lucky Dip

### For London Visitors

*Continued*

the rooms used by Queen Victoria were restored as far as possible to their original appearance. Even the chintzes and the pretty sprigged wall-papers were reprinted from the original blocks. The enchanting collection of Royal personal objects includes a stiff little white satin sofa, the tulipwood piano used by Prince Albert, and some fascinating toys, such as Queen Victoria's own doll's-house. Her bed-room, with its bird-patterned wall-paper and magnificent pair of papier mâché firescreens, possesses the added interest of having been the room where another great and beloved Queen was born—our own Queen Mary.

(Open Saturdays and Sundays only, admission 6*d.*)

### Music in Bloomsbury

Forgotten and lost to history for more than two hundred years stood Old Devonshire House, amid the squalor and dirt of a narrow Blooms-bury street, now re-named Boswell Street. Built in 1667 by the third Earl of Devonshire, it passed through many hands before being bought in 1934 by the present owner, Major Benton Fletcher. Now, carefully furnished with seventeenth-century furniture, which is in its accustomed place and in daily use, this lovely dwelling houses the owner's unique and beautiful collection of harpsichords, clavichords, virginals and spinets. The instruments are frequently used for practice and lent for public perform-ances of early eighteenth-century music. Portraits of various contemporary composers, such as John Blow, Dr. Arne, Purcell and Handel, as well as those of former residents, may be seen on the walls.

(Open 10 a.m. to 1 p.m. daily, admission 1s. 6*d.* Information about forthcoming con-certs will be sent on request.)

MRS. MARK LUBBOCK.

## Answers

### Spot the Twins

Nos. 3 and 5.

### Crossword Solution

*Across :* 1. Ships. 3. Stamp. 7. Rations. 9. Eden. 10. Ta-xi. 11. New. 13. Duce. 14. Oslo. 16. Tin. 19. Aces. 21. Free. 22. En-cores. 23. Slope. 24. Cross.

*Down :* 1. Siren. 2. Plan. 4. Tent. 5. Paris. 6. Fire. 7. Refugee. 8. Sailors. 11. Net. 12. Won. 15. Tanks. 17. Iron. 18. Lewis. 20. Snap. 21. Fear.

### Associations

1. Belfast (born there). 2. Carisbrooke Castle (imprisoned there). 3. Margate (wrote about it). 4. Conway Castle (abdicated there). 5. Coniston (lived there). 6. Dunfermline (born there). 7. Bognor Regis (convalesced there). 8. Burn-ham Thorpe (born there). 9. Caister Castle (reputed to have built it). 10. Brighton (lived there). 11. Lyme Regis (landed there). 12. Norwich (lived there).

### How Do You Rate ?

Count one point for each correct answer. If you score 8–9 points, count yourself an excellent parent, son or daughter ; if 5–7, average ; if under 4, start to reform yourself !

*Parents :* (1) No. (2) Yes. (3) Yes. (4) Yes. (5) Yes. (6) Yes. (7) Yes. (8) No. (9) Yes.

*Sons and Daughters :* (1) No. (2) Yes. (3) No. (4) No. (5) Yes. (6) No. (7) No. (8) No. (9) No.

### Stamp Quiz

(1) Black. (2) Malta. (3) 1 cent. British Guiana of 1856 (which fetched £7,500 in 1935). (4) ½*d.*, 1*d.*, 1½*d.*, 2½*d.* (5) By a black border. (6) Hungary.

### Who Are They ?

(1) John Masefield. (2) Clemence Dane. (3) H. G. Wells. (4) I. A. R. Wylie. (5) George Bernard Shaw. (6) Lady Eleanor Smith.

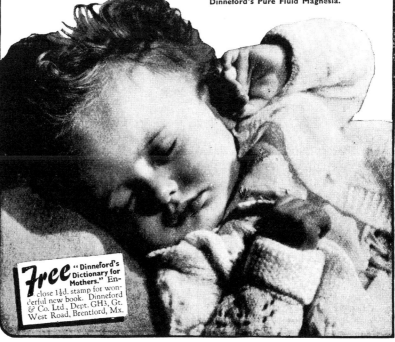

# THE "Budget" NURSERY

## Decorate the Nursery Yourself

ECONOMY is a stern word to apply to the nursery, where you would like to spend freely on decorations and the purchase of lovely furniture. If, however, the budget for your baby has to be cut down drastically you will find plenty of compensation in decorating the room yourself and in making it delightfully fresh and pretty at a small cost.

To begin with, the requirements for a new baby are very small, and only a minimum of furniture is necessary. To house his clothes he will need a chest of drawers and perhaps a hanging cupboard of some kind. An old millinery chest can be converted into a very satisfactory nursery wardrobe by removing the shelves and fixing a rod, or a unit pedestal cupboard can be equally well adapted. There is possibly a chest of drawers in the house which is shabby but could be " done up " to look very attractive. Rub it down with fine glass-paper and then paint with one or two coats of enamel paint. To make it very decorative, gummed transfers in flower or animal designs can be bought cheaply, or a line of contrasting colour can be picked out in the mouldings and on the handles. Perhaps you will be lucky in obtaining some inexpensive whitewood or unstained oak furniture which you can then paint or stain yourself.

A low nursing-chair is essential, and if you cannot afford one of the very nice ones with a roomy drawer underneath for holding napkins, etc., cut down the legs of any comfortable wood or cane chair and ename. it to match the furniture.

Baby needs a draught screen for his toilet, and an excellent type for the nursery is one of cretonne or print on a wood frame, which is made so that the fabric is easily removed for laundering. You can buy the ready-made frame and cover the screen yourself with the material which you have chosen for curtains.

The floor must be hygienic, and rubber is kind to baby when he starts to crawl, as it is warm and resilient. If you must have something less expensive, lay linoleum. In either case choose a jaspé or marbled pattern which does not show every footmark, and have one or two tufted wool rugs with animal designs. These are made in delightful colours on a white background, and will stand any amount of laundering.

Like everything else in the nursery, the walls must be washable, and a good enamel paint is the best choice for decoration, but if you intend doing the work yourself and must cut cost down to a minimum, distemper the walls instead, and apply a coat of varnish over the distemper. This will give a glossy finish which can be washed.

You will, of course, choose as airy a room as possible for the nursery, and if it faces south so much the better. In this case paint the walls and woodwork a cool green and the furniture white. Warm biscuit jaspé flooring and coral and white or peach hangings would look charming. If the room is not so bright, choose apricot for the walls and yellowy-cream with touches of pale blue for the furniture, and have blue and cream curtains.

## Solving the Nursery Black-out Problem

1940

CURTAINS of printed cotton or linen with Beatrix Potter or Walt Disney designs, or flowered Cubaleen—a satiny fabric which can be laundered more easily than glazed chintz—are a pretty finish to the nursery scheme. Make the curtains with a dainty frilled valance or, for the sake of hygiene, a painted wood pelmet, which can be cleaned so easily.

The question of black-out presents a real problem in the nursery. Fresh air at night is all-important, and yet it is not safe to take down the black-out curtains after baby is asleep, in case he needs attention quickly during the night. We suggest, therefore, that you line the curtains with a closely woven coloured casement or sheeting (no black for this room), and see that they are amply full, so as to leave no gaps in the centre or at the sides. Then fix to the window a ventilating device (costing less than £1), which enables the curtains to be drawn, yet gives free access of air to the room. A specially designed ventilating pelmet is also available, but this is a rather more expensive fitting.

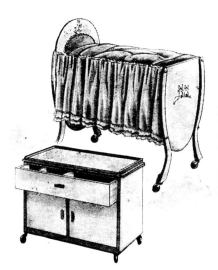

## Now for the Cot and Hamper

IF you are going to be very modern and practical, you will dispense with frills on the cot. Dainty though they are, they do need frequent washing and make extra work. But perhaps you do not want to sacrifice all sentiment to the merely practical, and in this case you will like the cot we are illustrating, which can be effectively trimmed with a simple valance on each side. The sides are ventilated and every part is detachable and washable. Also it can be taken to pieces for travelling and storage.

Perhaps someone will make you a gift of a hamper, prettily lined with pink or blue organdie. If not, we suggest the more utilitarian trolley cupboard on wheels. This holds everything required for baby's dressing and toilet, and nothing could be more hygienic.

## Baby's Laundry

A BABY in the house is going to mean a great deal of laundrywork, which will present a daily problem if you are a flat-dweller, with no garden in which to dry and air the clothes. Your list of equipment is not therefore complete unless it includes some provision for this, and a moderately priced electric clothes dryer would be a really practical purchase. The Institute can recommend one which costs only £4 10s., takes little space and is equally efficient for drying or airing clothes indoors.

## Scales for the Nursery and an Economy Bath

YOU must have scales to check up on baby's development, but it is most important that they should be reliable. Many unnecessary alarms and anxieties have been caused by inaccurate scales, so much so that doctors and nurses often advise mothers against weighing their babies at home. This is a pity, especially when it is possible to get a good pair of scales which can be used in the kitchen, and cannot therefore be considered as an unnecessary expense and debited solely to baby's budget.

The Institute can recommend an excellent " Dual Purpose " balance supplied with an interchangeable basket for baby and a white enamelled pan for the kitchen.

An idea that is a real economy, both in outlay and labour, is a folding rubber **bath** which just fixes over the big bath and is filled from the water taps. It is made with a plain wood enamelled frame and has a towel rail. All the work involved in carrying water to and from the nursery, and the extra paraphernalia required, are avoided. The cost of the bath is only about 10s.

1941

1941

*The Good House-keeping Children's Doctor deals with a problem that confronts most mothers at some time or other*

# Diets

## FOR SMALL INVALIDS

DIET in illness is always rather a problem, partly because the appetite is impaired or lost, and partly because the patient resents being disturbed to take nourishment which he does not want. In children these difficulties are accentuated, because they are not old enough to understand the need for making the effort to take nourishment, and also they stand lack of food less well than adults because of their rapid growth and the fact that they have not as large food reserves. During acute illness, when food intake is low, the body tissues are broken down rapidly and the fats are incompletely burnt, causing acidosis. To combat this, one must give little fat and plenty of sugar, to help the patient to burn up fats completely.

It falls to the mother, therefore, to see that adequate and suitable nourishment is given. She must know what kind of food is most suitable to give in the various illnesses, and in what form it will be most easily taken.

With a sick child any form of struggle must be avoided, and a certain amount of spoiling is inevitable. A mother must rely on persuasion and tempting dishes to attain her ends in the sick-room. She cannot follow a strict routine; often, for instance, the child will fall asleep when his food is due, and it must be put off till he wakes, or he will call for porridge when his mother offers him some specially nourishing dish she has prepared. In this instance it is wiser to make him some porridge, as he will

digest better a food he wants than one he doesn't fancy. One must exercise great patience and ingenuity to get the necessary nourishment taken.

During infancy, before weaning has started, diet for a sick child is comparatively simple. The essentials are to give plenty of sweetened fluids and to restrict fat. In an attack of diarrhœa and vomiting, for instance, whether due to an infection or to over-feeding, the rule is to stop all milk feeds for twenty-four hours and to substitute the following fluids, given at body temperature in small quantities ($\frac{1}{2}$ oz.–1 oz.) at frequent intervals. Plain water and glucose; diluted, strained orange juice and glucose; albumen water (this helps to control the diarrhœa); sherry whey. These may be given in rotation in increasing quantities as the symptoms subside. During the next twenty-four hours, if the child is keeping these fluids down, you can start giving him a diluted milk feed; in the case of a breast-fed baby it is simplest to express the milk and give it to him well diluted with water. A little glucose should be added to the feed. Cow's milk must be skimmed, to remove the excess of fat, and citrated to render the curd more digestible. The milk feeds are substituted for some of the water-feeds and gradually increased in strength and quantity, and given at less frequent intervals, till the baby is back to his normal feeds. The number of stools and the vomiting should be the guide as to when to increase the feeds. If at the end of the attack the stools

remain rather pale in colour, you should still limit the fat intake.

With older children the diet becomes more complicated. As a general rule the feverish part of illnesses such as measles, chicken-pox, whooping cough, influenza, tonsillitis, bronchitis, etc., can be treated with the same diet, i.e., one to combat acidosis. Plenty of sweetened drinks, such as orange, lemon, pineapple and grape-fruit juice, must be given. Diluted skimmed milk may also be used by itself, or with a milk food. Children often like milk and soda water. It is a good thing to add a tiny pinch of bicarbonate of soda to the drinks. With heavy colds and bronchitis the fruit-juice drinks should be given very hot, as the steam is soothing to the air-passages. Barley water is another fluid which may be given. This is especially beneficial in disease of the kidneys or bladder.

In the case of tonsillitis, or after operation for removal of the tonsils, cold drinks are most comforting. Simple water ices are especially useful, as they are more easily swallowed than liquids and contain plenty of sugar. During fever, as a change from drinks, simple jellies or milk shapes can be given, and are often more tempting than drinks.

When the temperature is very high, stimulating drinks such as beef tea or chicken broth are not advisable, but they are invaluable when the fever starts to fall. They must be carefully made, so that there is not too much fat present, and suitably diluted. Chicken, veal or calves'-foot jelly may now be added to the diet, as well as simple milk puddings.

When the mouth or tonsils are ulcerated, milk should not be given, as it is apt to stick to the sore parts and make the mouth dirty.

Diet during convalescence from all these feverish illnesses should be simple, easily taken and easily digested. The patient will now be able to take a little fat, so that soups, eggs and fish may be started. No fried food should be given, and eggs only when lightly boiled or poached. Fish should be given steamed. As the child's appetite returns the mother should gradually get back to normal meal-times and normal food. The last type of food to be added should be meat and vegetables, as these are the most difficult to digest. Plenty of sugar or glucose should be given with food and drinks, or even in between, as boiled sweets or barley sugar.

A diet for "liverish" attacks is often asked for. This is a very vague term, and may be said to cover any "tummy" upset. Occasionally, of course, the liver is the direct source of the illness, as in catarrhal jaundice. Some children, too, have a tendency to attacks of acidosis. In all there is a difficulty in digesting fat, and the diet in consequence must be one which includes little or no fat, and plenty of starch and sugar to aid in the burning up of the partly used fats in the body. For the first few days no milk, eggs or butter should be given.

# Dear Seventeen . . .

With Matric safely behind you, you have got a post at one of the Ministries and are starting life as a wage-earner, in a short week's time. It's hard luck that there is a war on and that, therefore, mother cannot spend as much as she thought on your new outfit, but perhaps it is a blessing in disguise! From now on you will be buying your own clothes, and it's never too early to learn to budget and to spend wisely.

First of all, try to get a picture in your mind of the new YOU that you want to be. With gym tunics and black stockings so recently left behind, you may long to look sophisticated and to go in for the nonsensical little hats and the rather extreme styles you've admired on others. Don't do it! In this case mother does know best when she insists on simple, youthful clothes. Remember you will be very much of a new girl in your fresh life and that if you look the part and act with a becoming modesty and diffidence, you will be more likely to endear yourself to those in authority, than if you appear too grown up and experienced. In American magazines and on the films, you have probably seen pictures of American college girls' clothes. These smart young people of eighteen to twenty-one affect camel coats, sweaters and skirts, simple shirt frocks, moderate-heeled shoes and plain sports-type felt hats for everyday. When they go to parties, they dress up a bit, as you can, but you will be very wise to follow their example in choosing clothes that are businesslike, and free from frills and bows, for the important nine-to-six hours.

Having made up your mind that you won't try to put five years on your age straight away, take a good look at yourself in the mirror and get to know your own good and bad points. Most seventeen-year-olds tend to be either rather thick round the waist and hips, or else to be very thin and immature-looking all over. Should you come into the first class, decide to improve your figure by the right kind of exercises and by going slow on cakes and sweets, and also to be strong-minded about wearing a girdle that really will make that hip-heaviness less apparent. At the same time don't hanker after fitted princess lines: they will only make you look bigger. A casual swing-back coat and a tailored shirt-frock will prove far more becoming to you than a reefer coat or a costume.

If, on the other hand, you are one of the " leggy " type, with thin, angular arms, narrow hips and small bust, a princess coat is a good idea. It will show off your small waist and make you look broader by reason of its squared shoulders, and wide hem-line. Choose flared skirts to your dresses, and if you have a costume, have one with a double-breasted jacket with a high fastening and a gored skirt. Long sleeves will generally prove more attractive than short ones, which tend to show up angular elbows. Close-to-the-throat necklines will also prove smartest.

You won't need a very firm girdle, but since your job will probably involve a good deal of sitting down, it will pay you to have a roll-on or two-way stretch belt that comes fairly well down over your " sit-upon " rather than to rely only on a little suspender belt. Even if you are small, it is easy for the back to broaden, and you don't want to swing behind when you walk!

Brassières are just as important when your bust is small as when it is heavy, because you do want to support the tender muscles so that your bosom develops to a really good shape.

About colours : after a lifetime, it seems, of brown and navy, there is a great longing to get into black. Black is grand if you can afford a fairly good quality, otherwise it tends to look shabby more quickly than navy. Also, if you are thin, black makes you look thinner. For the biggish girl, black, brown, or navy for the top-coat and dress, is a sound idea, providing you have some relief on the dress. For you who are rather thin, though, I think that a lighter-coloured coat, say, an Air Force blue, or a wine-red, or a natural camel colour, will prove more flattering and just as useful, providing you are careful and brush it well every time you come in, and watch out for spots.

When choosing a dress, or suit, try to find a neat, but not too bright, plaid or check if you are thin ; it will round you out a little. Since patterns do tend to add to the apparent girth, they should be avoided by all of you whose hip measure is bigger than you would like. Be careful, too, of those wide, swinging skirts gathered in at the waist. A gored skirt, or one with a few pleats, will prove much more helpful, and look just as gay. If you must have a pattern on your dress, have a small design, or have stripes going down.

1941

A touch of colour is a great help in cheering up one's spirits and also in making one frock look like two, but remember that in the winter lingerie touches, although always very smart, are a bit difficult to keep nice. A good plan is to have two or more bright-coloured leather or petersham ribbon belts, with simple choker necklaces or tuck-in hankie-scarves at the neck to match. The permanently stiffened small collars that clip on at the neck by their own band are also a good idea, as they keep clean much longer than the ordinary soft ones.

Providing you're not too hefty, knitted jumpers are a great standby for winter. They look gay, are lovely and warm, and if you make them yourself, don't come as too great a shock to the budget. Keep to fairly simple designs, they are much the best style, and if you can, knit gloves and ankle-socks to match. Knitted gloves, either in wool or string, do cheer up a dark outfit, and since they are easy to wash, are warm, and not expensive, they're really an excellent proposition. A couple of years ago, ankle socks in town were *not* smart, but now that we have all got to make stockings last longer, and that low heels are the more fashionable, they're not only permissible but advised for all except dress-up occasions. Remember, though, ankle socks with high heels *aren't* right.

Hats generally prove a problem. The pull-on sports type are safe, of course, but maybe they don't go too well with your coat, or you are just tired of them. Well, berets of all kinds, Scotch caps and pillboxes are all good winter types. They can have great style and yet look sufficiently youthful. Veils are best left alone for business hours. They tend to get in the way and look a bit too elaborate. Have one on the special party hat you save for the occasions when you go to a week-end tea-dance with the boy-next-door home on leave, but no more.

*Below : A good suit for any figure. " Boxy " jacket, lined contrasting shade : Harrod's Junior Miss Shop, 6½ gns. Cashmere sweater to match jacket lining : Girls' Shop, 29s. 6d.*

A best dress is easy to choose, and fun, too. Velvet is gay if you are thin, and the jewel colours are much better than black. Bigger girls cannot do better than a heavy, flat crêpe, and for them black makes a good choice. Fight shy of " bits," and remember never to choose a style that accents your bad points ; for example, fitted-in waists and full-gathered skirts are forbidden to those who are big round the middle (the new bloused back warrants inspection) and narrow, slinky skirts are a " don't " if you are thin.

That gives the main points, I think, but do write to me with your own personal dress queries if you care for individual advice. My address is " The Clothes Consultant," Good Housekeeping, 28-30 Grosvenor Gardens, London, S.W.1. Be sure to enclose a stamped and addressed envelope.

*An open letter from the Clothes Consultant*

# CRUSHES

**FRANCES WARFIELD gives some sound advice on a common adolescent problem**

DOES your adolescent daughter have an almost unnatural affection for some member of her own sex—for her Guide Captain, or the new librarian, or even the girl who sits in front of her at school? Is your child's adoration of this person becoming exaggerated? Are you beginning to worry about it?

If such is the case—and such is often the case with girls in their early 'teens—you will be interested to know what psychiatrists have to say about schoolgirl crushes. Interested, and relieved, for a psychiatrist will tell you that in adolescence a crush is perfectly normal; that it doesn't always happen, but is to be expected; that what to do about it is very little.

A psychiatrist defines a crush as "a natural development in an individual's effort to make new relationships." He groups crushes informally under three general headings—the idol type, the confidante type, and the attraction-of-opposites type.

For the first type of crush, school-teachers, librarians, club leaders and actresses are among the adolescent girl's logical targets. The girl may hover close to her idol or worship from afar, according to the circumstances. In either case, she copies her idol's walk, dress, mannerisms, opinions and hairdo as best she can. She treasures each word the idol speaks, each object the idol touches. Both awake and asleep, she dreams of growing up to be exactly like her.

The second type is the attachment of an adolescent girl for another girl of her own age—a girl who is more or less her equal. Giggling and whispering and the exchange of secrets and of valued possessions characterise this crush; also letter-writing, possibly in private code. Each girl tries to shine in the other's eyes, though not to surpass her. Both tend to exclude all other close friendships for the duration of the crush.

The third type is the attachment of one girl to another who is conspicuously her opposite—the attachment of a very pretty girl to a very homely one; of a brilliant girl to a dull one; of a prim girl to a hoyden; of a nicely brought up girl to a girl who may not be actually delinquent, but certainly knows more than is good for her. It is this crush, when it occurs, that makes dismayed mothers exclaim: "What can my child see in her? I can't understand it! What causes these crushes anyhow?"

Nature causes them, says the psychiatrist. Crushes are as much a part of adolescence as spotty complexions, and, like the spots, are reasonably certain to disappear.

In adolescence the child first begins to break away from the family and become an independent individual. She knows instinctively that she cannot stay, protected, inside the family circle for ever, that she must enlarge her world, shift the feelings she has for members of her family to individuals outside. That now is the time to begin.

But just look at your darling daughter. Unorganised, insecure and gawky. Bands on her teeth, inferiority in her soul. Nature is telling her she's growing up, that she must win friends and influence people, go to parties, get married eventually. The idea makes her shriek with laughter. Then it makes her want to sink right through the floor.

You know her personality will crystallise out some day; but she doesn't know it. And she can't talk to you very easily about the things that are getting her down. Why? Because this is the stage in which she is trying to break away from her parents. It is typical of this phase, the psychiatrist says, that in her effort to break away the child goes too far in the opposite direction and rejects her parents entirely for the time being. She becomes hypercritical of them, wants to be as unlike them as possible.

**\* Keep your Tooth-paste Tubes to help make Torpedo Tubes.**

1942

---

## THE LADY WOOLTON SCHOLARSHIP IN CANTEEN COOKERY : VALUE £75

### To cover cost of fees and a grant towards the winner's living expenses while studying in London

*If you are anxious to take up Canteen Cookery as your war work, you are invited to apply for this Scholarship. Fill up the attached form and return it to The Director, Good Housekeeping Institute, 28–30 Grosvenor Gardens, London, S.W.1, together with a letter of not more than 250 words, stating why you wish to enter for the Scholarship and explaining why you think you are entitled to receive it.*

*Selected candidates will be asked to attend Good Housekeeping Institute for an interview.*

Date of Birth ..........................

Name ....................................................................

Address ....................................................................

....................................................................

Present Occupation ....................................................

Education ....................................................................

....................................................................

....................................................................

Qualifications and Experience ................................

....................................................................

....................................................................

---

## Crushes

She decides they are old-fashioned or dull or too severe, and that anyway she is probably really an adopted child (preferably of royal or gypsy blood).

Yet she desperately needs help at this stage in her life. Perhaps she wants a model—some poised, beautiful, successful person who is all she dreams of becoming herself and all she so depressingly is not. In that case an idol crush may develop. Or perhaps she wants the comforting assurance that she is not facing the grown-up world alone, that another girl shares her yearnings and her bursts of shaky joy. That is the foundation for the confidante crush. Or perhaps she wants to build up her faltering ego by feeling superior to, or even protective towards, another person. In that case the result is likely to be a crush of the third kind, based on the attraction of opposites.

Whatever the type of crush, the psychiatrist says, it is normal for it to occur. It is also normal for it to end. Parental interference may prolong it; so try to be tolerant. Don't criticise the idol, make fun of the confidante, or snub the girl you disapprove of. If you do, your daughter will cling to her all the more.

Encourage her indirectly to compare her crush with some of the other girls. Suggest indirectly that to play with the other girls might be fun, too.

Given half a chance, the child will work the crush out by herself. How well and how quickly she works it out depends largely on you. Ask yourself honestly why you object to the crush. Is it really objectionable? Or are you simply unwilling to give up your own place as the centre of your daughter's universe? If it is really objectionable, try to discover why your daughter has formed this particular attachment. The chances are that it springs from some cause you can correct.

If your daughter has chosen a bosom friend who is obviously her inferior, for instance, she is simply showing you that you have failed to give her enough attention, that she is so insecure she has to feel superior to someone, even a girl with whom nobody else wants to be seen. In that case, your job is to start giving your daughter as much unobtrusive attention as you possibly can.

The important thing is to encourage the child to talk.

Parents, psychiatrists say, should make it plain that they are ready, willing and able to discuss anything under the sun their children want to discuss. They should find out what the child's worries are and tactfully put them at rest.

Some of these worries will be apparent. "What makes me so clumsy?" "What shall I talk to the boys about?" "What if no one dances with me?" A mother can talk to her daughter about those things without being asked. Other worries may go deeper; but they are fairly trivial, even so. Make it plain to your daughter that she is not different from other girls, that the things she is experiencing are simply a part of growing up, and that everybody has been through them.

In certain rare cases actually abnormal attachments may be formed —usually in later years. This article does not pretend to cover such cases. When they occur, the parent should consult the family doctor or explain the situation to a competent psychiatrist.

As an average mother, however, you need not worry about such eventualities. Nor, if you establish a basic understanding between your daughter and yourself, have you anything to fear from any passing schoolgirl crush.

**\* The Nation's Arsenals need Bone and Metal scrap.**

1942

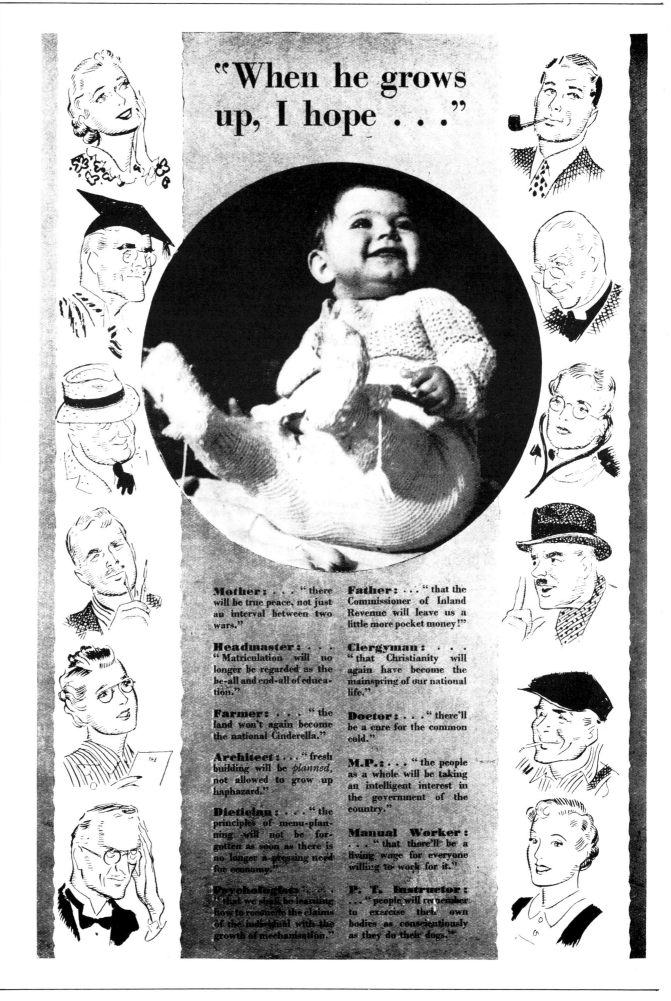

# "When he grows up, I hope . . ."

**Mother:** . . . " there will be true peace, not just an interval between two wars."

**Headmaster:** . . . " Matriculation will no longer be regarded as the be-all and end-all of education."

**Farmer:** . . . " the land won't again become the national Cinderella."

**Architect:** . . . " fresh building will be *planned*, not allowed to grow up haphazard."

**Dietician:** . . . " the principles of menu-planning will not be forgotten as soon as there is no longer a pressing need for economy."

**Psychologist:** . . . " that we shall be learning how to reconcile the claims of the individual with the growth of mechanisation."

**Father:** . . . " that the Commissioner of Inland Revenue will leave us a little more pocket money !"

**Clergyman:** . . . " that Christianity will again have become the mainspring of our national life."

**Doctor:** . . . " there'll be a cure for the common cold."

**M.P.:** . . . " the people as a whole will be taking an intelligent interest in the government of the country."

**Manual Worker:** . . . " that there'll be a living wage for everyone willing to work for it."

**P. T. Instructor:** . . . " people will remember to exercise their own bodies as conscientiously as they do their dogs."

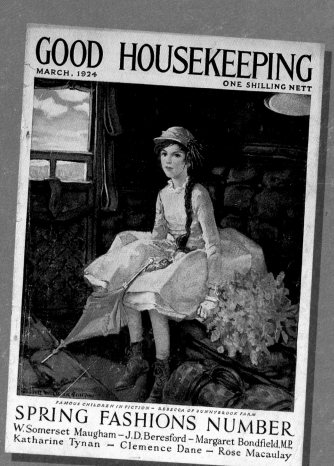

**GOOD HOUSEKEEPING**

MARCH, 1924    ONE SHILLING NETT

*FAMOUS CHILDREN IN FICTION – REBECCA OF SUNNYBROOK FARM*

## SPRING FASHIONS NUMBER

W. Somerset Maugham – J.D. Beresford – Margaret Bondfield, M.P.
Katharine Tynan – Clemence Dane – Rose Macaulay

**Good Housekeeping**

OCTOBER 1934    ONE SHILLING NETT

## AUTUMN FURNISHING NUMBER

*Rafael Sabatini · Marion Cran · Princess Troubetzkoy
Helena Normanton · St. John Ervine · Winifred Holtby
Ethel Smyth · Christine Jope-Slade · Lorna Rea*

**Good Housekeeping**

AUGUST 1934
ONE SHILLING
NETT

## SUMMER HOLIDAY NUMBER

Diary of a Cruise by Lorna Rea

*Clemence Dane · Beatrice Kean Seymour · Beverley Nichols*

**Good Housekeeping**

JULY 1935

ONE SHILLING
NETT

## NEW SHORT SERIAL by DOROTHY WHIPPLE

Sinclair Lewis : This Golden Half Century

Robert Bernays — Phyllis Duganne
Dr. W. Howard Hay — Sewell Stokes — Neil Bell